PRAISE FOR CASSELMAN'S CANADIAN WORDS

"For a full appreciation of how and why Canadians came by their unique linguistic heritage, there can be no better guide than Bill Casselman."

MOIRA FARR, EQUINOX

"Funny and literate. Well done, William!"

BILL CAMERON, CBC TV'S "MORNING NEWS"

"I laughed and laughed. You are funny, Casselman."

VICKI GABEREAU, CBC RADIO

"A work of humour and scholarship"

CANADIAN GEOGRAPHIC MAGAZINE CATALOGUE, FALL & WINTER 1995-96

"Gopher, pablum, bangbelly, shanty, Imax, and fuddle-duddle. Sound like fun? It is."

HALIFAX DAILY NEWS

"Casselman is a refreshing antidote to the dreary word cops and tired language pedants. He is funny, relaxed, and wonderfully entertaining."

MICHAEL ENRIGHT, HOST OF CBC RADIO'S "AS IT HAPPENS"

CASSELMANIA

MORE WACKY
CANADIAN WORDS & SAYINGS

BILL CASSELMAN

LITTLE, BROWN AND COMPANY (CANADA) LTD.
BOSTON · TORONTO · LONDON

CANADIAN CATALOGUING IN PUBLICATION DATA

Casselman, Bill, 1942–
          Casselmania : more wacky Canadian words and sayings

ISBN 0-316-13314-0

1. Canadianisms (English).   2. English language -
Etymology.   I. Title.

FC23.C36 1996   422   C96-931409-4
F1006.C36 1996

Cover design: Tania Craan
Cover artwork: Susan Leopold
Printed and bound in Canada by Best Book Manufacturers

Little, Brown and Company (Canada) Limited
148 Yorkville Avenue, Toronto, Ontario, M5R 1C2

to the most loving teachers I had,
my mother, Margaret Jane Casselman, née Gordon,
and my father, Alfred Merkley Casselman

piam in memoriam

TABLE OF

PREFACE

"Would that varlets from some northern hinterland across the ocean claim not my ey!"

Geoffrey Chaucer

o ahead; use tooney to refer to the two-dollar Canadian coin. Just remember that on the sunny isle of Trinidad, tooney or tuney is a slang word for 'vagina.' Sneak a peek at chapter two for details. Or look at the opening chapter on Canadian weather rhymes to discover that the flap of a butterfly's wings in Ontario might change the course of a storm in Nova Scotia a week later! Are Canadians connected or not? If you've ever watched aspen and poplar trees turn their leaves up before a storm, you'll understand this Ontario weather rhyme from my childhood summer camp in Muskoka: "When poplar shows its underwear, the clouds do rain and thunder bear." Or probe the validity of this weather jingle from Nova Scotia: "A summer fog for fair, a winter fog for rain, a fact most everywhere, from Canso right to Maine." You think we invented that persistent marker of Canadian speech, "eh"? How come English poet Geoffrey Chaucer used it in the form *ey* in his *Canterbury Tales* written between A.D. 1387 and 1400?

West coast Canucks have dubbed the Kitsilano area of Vancouver with the playful tag *Kitschilano*. Halifax is Slackers. Vancouver had the first Skid Row in Canada. A block of Toronto's Bloor Street housing Hungarian restaurants is called The Goulash Archipelago by University of Toronto student customers. Parkdale in Toronto's west end was once known as Perkdale, because the prostitution and street drug trade made Percodan pills a medium of exchange. These and other neighbourhood words pop up in chapter four.

Theft of a pomaceous comestible

This book features the inauguration of The Canadian National Museum of Gobbledygook and Bafflegab. Do take the tour to learn about political doublespeak, about how pussyfooting officials in many professions try to hide the truth by coating Canadian English in a rich syrup of unctuous bunk. You don't bring an apple to the teacher anymore. You transfer a pomaceous comestible to the on-site facilitator of pupil learning. My pet annoyance is a word of bamboozlement entirely Canadian in origin, "nordicity," used by no less a master of plain speech than Joe Clark. I take nordicity into the word morgue and apply a scalpel to its pompous corpus. The autopsy report's at the end of chapter five.

Fans of broadcaster Vicki Gabereau ought not to miss the chapter about Canadian words of greeting, and the story—the only shaggy dog story in this book— about a canine named Chimo after the common greeting and toast used up north. We Canucks hail one another with a multilingual spritz of salutations: *aksunai*!, *bitaemo*!, *bojo-bojo*!, the Algonkian *nitchie*!, the Chinook Jargon *klahowyah*!, the Cree-based *wachee*! They bid you welcome in chapter seven.

On the trans-Canadian toboggan ride of chapter eight, meet words and phrases coined in every province and territory. Have you ever had to put up with a jill-poke? In the jargon of New Brunswick lumbering this noun named a major nuisance for log drivers: a timber pole that had one end stuck in the mud of a riverbank and the other projecting dangerously out into the current. Jill-poke was also heard in early Maritime lumber camps as a label for anyone in camp who was a "pain-in-the-ass." "Get that drunken jill-poke's face out of the molasses!" It's a nifty, jabby chop and should be resuscitated for use in political invective. I confess to engaging in a tad of invective myself in chapter eight where the word "Atlantica" is offered by some for the silly notion of Maritime union. Prince Edward Island has a vivid synonym for diarrhea, "the flying axehandles." In Ontario, Caribbean English prompts a probe into the origins of "mas." You'll discover what part of Ontario lays claim to "haw-eaters." Manitoba's Bungee language speaks again. And we toast Winnipeg with the phrase, "Here's a Ho!" We travel down Saskatchewan's "grid roads" to a meditation on the word "prairie" itself, and some of the phrases sprung from it, like "prairie itch," a dermatitis produced by contact with nasty micro-organisms called fresh-water polyps of the genus *Hydra* found in prairie potholes, ponds, and ditches. In W. O. Mitchell's *Jake and the Kid* a character "had the measles and the prairie itch once and the mumps on both sides."

Can any word be more Albertan than hoodoo? The word "hoodoo" comes from Africa. Hoodoos are oddly shaped pedestals of earth or pillars of rock that develop through erosion by wind and water, especially in areas where the sedimentary layers alternate between soft and hard material, for example in horizontal strata of shale and sandstone. In the eighteenth and nineteenth centuries, African people of Hausa origin brought with them to their enslavement in the American South a distinct magic practice called hoodoo. The word comes directly from the Hausa language where the verb *hu'du'ba* means 'to arouse resentment, produce retribution.' How did a word for African magic get plastered on Alberta rock formations? See chapter eight. Northern words like bruck, catskinner, and cheechako are on parade there as well. In the same area the inquiring scholar will find that shit-disturber and shite-poke are Canadianisms. If you have ever been offended by slang phrases that refer to the *derrière* of a cooked fowl, namely: deacon's nose, parson's nose, pope's nose, then the final section of chapter eight will assist you in providing the correct technical word in ornithology for the fleshy protuberance on a bird's butt that supports the tail feathers. Just part of our service, folks.

Chapter nine concerns brand-names and trademarks like "Horned Toad"—a new beer, "Anti-Flirt" underwear, "Rotting Grape" wine—I kid you not, and "Dead Cow" leather gloves and mitts. What will they try to trademark next? I guess the word "Canada" is safe, eh? Think so? Did you know that at EXPO 86 in Vancouver, British Columbia, during the preparation of our national pavilion on Canadian soil the federal government of Canada was not allowed to use the maple leaf logo and the name Canada until it had humbly applied for permission from the Ace Novelty Company of Seattle, Washington? The good folks at Ace Novelty had been granted exclusive use of the name Canada and the maple leaf logo at the exposition. Now there's word-watching with a vengeance. Interesting, how in specific venues a country might not own the rights to its own name! We chronicle other audacious trademarkings too.

Chapter six is the first extensive study of Canadian surnames ever published. Our first and last names have sprung from the tongues of first peoples and hitched rides to Canada from almost every language on earth. English and French predominate, of course. But consider movie star and Canadian Keanu Reeves who has a given name that is Hawaiian and means 'cool breeze.' *Ke-ahe-anu* is literally 'the breeze cool.'

Eileen "Shania" Twain, the million-CD-selling country-and-western singer-composer, grew up in Timmins as Eileen Twain and got her start singing at Ontario's Deerhurst Inn. She won several awards for her

work at the 1996 Grammies. Shania was the name of a
girl she worked with at the Deerhurst Inn, and, when it
came time to confect a show-biz name, she chose
Shania (pronounced sha-NYE-a) which is Ojibwa for
'on my way.'

There are many books about family names, but
only chapter six of this book explains how some first
and many last names work by using surnames important
to Canadians. Singer, dancer, theatre director, and
choreographer Jeff Hyslop has a name describing where
an ancestor lived, in an Old English *hæsel-hop*
'hazeltree-valley.'

Tatanga Mani, the Stoney Indian leader, statesman,
and philosopher (1871–1967), born in the Bow River
Valley of Alberta, had the English name of George
McLean. *Tatanga Mani* in the Stoney language is liter-
ally 'buffalo walking.' Canadian aboriginal actor
Graham Greene has a memorable scene in the film
Dances With Wolves trying to guess the charade as the
Kevin Costner character imitates a buffalo—badly—but
Greene's character does understand and says, "Tatonka!"
which is the related word for 'buffalo' in the language
of the Lakota Sioux.

Tatanga

There's a fascinating surprise behind almost every
surname borne by Canadians. And even if you don't
know the original meaning of your family name, it is
still precious, personal, and not to be defiled by coarse
lips. I still recall the sting of a taunt by a Grade 5 class-
mate who called me "Cat's-ass-elman." The same little
Torquemada-in-training then tiptoed after me around the
recess yard, singsonging "Silly Billy. Silly Billy. Silly
Billy." An iced snowball to his protuberant mandibular
region caused him to reconsider singsong as a career.

Don't mess with my name. And so say all of us.
Names have a ritual sanctity that is made plain at bap-
tism. But there's fun and enlightenment and astonish-
ment galore in the story of Canadian surnames.

The names we inherit at birth are the most personal gifts life offers. Yet how many of us know much at all
about the meaning of our last names? Have we asked
our mother and father their meanings? Did we question

a grandfather or grandmother about the origin of our family names? And, did gramps and grammy get it right? I remember a Canadian family called Griggs who had been convinced by several generations of wise elders that their name meant 'grasshopper' until research showed that Grigg was a Cornish pet name for any man named Gregory, so that Griggs meant 'descendant of a Cornish man named Gregory.'

One of the most widespread mistakes about the meaning of a last name happened in Québec. During his years of political power, a hoary folk etymology, very common and very wrong, made the rounds about Pierre Trudeau. You could have asked many on the street in Québec and have been told that Trudeau was, *bien entendu*, from *trou d'eau*, a supposed old term for water-hole. And of course there were vulgar jokes told that depended on this spurious etymology. Trudeau as a surname goes back to an ancestor who bore the Teutonic warrior name *Trudo*. The root is Old High German *drud* which meant 'strong, hardened, tough, mighty.' So frequent a first name was it in very early French that we even find it in ancient church records with a full Latin declension: *Trudo, Trudonis*, etc. Quite the opposite with our little water-hole *trou d'eau,* which is **never** found in early French print. *Trou* was simply not used like this in early French. *Trou* indicated always an absence, a hole that was empty. Even in the most recent French coinages using the word, this holds true. For example, the English astronomical term "black hole" is translated in current French by *trou noir.*

You'll find Canadian names here from Arabic, Belgian, Czech, Danish, English, French, German, Hebrew, Irish, Italian, Russian, Scottish, Ukrainian, and many other sources. It's the chapter of this book I most enjoyed writing and most want you to read.

I also had fun selecting the nineteenth century woodcuts and engravings I use in this book to provide visual refreshment for all us text-tourists. Time has brushed away the names of many of the artists who made these illustrations. But, anonymous or not, the old

cuts are more piquant than photographs, and more useful for mildly satiric purposes.

Had a laugh about *anything* Canadian lately? I
think you will in reading chapter three where I have collected almost five hundred Canadian folk
sayings and categorized them by topic in
dictionary form. Of a dull knife, eastern
Canadians say: "You could ride to Halifax
on that blade." Dutch immigrants brought
their version of "a girl for every boy" to
Canada, now translated as the somewhat
sexist "every pot finds its own cover."
From the late nineteenth century is this
Canadianism: "All dolled up like a barber's cat." A reader in Sault Ste. Marie,
Ontario, heard this one in the 1940s: "You
smell better than a dime whore on nickel
Tuesday." A localism from Prince Edward
Island describes a very small crowd:
"There were thousands and thousands
from Tyne Valley alone." From Three
Hills, Alberta, comes: "He's lower than a
snake's belly in a wagon rut."

Not all our folk expressions hark
back to a rural past, although some of the
best do. An ecologist from British
Columbia said of a dull companion: "He's
got his solar panels on the north side."

"All dolled up like a barber's cat."

When an audiophile breaks wind, he might hear: "Not
bad for a half-inch woofer." "They eat like gannets" say
people on Cape Sable Island, Nova Scotia, to describe
those who bolt their food whole, as gannets swallow
fish whole. An Albertan outdoors guide, asked how
things are going, replies, "Slicker 'n a brookie!"
Brookie is a Canadian diminutive for brook trout. A
well-known Canadian hockey star, speaking of his
childhood in western Canada, always says, "Poor?
Listen, we were so poor that if you didn't wake up in
the morning with a hard-on, you had nothing to play
with all day." Canadians are adept at sexual folk sayings. "Noisier than inbreeding on a cornhusk mattress."

"With him, every night was like hormone day at a mink ranch."

"He has a one-track mind, and that's narrow gauge" runs an old Canadian railroader's insult. In Saskatchewan, a storm prompted: "That wind is strong enough to blow the nuts off a gang plough." A north wind streaming south off Georgian Bay summons the comment: "It's blowin' a gagger."

Inside, I know you'll find Canadian words and sayings to startle you and to be enjoyed. Now I've written enough of this prefatory sampling. Am I tired? Well, if my arsehole drags any lower, I'll have to stick it in the cuff of my pants.

205 Helena Street,
Dunnville, Ontario, Canada N1A 2S6
September, 1996

ACKNOWLEDGMENTS

dam Gilders, M.A., this book's indefatigable and tenacious researcher, gets first thanks. His computer-assisted burrowings in the warrens of Canuckiana unearthed many a gem, and I wish him the best as he pursues a doctorate in English studies at the University of Toronto. Pamela Erlichman edited this book, laser-gunned the verbal debris, and spritzed clean my messier sentences. With brio and panache, Scott Richardson designed this book using his customary typographic savvy. For enlightenment and correction on matters artistic and for the joy of his witty company, I thank my friend, Gary Michael Dault. Darren Hagan again helped me index the work and was a walking reference text on Canadian slang. My Winnipeg buddy, Jack Farr, assisted by contributing Manitoba lore. For early and thorough perusal of the manuscript and for his many helpful suggestions and corrections in matters etymological, my gratitude goes to Jon Simpson of Quispamsis, New Brunswick. Keith Thomas viewed with Attila-the-Hunnish hauteur my efforts to write in scientific mode, and as a friend corrected passages that did not pass muster. Let me say in my defence, however, that these same passages did—as I once heard a soldier say—pass mustard. I relish all their help.

Judy Brake, *amiga di mi corazón*, has been a loyal friend always. She has given and does give support as my adviser, sometime employer, and constant idea source. Judy puts the brake on my excesses of ego and then restores the remnants with her critical intelligence. Even during times—surely brief—when I prove a "high-maintenance" friend, Judy Brake has been there for me. Back to you, J.B., with love and affection.

My agent, Daphne Hart, of the Helen Heller Agency, used her clever verve to bring this book to the attention of my new publisher. And I thank Kim McArthur and Sarah MacLachlan for their enthusiastic welcome to Little, Brown.

Many Canadians wrote to add Canadian sayings, new to my files. Many phoned in to radio and TV shows, and several buttonholed me at book signings to offer suggestions for this book. I thank you all. Some who helped are mentioned by name beside their contributions at various places throughout the book and particularly in the chapter on folk sayings. For taking special interest in my database of Canadian folk speech, I thank the following: Lew Gloin, Margarita Hill of Prince Albert, Mr. E. C. Lougheed of Guelph, Ontario, and his brother Mr. G. I. Lougheed, Sandra Mitchell of Charlton Station, Ontario, and J. H. Toop, of Windsor, Ontario.

Les Nirenberg bought the first prose I ever sold. A nervous nerd uncertain of any life direction, I was in Grade 11 at Dunnville High School. Les was the editor and sole proprietor of *The Panic Button*, a Canadian satirical magazine of the late fifties and early sixties, which he published out of a variety store on Weston Road in Toronto called The Co-existence Candy Shop. He paid me twenty dollars for a 400-word piece, and more for subsequent submissions. I was in writerly ecstasy for weeks. Across all the years, for that happy beginning, thank you, Les.

CHAPTER ONE

CANADIAN WEATHER RHYMES

"Red sky at night,
sailors' delight.
Red sky at
morning, sailors take
warning."

t is a weather rhyme familiar to most Canadians. But how old is it? Well, Jesus knew it. The Gospel according to Saint Matthew (King James' version, 16:2–3) reports that Christ began his rebuke of the Pharisees with these words: "When it is evening, ye say, it will be fair weather: for the sky is red. And in the morning, it will be foul weather today: for the sky is red and lowring. O ye hypocrites, ye can discern the face of the sky; but can ye not discern the signs of the times?" With no wish to profane Holy Writ, we today might fling that line—at a TV weather person after some spectacularly inaccurate forecast. Just how old is the Gospel according to Saint Matthew? Some scholars say Matthew attained its present form, the koine Greek version, about A.D. 70. But we can find that very same red-sky weather saying more than four hundred years earlier, in fragments of the West's first book of weather forecasting written around 340 B.C. by the Greek philosopher Theophrastus.

So this red-sky weather rhyme is old. How accurate is it? Sundry professors who teach meteorology and climatology dismiss most proverbial bits of weather lore. The rhymes have no general scientific validity because the weather rules they state have no universal application. Many a red-faced twilight has turned to rain. Many a rosy-fingered dawn has been the herald of a sunny morning. Weather systems are too complex to predict accurately and fully in every instance.

CHAOS THEORY & OUR WEATHER

Much of our natural world, including weather systems, is turning out to play by rules that are not linear, not always obedient to the laws of Newtonian physics. Chaos theory and the new science of complexity brand such systems as non-linear. The millions of variables that help make up these systems obey strange rules which scientists who study complexity are just barely beginning to understand. In chaos theory one such factor is called "sensitive dependence on initial conditions." It is impossible to measure weather conditions without some small errors. But in non-linear systems, as the equations play out in time, the magnitude of the initial small errors increases exponentially. M. Mitchell Waldrop, in his book *Complexity: The Emerging Science at the Edge of Order and Chaos*, gives this memorable example: "The equations that governed the flow of wind and moisture looked simple enough...until researchers realized that the flap of a butterfly's wings in Texas could change the course of a hurricane in Haiti a week later." Even powerful computer simulations of weather patterns, with thousands of variables fed in as data by the second, cannot produce totally accurate forecasts. Nor do weather systems behave in tidy obedience to all previous meteorological observations.

Have we roved too far from simple weather rhymes? I don't think so. For now we can be more sympathetic to the hapless TV weather guru whose computer-animated maps help but never tell all. Although casting a mildly skeptical eye on weather rhymes, we can still enjoy them for their tang and folksy resonance.

Few of the rhymes in this chapter are Canadian in origin; all are Canadian in use. As the ancient roots of the red-sky saying show, some of the rhymes are thousands of years old. Others still heard in Canada were brought here by emigrants from the British Isles, although English cannot claim to be the originating tongue. Consider this weather maxim: "Under water, famine. Under snow, bread." In the temperate zone of the northern hemisphere where this truism holds, variant expressions include "A year of snow, a year of plenty" and "A year of snow, crops will grow." But the saying did not originate in English. We have it in medieval Italian and in this current Italian form too: *Sotto la neve pane, sotto l'acqua fame.* Earlier still is the Late Latin version: *sub nive panis, sub aqua fames.*

These folkisms are remembered and passed down to sons and daughters because people who depend for their livelihood on weather, principally farmers and fishermen, have found them useful and psychologically comforting. In a world of climatic turmoil, even false surety propels the sower to cast his seed and the sailor to cast off. So shall we now, on a weather-rhyme tour of our dear Dominion, beleaguered as it is by the "neverendum" referendum. Our national days may be in the sere and yellow leaf, but there's colour in the old maple yet.

Nautical aphorisms abound on the bounding main. These are my favourites.

A high dawn, look to your reef points.

A red sun got water in his eye.

UNDER WATER, FAMINE. UNDER SNOW, BREAD.

"Under Snow, Bread." Ukrainian-Canadians sleighing over the prairie, 1893.

NEWFOUNDLAND

When rain comes before the wind,
Halyards, sheets, and reef-points mind.

When the rain comes from the south,
It blows the bait in the fishes' mouth.

Mackerel sky and mares' tails,
Warning sure for reefing sails.

The rhyme above is a variant of the British one below.

Mackerel sky and mares' tails
Make lofty ships carry low sails.

A "mackerel" sky is blotched with altocumulus and cirrocumulus clouds in patterns resembling the dorsal scales of that fish; "mares' tails" are long, slender cirrus clouds.

"Sea birds keeping near the land, tell a storm is near at hand."

Sea birds keeping near the land,
Tell a storm is near at hand.
But flying seaward out of sight,
You may stay and fish all night.

When a snipe bawls, the lobster crawls.

When herring rush to the shore,
The wind will blow some more.

When caplin eat sand,
Their bodies to ballast,
Then heavy seas stand,
And the fisher's hand—is callused.

When the sun is drawing water,
Bide home with wife and daughter.

Patrick Devine in *Devine's Folklore of Newfoundland* explains the last maxim: "When the yellow streamers called 'sun hounds' surround the sun after its rising and extend right down to the surface of the ocean the fisher-

men say: 'The sun is drawing water and a storm is
pending.' "

Some of the weather rhymes I first heard from Islanders
are of course found in other parts of Canada. This holds
true for most of these widespread sayings.

PRINCE EDWARD ISLAND

When the wind is west, the fish bite best.
Even from away, put a boat in the bay.

From Rustico to Summerside,
A moon-ring will rain betide.

The gull comes against the rain.

When the wind is in the north,
The fisherman goes not forth.

If the sun goes pale to bed,
'Twill rain tomorrow, it is said.

NOVA SCOTIA

A summer fog for fair,
A winter fog for rain,
A fact most everywhere,
From Canso right to Maine.

Snails on the road, water for the toad.
(It will rain tomorrow.)

When the mist creeps up the hill,
Fisher, out and try your skill.
When the mist begins to nod,
Fisher, then put up your rod.

Rain before seven,
Lift before eleven.

If the goats come home in files,
Get your fish in covered piles.

Rainbow to windward, foul fall the day.
Rainbow to leeward, damp runs away.

NEW BRUNSWICK

Pale moon rains,
Red moon blows,
White moon neither rains nor snows.

Compare the rhyme above with this one from
nineteenth-century Italy and still heard in the Italian
countryside:

Luna bianca, tempo bello;
Luna rosa, vento;
Luna pallida, pioggia.
'A clear moon, nice weather;
A pink moon, wind;
A pale moon, rain.'

Onion skins very thin,
Mild winter coming in.
Onion skins thick and tough,
Coming winter cold and rough.

When the stars begin to huddle,
Soon the earth will be a puddle.

This implies that when a high mist obscures the smaller
stars and makes the large ones blurry, almost like a
cluster of stars, then rain is on the way.

Sound travelling far and wide,
A stormy day will betide.

QUÉBEC

Le diable est aux vaches.
'The devil in the cows' portends a change of
weather.

ONTARIO

> When the woods murmur, and the Great
>   Lakes roar,
>   Then close your windows, and stay on shore.

> When poplar shows its underwear,
>   The clouds do rain and thunder bear.

On the approach of a storm, aspens and poplars do turn
their leaves up due to changes in barometric pressure
that cause alterations in water pressure within the vas-
cular system of the leaf. I first heard that little scamp of
a rhyme at a United Church summer camp in Muskoka.

> When the dew is on the grass,
> Rain will never come to pass.

> Where the firefly lights his lamp,
> The air is always warm and damp.

But this saying is disproved by dry midsummer
nights in Ontario when the winged nocturnal beetles
of the Lampyridae family produce their flickering flash-
es by the intermittent oxidation of the biochemical
luciferin. They flash to attract mates. Of course, rubbies
in old overcoats are said to do likewise—futilely. If
human genitalia lit up during arousal, and fishnet clothing made a big comeback, think how unstressful dating
might be!

> When the glass falls low,
> Prepare for a blow.
> When it rises high,
> Let kites go fly.

That barometric ditty has meteorological verisimilitude
on its side. Perhaps that's why it is so obscure and infrequently quoted.

> If you don't like the weather in Toronto, blame
> the Tories.

MANITOBA

If you don't like the weather in Winnipeg,
you're out-of-luck.

When the grasshopper sings near,
The weather will be hot and clear.

When fleas do very many grow,
Then surely it will rain or snow.

A field has four needs: good weather, good seed,
good feed—and a farmer who knows his arse
from a gopher-hole.

All signs fail in dry weather.

SASKATCHEWAN

If twilight's ducks and rabbits,
Don't let them bring bad habits.

Fluffy cumulo-nimbus clouds (ducks and rabbits) in the late afternoon sky make the harvesting farmer stop work early (a bad habit), because ducks and rabbits foretell a glorious day tomorrow. But the weather proverb reminds us how quickly changeable prairie weather may be. Is it valid for Saskatchewan? I can't say except to note that that rhyme was first quoted to me in the cafeteria at CBC Regina.

Calm weather in June sets corn in tune.

For weather, go to heaven; for company,
go to hell—sir.

No weather's ill if the wind be still.

ALBERTA

When Chinook blues above the foothills show,
Then soon warm winds will melt the snow.

Chinook "blues" are the arch-like cloud formations, often seen as a bright blue strip over the Rockies that stands out from the darker, overcast conditions that surround it. The Chinook is a dry, moderating, westerly wind, common in winter and spring, especially in the eastern foothills of the Rockies from Peace River country all the way down to Colorado, and occasionally over much of our prairies. Following a long tradition in the burgeoning of the English wordstock, the noun has become a verb. "It chinooked last night, went up 40 degrees in two hours. Had to toss all my blankets off. She was blowin' warm as summer."

BRITISH COLUMBIA

If you don't like the weather in Vancouver, wait a minute.

If God had really wanted people to live in the Lower Mainland, we'd have been born with umbrellas sticking out of our heads.
(Heard on the street in Richmond, B.C.)

So ends our rhymster's gallivanting across weather-rich Canada.

THE OLDEST WEATHER RHYME?

For those of antiquarian bent, the oldest weather rhyme I have found is this one:

> *Quando sol est in Leone*
> *pone mulier in cantone*
> *bibe vinum con sifone.*
> 'When the sun is in the Lion,
> put your wife in a corner,
> and suck wine through a straw.'

A piggish little recipe is this, for the hot days of July, when in ancient times the sun was in the house of the Lion, that is, in the constellation of Leo. Note the oink of male chauvinism in its second line. This misogynist ditty is so old it is recorded in ninth-century street Latin, giving us a glimpse both of Latin as it was spoken then, and of Latin on the brink of its transformation into the Romance languages including Italian. True, weather proverbs occur in ancient Greek. I found none that rhymed. Comments on climate echo in Egyptian hieroglyphics on sunned stone, and perhaps at Sumer and Akkad, but they do not chime with the jingly mnemonic of rhyme.

To conclude this chapter here is a general rhyme to keep in mind: Some are weather-wise, some are otherwise.

The sun in the house of Leo. The Latin reads: "The sun, whose home is in Leo, is the middle and the greatest of the planets."

CHAPTER TWO

POP! GOES THE TOONEY — THE BIRTH OF A CANADIAN WORD

old. Silver. Doubloons. Pieces of eight. Arrr, matey. Psychiatrist Sándor Ferenczi, disciple of Freud, theorized that the miser's hoarding of coins and the numismatist's joy in collecting, handling, and trading coins were—in part—the manipulation of symbolic excrement. Ferenczi considered such coin-hoarding the expression of long-repressed memories of the infant's pleasure in his own feces, a mercifully brief episode which usually ends when the child has internalized the parental taboo against such inappropriate sculpting. Ponder that, you emptiers of vending machines.

Should you deem that psychiatric metaphor too far-fetched, consider the often childish names we bestow on our coins: doubloonie, looney, tooney. "The word 'tooney' has too much of the nursery about it, but commends itself on grounds of accuracy (two loonies)..." wrote Warren Clemens, the *Globe and Mail*'s "Word Play" columnist. At least Clemens was interested in the names we might give a new coin in this coign of the realm. Quite testy was the same paper's art and architecture critic, John Bentley Mays, who pouted that he was "bored silly by the wacky squabbling over what nicknames to give it." Johnikins, you are excused from this chapter.

The two-dollar coin is, stated the Mint, Canada's first bimetallic one, with an outer ring made of nickel, and a centre made of aluminum-bronze. But bronze is an alloy of copper and tin, which seems to indicate that the tooney is made of four metals. Therefore the more cumbersome neology of *quadrimetallic* is fitting. In any case, one side of the centre features a bust of Queen Elizabeth the Second. On the other side is a polar bear. So, ran an early joke, it should be called the moonie, since it shows the Queen on the front with a bear behind.

A BORDEN

What would we call this new coin in popular speech? Paper currency and coinage attract nicknames. I heard a tangy one not so long ago at a used car lot in Hamilton, Ontario, where the salesman, looking remarkably like Oilcan Harry from the old Mighty Mouse cartoons, was about to foist a flivver on some innocent buyer: "So, good-lookin' set of wheels, eh? Tell yuh what. $4,000 is the list. I'll knock off a couple of Bordens. You'll take it." Former Prime Minister Robert Borden appears on the Canadian one-hundred-dollar bill.

A BLOONEY?

The Royal Canadian Mint officially introduced the tooney on February 19, 1996. A year earlier when plans to discontinue the two-dollar bill hit the media after Finance Minister Paul Martin announced it in his 1995 federal budget speech, the most popular name for the planned coin was doubloon, for "double looney." But that did not stick. Neither did blooney. Apparently both were too piratical.

But a minor doubloon rush did occur at the Canadian Intellectual Property Office in Hull, Québec, where new brand-names must apply to be trademarked. The federal registry then publishes them so that any objections to new brand-names may be stated. In the August 2, 1995, issue of the *Canadian Trademarks Journal*, Hagemeyer Canada Inc., maker of candies and chocolates, filed an application to trademark

"Doubloon" and "Double Loon." Imperial Oil Ltd. sought to trademark "Dubloon," also as a chocolate and candy. A few weeks later in the *CTJ* an enterprise called Triple-C Inc. applied to trademark "Toonies" as a chocolate confectionery. "Twonies" was listed in the *CTJ*, too.

In late February and early March of 1996, newspapers were referring to it formally as the polar bear coin. In the streets one heard "bear, bear buck, bearback, bear butt, Teddy, Yogi, and Winnie." The looney weighs 7 grams and the tooney 7.3 grams. This extra burden had fussbudgets fretting that their pocket seams would burst. They dubbed the weighty newcomer "Unbearable" and "Pocketbuster." In fractured *franglais* one waggish Montrealer offered "deuxbear" because it was too heavy *to bear*.

At the February launch of the tooney in Montréal, federal Public Works Minister Diane Marleau was tuning her tonsils in an introductory address when a Greenpeace protester costumed as a polar bear drowned her out by screaming: "Help me, help, I'm an endangered species." Other Greenpeacers at the ceremony passed out pamphlets pointing out the decline in the polar bear population and predicting that the new polar bear coin, with a life in circulation of twenty years, just might outlive the polar bear itself.

Nanuq

In Ottawa the Commons heritage committee heard a proposal in mid-March from Jack Iyerak Anawak, the MP from Nunatsiaq, a riding in the eastern Arctic, to bestow the official name of *nanuq* on the new coin. *Nanuq*, or in the older and less precise spelling *nanook*, is one Inuktitut word for 'polar bear.'

Deuce, deuxsy, doozie, double burden, double

loon, doubloon(ie) were slangy monikers. So was doughnut, because some of the toonies, fresh off stamping machines at the Mint's Winnipeg production facility, popped their centres and thus had a hole like a doughnut. In a brief attack of late-winter cabin fever, frenzied Canucks took to bashing and smashing the tooney. People dropped it off skyscrapers, plunged it into liquid nitrogen, blow-torched it, and whacked it with hammers and chisels. In Mississauga, Ontario, a nine-year-old boy popped a tooney into two parts and used the doughnut-shaped outer ring as just that, a ring for his middle finger. The boy could not remove it. Alarmingly, his finger began to swell. The boy's father went to the school and cut the tooney off with tin snips. Said the inquisitive lad's mother, "The government recalls dangerous toys—what about dangerous coins?" At another school, firefighters carefully hacksawed a tooney's outer ring from the pinkie of a junior scientist and restored his digital dignity.

COIN CRIME

While the tooney was designed to withstand 60 to 80 pounds of pressure per square inch, it is quite illegal to tamper with, damage, or deface Canadian coinage or paper currency. The Criminal Code offence provides for the convicted miscreant a $2,000 fine and/or six months in the slammer. Is that, milord, payable in toonies?

Popping the coins in two brought forth a new nickname too: the splittoon. The smallest change, even in small change, is still change, and seems to unsettle some people momentarily. A new piece of pocket change jingle-jangles the nerves. Novelty and damp armpits go together. So even at the birth of a new coin, strident midwives were everywhere. "It's a monstrosity!" yelped some bank tellers who opened tooney rolls to find the occasional blank. Now the Mint did issue fifty-five million tooneys by March 31, 1996. As with any new mass-produced object, a few blanks occurred as quality control in the manufacturing process was fine-tuned. So the numismatic neonate was imperfect. Gadzooks! It was not in mint condition. Heaven forfend! The brouhaha abated in the following weeks as the Mint's publicity department gushed bumf explaining the tooney's raison d'être.

FED PROFITS

Foremost were government savings and profits on the coin. The gain to federal coffers by March 31, 1996, was estimated to be $100 million! Not too shabby a wad in these times of deficit reduction mania. Over the next twenty years, soothed the Mint, replacing two-dollar bills with the coins could save us $250 million, maybe $500 million. This will happen partly because the issuance of paper money and coins are treated quite differently in government account books. For example, a two-dollar paper banknote is in fact a promissory note issued by the Bank of Canada payable to the bearer on demand, and must therefore show on their account books as a liability.

SEIGNIORAGE

Coins, however, are bought by the federal Finance department, at cost from the Royal Canadian Mint. A tooney costs 16¢. Finance sells them to chartered banks for the face value of $2. That's a wacking good profit of $1.84 each. This profit has an interesting name derived from feudal times: seigniorage, the margin between the face value of coins and their production cost. In late Middle English, seignorage or seigneurage (these are variant spellings) was any prerogative claimed by a feudal lord or monarch. Then in England it referred to the Crown's right to keep a certain percentage of any gold bullion purchased by a mint to make coins. Now seigniorage is the technical financial term for profits on coinage.

TOONEY DESIGN

The tooney is a bonanza for the government but less of a windfall for the artists who designed it. The portrait of Queen Elizabeth the Second, stamped on all Canadian coins since 1990, is by Canada's most honoured medalist and medallion designer, Dora de Pédery-Hunt. The winning polar bear motif on the two-dollar coin was commissioned in a closed competition from Brent Townsend, a wildlife painter from Campbellford, Ontario, who received the semi-measly sum of $5,000.

It seems the Mint only invites submissions from draughtspersons who draw and paint in a "magic-realism" style, with emphasis on the realism, and less on the magic.

By April of 1996 it was clear the tooney for most Canadians was an esthetic flop. It was "plain, boring, unexciting." Christopher Hume, the art critic of the *Toronto Star*, had said in a March 21 column that "the latest addition to our currency has gone from a state of abuse to indifference." Hume thought the new coin looked like "a souvenir" or "a locker token." After a month in circulation, "the new coin has failed to grab the public consciousness. It's not so much a question of ugliness as emptiness. The proportions are wrong and the imagery not large

Like the tooney, the canoe-sleigh was a Canadian invention of high hopes. But sometimes ingenuity is not enough.

enough." The Queen's head and the polar bear were too tiny, Hume decided, having been confined to the core piece. There was a lack of detail. Even the current and much-hated penny had more numismatic verve than the tooney. "Without the accumulation of such elements [of design], no matter how small, to fill the surface, add texture, reflect light and, ultimately, to impart value, the toonie falls flat," wrote Hume. Canadians polled at random agreed with him.

Another reason for replacement of the Canadian two-dollar bill is that the average deuce banknote of late has looked tattered and rather ratty, because it has been used more frequently since 1987 when our one-dollar bill went bye-bye and the looney was introduced. The Canadian two-dollar bill also had some historical opprobrium attached to it, especially in our Prairies where in yearning days of yore it was the standard wages of sin, being the fee paid for the services of a prostitute. Some businesses in our West used to refuse to take a deuce note at all. The deuce was also the devil. Other prairie establishments sneered at the two-dollar bill as a "B.C. buck." Early in their history, many Americans had disliked their two-dollar bill so much that it was discontinued. A deuce was vulgar. It reeked of the racetrack tout and the cheap bet in some iniquitous den of Las Vegas.

TOONEY OR TOONIE?

Such were the ephemera attendant on the creation of the tooney. The spelling "toonie" was in print early in 1995, long before the debut of the fissionable fiasco. There were variants. On Tuesday, February 27, 1996, a front-page headline in the *Toronto Star* spelled it "toonie" while that same night CFTO-TV in Toronto supered it as "twoonie." In less than two weeks, the orthographical variants largely disappeared, and most media used "tooney" to conform with "looney" in both sound and spelling. Will tooney suffer the same sea changes as looney which one stills sees as loony and loonie? Perhaps. But the acceptance of new slang is severely practical. If a new word is short, easy-to-remember, easy-to-spell, not likely to be confused with a word already in use, and based on a past word, it quickly gains favour. The potency of all of the puns and one-shot, cheap jokes waned with repetition. "Twosince" rhymed with nuisance, and disappeared.

NOT TWOONIE!

Twoonie or twooney could be mistakenly pronounced *tuh-woony*. Those in favour of the spelling t-w-o-o-n-i-e point out that we don't say *tuh-woo* for two. Nevertheless, twoonie was too complicated, and gave way to tooney. But not in the pages of the *Globe and Mail*. As a national newspaper, the *Globe and Mail* plays a legitimate and major role in determining the spelling of new Canadian words. When there are variant spellings of a new word, what the *Globe* chooses often becomes the standard. By March 23, the *Globe and Mail* style mavens had decided on the clumsy but clear twoonie and put it in a sub-head. Leaving the *w* of twoonie in the word is logical, but many other newspapers and print media selected tooney to jibe with looney. Then on March 30, a *Globe and Mail* editorial sniffed that twoonie was "an alloy so cute it makes us [Canadians] sound like a stuffed puppet kingdom at the end of the miniature railroad in Mister Rogers Neighbourhood. Money is not funny. Money is grand and solemn, serene, sublime." The editorial concluded by bestowing its approval upon *nanuq*, Inuktitut for 'polar bear.'

Tooney does have a homonym in the patois of Trinidad and some other Caribbean islands, where "toonie" is a slang word for vagina, much like pussy. Folk etymology claims it is a diminutive of tuna. This is similar to a term in talkie-talkie, a patois of Guyana, where "fish" refers to female genitals. In talkie-talkie, a prostitute may say to a customer, "You want muh fish, mahn?" While this similarity got a few laughs from Canada's Trinidadians, it was not broadly enough known to scupper the nickname tooney. But the Trinidadian *toonie* originated in one of the aboriginal Caribbean languages. Its root is *tune*, a modern variant of *t'una* 'girl, young female, daughter' in Proto-Amerind, an ancient mother tongue from which developed literally hundreds of aboriginal languages in North, Central, and South America.

And for the future? The government of Canada is considering the introduction of a five-dollar coin. When I heard that, my heart *cinq*.

MONEY TERMS

Although they are not Canadian, we use words like coin, dollar, mint, money, and penny every day, and they have interesting sources.

$ Most contested is the origin of $, the dollar sign. Officially the dollar sign has one vertical stroke, but it is often written with two. Print a capital *U* and then print a capital *S* directly over it. It began as a bankers' short form, so that U.S. 10.00 became $10.00 with the bottom of the loop of the U being dropped to speed the writing of the superimposed form. A Boston newspaper printed this explanation as early as 1847. Some claim it was Thomas Jefferson's personal abbreviation for denoting American currency. Others guess that it was a fancy figure-8 modified from the way it was struck on old Spanish coins called in English pieces of eight (see Dollar entry below).

COIN

Coin derives from Old French *coing* 'angle, corner, wedge, metal stamp' and referred first to a die used for stamping money that did resemble a wedge, then the meaning was transferred to the stamped impress on the money, and finally to the piece of money itself. OF *coing* came from Latin *cuneus* 'wedge.' When the ancient Assyrians wrote in unbaked, wet clay they impressed their letters in wedge-shaped strokes which later linguists called cuneiform.

DOLLAR

In A.D. 1516 there was a silver mine in northwestern Bohemia in the valley of St. Joachim (now Jáchymov in the Czech Republic) which produced sufficient ore that silver coins could be minted there. In sixteenth-century German, the coins were called *Joachimsthalern*. In the singular this was *Joachimsthaler*. German Tal or Thal 'valley' is akin to our English word "dale." The Germans abbreviated the coin's name to Taler. Plattdeutsch and Dutch changed the *t* to *d* giving *daler*, and it was this form that English borrowed. By the eighteenth century it was spelled *dollar*. Meanwhile, as Spanish *dolar*, the name had been transferred to the Spanish peso or "piece of eight" so-called because it was worth eight *reales*. By the time of the American War of Independence this Spanish dollar was the most widely circulated coin in all the British colonies. Thomas Jefferson wanted nothing to do with the British pound sterling. In 1782, he suggested in *Notes On a Money Unit for the United States* that the Spanish dollar was "the most familiar [coin] of all to the mind of all of the people. It is already adopted from south to north." And thus by the Coinage Act of 1792, the dollar became the basic unit of U.S. currency, and was later adopted by Canada, Australia, New Zealand, and many other countries.

MINT & MONEY

Both mint and money stem from the same Latin root. The queen of the gods in the Roman pantheon was Juno. Greek and Roman gods had many by-names; one of hers was Juno Moneta, which the Romans glossed as Juno The Warner, seeing in *moneta* their verb *moneo* 'I warn.' Admonish and monitor hold the same root. In the Roman mythological scheme of things, Juno did warn women and girls of various dangers. To later etymologists, it appears that Moneta may be the remnant of an Etruscan name that predates even the founding of Rome.

In any case, around 384 B.C. a worthy gent named Camillus had cornered the silver bullion market in ancient Rome. He paid for a huge temple to be built to honour Juno Moneta, and just coincidentally attached the first Roman mint to the temple. Ever accommodating in the goddessy responsibilities she would take on at the drop of a toga, Juno became guardian of Rome's finances. On some Roman medals and coins, Juno carries the tools of the coin-maker: hammer, anvil, pincers, and dies.

Several hundred years later, certainly by the time of Cicero, *moneta* was the Latin noun for 'place where coins are made' and then for 'coinage.' The Latin word became *moneie* in Old French, and English borrowed it around A.D. 1290 as money. But earlier Anglo-Saxon monks knew *moneta* directly from their Latin studies, and put it into Old English in the eighth century as *mynit* 'coin, money,' which by Middle English was *mynt* 'place where money is coined' and the spelling evolved into the current "mint."

Juno has checked the Mint's account book. She is not amused.

PENNY

A penny is a mere flash in the pan. Old Norse *panna* 'cooking bowl' and Old High German *pfanne* 'broad, shallow, and usually open cooking vessel' probably are ultimate sources of the German word *pfennig* 'a penny'. Some linguists dispute this origin. But I think it's correct. Betcha a tooney!

CHAPTER THREE

CANADIAN FOLK SAYINGS

*"Politician! He's got
more tongue than a
Mountie's boot."*

n folk speech at least, a Mountie's riding boot has a very long tongue indeed, and that saying from Nova Scotia to describe a talkative person shows just how fitting folksy expressions in Canada can be. On a recent book promotion tour across our country, I collected almost five hundred Canadian folk sayings, some new to me, many never before published. In this chapter, which is the largest collection of Canadian-used folk sayings in print, I share my favourites with you.

But why, you may ask, should we collect these pungent chunks of Canadiana and keep them alive? Well, they are not mere *hick talk*. In an age where television threatens to make all of us speak exactly the same, in the pale, bland English of the TV newscast, it is no bad thing to keep in circulation these vivid reminders of what a dynamo English can be in the mouths of ordinary Canadians speaking without constraint, without the politically correct thought police hovering nearby.

How do we define a folk saying? Some parts of Canada call these multiword phrases "folksay." A folk saying then is a humorous idiomatic phrase or sentence defining some truism of our communal experience, often expressed in non-standard English in the form of a vivid simile or metaphor designed to startle listeners. Folk sayings are passed orally in a small community where life and work are shared. In this particular collection, a folk saying is not a riddle, a joke, a proverb, a weather rhyme, a folksong lyric, a charm, or a tall tale, although all these modes of speech are part of a people's oral tradition. And, yes, some folk sayings begin as jokes or statements exaggerated to elicit a laugh. A repeated joke passed down through several generations of a family is well on its way toward enshrinement as a folk saying. Gordon Schmidt of Toronto sent me this example in a grandfather's habitual greeting: "How's your old straw hat?" Generations of children and grandchildren were coached to respond with: "It's never been felt." As the children advance into early puberty, they start to recognize, with a giggle or two, the slightly sexual connotation of the reply, and that helps fix it forever in memory.

WEATHER

Some Canadian folk sayings arise from that which we cannot fully escape, namely, the weather. Weather caused much pioneer comment, and still does, as this gem from Saskatchewan makes clear: "that wind would blow the nuts off a gang plough." Also weather-wise is this saying, a direct translation from Ukrainian, which describes a fluffy snowfall: "the old woman is pluckin' her geese today." Consider this little asseveration of assiduity from southern Manitoba: "he works harder than a dog under a covered wagon." During the settling of the prairies, homesteading drylanders drove covered wagons along trails. The wiser dogs raced alongside in the shadow cast by the brown tarp covering the wagon. It was cooler there than in full sun, and the dogs could run farther without tiring.

ACADEMIC SNOOTINESS

Now, language scholars have, for the most part, looked upon these lively tags and wise saws as the babble of peasants, and left them out of their studies. In fact, Tom McArthur, a well-known Scottish linguist who is the editor of *The Oxford Companion to the English Language* (1992), pins the tail on this particular academic donkey-prejudice when he writes, "In the use by scholars of such terms as . . . *folk linguistics* there is often a dismissive quality implying that 'folk' movements inherently operate at a lower and therefore less significant level than the traditions to which the scholars themselves belong." Such snobbishness is utter flapdoodle, piffle, and poppycock, for folk sayings give insight into occupations and origins of a community. Folk sayings often preserve in their verbal amber ways of social life, local history, and modes of popular thought. But Canadian folk sayings are not entirely historical. We're still coining doozies. Consider the British Columbia ecologist who says of a dull companion, "He's got his solar panels on the north side." Why, he might be a few sandwiches short of a picnic too. How strong was that Nova Scotia home brew? "The likker in that jar'd grow hair on a wooden leg in three days."

"The likker in that jar'd grow hair on a wooden leg in three days."

Canadian English has borrowed folk sayings too, from Amish and Mennonite German. For example, from the German of farmers near Kitchener, Ontario, comes *arm wie a Kirchemaus* 'poor as a church mouse' (in standard German *arm wie eine Kirchenmaus*) and *schlau wie die Hille* 'slow as the hills.' The last is probably a Mennonite dialect transformation, with attendant alteration of meaning, of the standard German *schlau wie die Hülle* 'sly as the veil.'

Even a few Canadian kilometres alter folk speech. Regan Warner of Sydney, Ontario, near Huntsville, sent me this observation about different sides of the Ottawa Valley. "On the west side, people might say: 'Lord

HOW SAYINGS BEGIN

Liftin' Jesus, that truck's got a lot of snot in 'er!' On the east side: 'Jesus H. Christ, that truck goes like stink!' And in Ottawa itself: 'Dear me, but that utility vehicle is rather powerful.' "

Sometimes we can trace the very beginnings of an expression. But it's only a guess whether or not it will spread from one particular family into the population. Take this expression: "You can't eat pickles in the basement." Dan Roscoe of Winnipeg writes, "My British grandfather, Herbert Parry, was very fond of pickles with his supper. They were normally stored in the basement where it was cool. It often happened therefore that the pickles were overlooked when setting the supper table. Grandfather would say, 'Pass the pickles, please.' Someone would say, 'Oops!' And the forgetful miscreant would be sent down to fetch them. The expression has come down now through two more generations of our family as a generalized saying that means 'what you want is not where you are.' " Who knows? If you read it here and use it, this nifty tag may go winging its verbal way across the whole of Canada.

POLITICALLY CORRECT—NOT!

Are folk sayings all pleasant? No, indeed. A plain but brave woman venturing into a lumber camp as a cook in southern British Columbia recorded in her diary in 1926 that she overheard this sexist description of her arrival in camp: "Seen the new cook? Ugly? She looks like a dog's ass sewn up with a logging chain."

It's human nature to delight in comic exaggeration of the faults of others. This *Schadenfreude* bristles in many Canadian folk sayings and is the psychological motive force that drives people to create some of them. No, they are not pleasant, but they are often what the speaker really feels, with all notions of political correctness ruthlessly removed. Nor is the language of folk sayings suitable for all company. But we are reporting the way real people talked, and still do talk, and so one cannot always gussy up these phrases in Sunday-go-to-meetin' clothes, because such editing out of unpleasant references robs folk expressions of their power. Thus we record these terse dismissals of cheapskates:

He would fart on a stone to save the grease.

He's tighter than a frog's ass, and that's watertight!

She's so cheap she avoids cold showers, 'cause goosebumps are hard on soap.

She's so cheap when she opens her purse, the Queen squints.

He's so cheap he wouldn't give you the droppings of his nose.

He'd give you the sleeves off his vest.

Tighter than a wet boot.

Money? Stuck to him like snot to a suede jacket.

So cheap he'd pick the pennies off a dead man's eyes, and then kick the corpse 'cause they weren't quarters.

He's so tight, when he farts, his ankles swell.

He's so stingy he wouldn't pay a nickel to see Jesus go over Niagara Falls on water skis.

Folk sayings may be off-colour, sacrilegious, mildly disgusting, hugely disgusting. So? It's the way lots of people talk. Other sayings are funny, witty, telling, or insightful.

The folk saying has influenced literature too. Mystery writer Raymond Chandler beefed up his tough-guy narratives by inventing new phrases modelled on folk sayings, for example in *Farewell, My Lovely*: "It was a blonde. A blonde to make a bishop kick a hole in a stained-glass window." P. G. Wodehouse (1881–1975), creator of the comic British butler Jeeves and spoofer of English stereotypes, spent much time in America, both in New York City and Hollywood. Wodehouse parodied

North American folk expressions many times in his work. For example, in his comic novel *Ukridge*: " 'Alf Todd,' said Ukridge, soaring to an impressive burst of imagery, 'has about as much chance as a one-armed blind man in a dark room trying to shove a pound of melted butter into a wild cat's left ear with a red-hot needle.' " Here Wodehouse has combined and tidied up two folk sayings he heard working in Hollywood in the 1930s. "Quick as a one-armed paper hanger" is blended with "He's got as much chance at that as he has of stuffing soft shit up a wild cat's ass with the narrow end of a toothpick." I prefer the North American originals, vulgar but memorable.

We Canucks are packrats. We collect everything: buttons, stamps, baseball cards, and even great bales of folk talk, which I now haul from memory's barn. I thank all the Canadians who have helped with the harvest by writing me, phoning in to me at radio and TV shows, buttonholing me at book signings, and just generally letting me know their own favourite folksy zingers. Keep 'em coming.

A DICTIONARY OF CANADIAN FOLK SAYINGS

For the reader's convenience, I have arranged the folk sayings in broad categories like Sex, Stupidity, Thinness, and Unpleasantness. These categories are numbered and listed alphabetically on the next page. If you know a nifty folk saying that is not listed in this chapter, please send it to me at the address given at the end of the preface to this book.

Why should you read a folk saying collection? For the laughter? For the sheer ecstasy of knowing? If those answers leave you tepid, nurture this notion: they make great little inserts to pep up a tired speech you may have to deliver. Sales reps find them efficient conversational ice-breakers. They pump vigour into flaccid newspaper copy. Writers of every stripe and persuasion will find ways to make comic points in this treasury of snappy old sayings.

THE CATEGORIES

1. All is well.
2. All is not well.
3. Anger
4. Appearance
5. Appetite
6. Bad and good odour
7. Bad luck
8. Bad mood
9. Baldness
10. Blabbermouth
11. Bodily faults
12. Burping
13. Canadiana
14. Certainty
15. Charity
16. Childishness
17. Children
18. Chutzpah
19. Craftiness
20. Craziness
21. Crowding
22. Death
23. Dismissal
24. Distance
25. Distrust
26. Dress
27. Drinking alcohol
28. Ease
29. Embarrassment
30. Equanimity
31. Evil
32. Excrement
33. Excuses
34. Fakery
35. Fatness
36. Fear
37. Flatulence
38. Food
39. Freckles
40. Fun
41. Gingerliness

Child and best friend

Gossip

42. Gossip
43. Haste and slowness
44. Hatred
45. Help requested
46. Honesty and dishonesty
47. Hunger
48. Know-it-alls
49. Loneliness
50. Liars
51. Machismo
52. Menstruation
53. Messiness
54. Nervousness
55. Nitpicking
56. Old age
57. Old jokes
58. Patience
59. Physical imperfections
60. Poverty
61. Quiet
62. Reputation
63. Responsibility
64. Runs in the family
65. Sadness
66. Sex
67. Sexism
68. Shyness
69. Singing
70. Skepticism
71. Sleeping-in
72. Snobbery
73. Stinginess

Sex as play

74. Stupidity
75. Surprise
76. Tea
77. Teeth
78. Tenacity
79. Thingamajigs
80. Thinking
81. Thinness
82. Threats
83. Ugliness
84. Unpleasantness
85. Untidiness
86. Utility
87. Various conditions
88. Vomiting
89. Weakness
90. Weather
91. Welcome
92. Work
93. The end

Work

1. **Everything's rosy when the goose hangs high.**
   That is, when harvest is in and the larder is full,
   this old British expression is apt.

2. **Slicker 'n a brookie!**
   Said in answer to "How'd it go?" by an
   outdoors guide in Alberta. Brookie is a
   Canadian diminutive for brook trout.

3. **Happy as a clam at high tide.**

4. *L'affaire est ketchup.*
   Everything's okay.

5. **He was grinnin' like a butcher's dog.**

6. **Happy as a pig in shit.**

7. **Schmeile wie ein Klosterkatz.**

1. ALL IS WELL

All is well.

'A smile like a convent cat' is a German-Canadian expression from Waterloo County in Ontario. In the old country, nuns and monks fed such cats.

8.   **Everything is jake. Everything is jakealoo.**
A number of Canadians remember when this response to "How are you?" was heard daily. Gordon Schmidt of Toronto writes, "Jakealoo was in quite common usage during the 1930s and 1940s in Hornepayne, the railroad divisional point town where I grew up in northern Ontario. Railroad boomers came from all parts of Canada in those times and brought their linguistic flavours with them....Jakealoo is a lovely word, understood immediately by all and with such a musical sound to describe a state of satisfaction or well-being." E. C. Lougheed, born in Thornbury, Ontario, in 1927 tells me "Expressions used by my father included 'jake,' as in the phrase 'everything is jake' and my father often added to the word using the term 'jake-a-loo.' "

"Everything is jakealoo."

The Merriam-Webster's dictionaries state that 1914 is the earliest American citation of "jake" in print. It then becomes much more frequent in America during the 1920s and afterward. It was never common in England, but jake and jakealoo are both heard in Aussie slang. Jakealoo does not appear in print in Australia until 1919. It seems likely that Australian and New Zealand troops extended the American jake (okay, fine) and then passed it to Canadian and American soldiers during the first World War.

In *A Dictionary of the Underworld: British and American*, Eric Partridge points out that jake also appears in print in 1914 in British criminal argot meaning 'familiarity with a secret, state of knowing' and suggests both shades of jake are related ironically to an American colloquialism "a country Jake" which was a synonym for a hick or rural fool. But how does a rube become "fine, okay, in good health"?

Superficially, jakealoo does not appear to be related to jakes meaning outhouse. But one recalls the dozens of languages in which a response to "How's it going?" is a playful "Shitty, and you?" For example, in German slang: *Wie geht's? Alle Scheiße!* 'How's it going? It's all shit!' But the answer is often given with a laugh. Thus it is by no means strange to find a word of excrementitious meaning used in everyday speech to signify fine or okay. Perhaps some reader who is privy to the authentic origin of jake will reveal it to us?

9. ***Pas un pet de travers***
    'Not a fart out of place,' that is, everything's in order.

2. ALL IS NOT WELL

1. **Up shit creek without a paddle**, or, in a purely Canadian euphemism: up the well-known stream without the necessary means of conveyance.

2. ***Baise-moué l'ail!***
    Kiss my ass! Literally 'kiss my garlic.'

3. **I feel like a dyin' calf in a hailstorm.**
    This expression describing the onset of a bad cold came from Vulcan, Alberta.

3. ANGER

1. **I'm so mad, I could spit rust.**

2. **I couldn't warm up to you, if we were cremated together.**

3. **She went up in the air like a homesick angel.**
    I collected this first from Hanna, Alberta, where it was used to describe a person who became angry very quickly. But ex-aviator Don Peters of Smiths Falls, Ontario, writes that it was originally used by

pilots to describe the climbing characteristics of fighter aircraft. "She climbs like a homesick angel" was used in comparing planes. If one had flown the CF-100 or the F-86, then one said it of the CF-101 or the CF-104. "Today's pilots," writes Don, "probably say it about the CF-18."

4. **I'll be gettin' hot tongue and cold shoulder.**
What a husband arriving home very late is served for supper.

5. **Ain't that enough to cramp a snipe!**
An expression of mild anger from New Brunswick.

6. **Mad as a bull at a five-barred gate.**
Heard in southern Alberta.

4. APPEARANCE

1. **The porch light is on, but there's nobody home.**
Said of someone who's good-looking but dumb.

2. **He had a smile on him like poison come to supper.**

3. **She's as pretty as a bald-faced heifer.**

4. **Yellow as a duck's foot.**

5. **Red as a spanked baby's arse.**
The implication of child abuse has sealed the fate of this folksy simile.

6. **Dirty as a duck's puddle.**

7. **Hard to tell from its looks how far a frog will jump.**

5. APPETITE

1. *J'ai le ventre pardessus de dos.*
'My stomach is over my back.'
A Québec saying contributed by Stephen Vermette that means 'I've eaten too much.'

6. BAD & GOOD ODOUR

1. **Stench? That would drive a buzzard off a dead cow.**

2. **That smell would gag a maggot on a gut wagon.**

3. Variant of 2: **So rotten it would drive a hound from a gut wagon.**

4. **You smell better than a dime whore on nickel Tuesday.**
   Heard in Sault Ste. Marie, Ontario.

5. **Go outside and blow the stink off you!**
   E. C. Lougheed reminds us of this dead-of-winter advice from the days when there was no running water in a home, and men's long underwear was changed infrequently.

6. **What are you smoking? Plank Road?**
   What's Plank Road? Horse manure and slivers.
   An interchange when someone smelled cheap, pungent tobacco.

7. BAD LUCK

1. **If it was raining soup, he'd be caught with a fork.**
   Said of the unlucky in Saskatchewan.

2. **"Tough titty" said the kitty, when the milk ran dry.**
   Contributed by Paul Whelan, Unionville, Ontario.

3. **He's got about as much chance as a one-legged man in an ass-kicking contest.**

4. **The devil owed her a cake, but paid her a loaf.**
   Worse luck than she anticipated came her way.

8. BAD MOOD

1. **Ornery as an old bear.**

2. **He rode in on an ugly horse.**
   Said in Alberta of a foul-tempered man.

ESTABLISHED 1801.

BARRY'S TRICOPHEROUS

FOR THE HAIR.

Since the year 1801, this invaluable preparation has been before the public, and, every year, as its excellencies become more extensively known, its popularity has increased. For removing dandruff, cleansing and restoring the hair, and for all ailments of the head, it is a sovereign remedy. It will keep the hair moist, thick, and lustrous, and is warranted to prevent it from ever becoming gray, thin, harsh, or scurfy.

3. **Mean? He wasn't born. He just sprang up one day after a buzzard jerked off on a hot rock.**
   Heard in Delta, British Columbia.

4. **She could start a fight in an empty house.**

5. **There's blood for breakfast.**
   Brought to Canada by British sailors, this saying was current by the 1890s in the British navy and originally referred to a captain's bad mood of a morning.

9. BALDNESS

1. **You can't grow hair and brains both.**

2. **You can't grow grass on a busy street.**

3. **Bald as a bladder of lard.**
   Heard infrequently in Nova Scotia, this is a mid-Victorian British expression. A bladder of lard was also used to denote a talkative person.

10. BLABBERMOUTH

Gramophone

1. **He's got more tongue than a Mountie's boot.**

2. **She would talk the ear off a tin pail.**

3. **Ask him the time of day and he'll tell you how to make a watch.**

4. **She was vaccinated with a gramophone needle.**

5. **Her tongue wags like the flapper on a goose's behind.**
   Contributed by Donna Tedford of Blue Mountain, Pictou County, Nova Scotia.

6. **His mouth flaps faster than a loose board on a truck.**

7. **That dog can bark a blue breeze.**
   From Nova Scotia.

8. ***Ferme ton gorlot!***
    A Québecois version of "Shut up" but literally
    "stop ringing your sleigh bell."

9. **Got a mouth on her that moves like a whip-
    poor-will's ass end.**

10. **He'd talk the hind leg off a mule, and then
    whisper in the socket.**

11. Joan Hazlett of R.R.# 3, Cookstown in Ontario
    writes: "My grandmother Minnie, of Irish descent
    from Donegal, when having a satisfying
    conversation would always say, **'We're having a
    good chin wag'** or 'you're a good chin-wagger,
    my dear.' When she first used the expression to me
    as a little girl, I didn't get it. She explained, 'Hold
    your chin with your hand and keep talking.' This is
    still lots of fun with young children."

"Having a good chin wag."

12. **He's got enough mouth for four rows of teeth.**

13. **Empty barrels make the most noise.**

11. BODILY FAULTS

1. **He looks like he was dragged through a
    knothole backwards.**
    Contributed by Cindy and Andrew Boughen,
    Aurora, Ontario.

2. **Has a face that would make a freight train take
    a   dirt road.**

3. **He looks like he just ate his Stick Deodorant.**
    Said in Northern Ontario of a wimp.

4. **He was so bow-legged, he couldn't trap a pig in
    a   ditch.**

5. **He's so wall-eyed he can lie on his back and
    look down a well.**
    Contributed by Wilson Kindred, Brussels, Ontario.

6. **He looks like he's been ridden hard, and put away wet.**
Contributed by Cindy & Andrew Boughen.

7. **He had an ass on him like a tame bee.**

8. **He won't lie out for lack of a handle to carry him in.**
Said of a large-nosed person. Contributed by John A. D. McLean of Belleville, Ontario.

9. **Her ass moves like two rabbits in a bag.**

10. **Don't stand there, smirkin' like a weasel suckin' eggs through a gumboot.**

11. **Don't be such a snivelling snuffle-buster.**
Brought to Canada from New Zealand.

12. **He had an eye like a stinking eel.**
From Shelburne, Nova Scotia.

13. **She's got a face long enough to eat oats out of a churn.**

14. **She wasn't behind the door when the feet (brains, B.O. etc.) were handed out, was she?**

15. **Deaf as a haddock.**

16. **Got sprogs like scows.**
Prince Edward Island expression for someone with big feet or wearing large shoes.

17. **You have mailman's eyes: one on the envelope, the other on the mailbox.**
Said of someone wall-eyed.

Me? Deaf?

12. BURPING

1. **It's better to belch it than squelch it.**

2. **Bring it up again, and we'll vote on it.**

1. **The CBC cafeteria is the place old flies go to die.**
From comedian Don Harron.

13. CANADIANA

1. **Sure as there's cold shit in a dead dog.**

2. **That'll show you where the bear stood in the buckwheat.**
In other words, that's proof of what I'm saying. Contributed by Doreen Andreson of Brandon, Manitoba.

14. CERTAINTY

1. **Charity begins at home, and usually stays there.**

2. **He'd lend you his arse and shit through his ribs.**
Said of one who is too generous. This expression came over with immigrants from Great Britain.

15. CHARITY

1. **That boy never did grow up. One day he just sorta haired over.**
Said when an adult behaves like a child.

16. CHILDISHNESS

1. **I didn't raise my Ford to be a jitney.**
Said when you are disappointed with your children. Contributed by Marjorie Andrews. A jitney was a ramshackle bus of early twentieth-century America that carried passengers for a cheap fare, usually 5¢.

2. **Get out of my way, small change, or I'll spend you.**
Said to bothersome children, this slangy use of small change to mean 'children' is common to many languages. There was a Puerto Rican teenage rock group once called Menudo, which means 'small change' to *puertorriqueños*.

17. CHILDREN

3. **Every crow thinks his is the blackest.**
Said to parents who boast endlessly about their children.

4. **Keep yer hand over yer ha-penny.**
This is Scottish advice to girls going out on their first date. Brought to Ontario by Scottish immigrants, contributed by Morag Condon, London, Ontario. Ha-penny here means pudendum.

5. **Oh, go find some snert!**
In southern Saskatchewan, pesky children are sent on a snert-hunt by adults. The child is not told what snert is immediately. Snert = snow + dirt.

6. **Your eyes are too near your bladder.**
Said to a crybaby child.

7. **A silver know-nothing with a whistle on the end.**
When elders are asked by children what they want for Christmas, the adult gives this reply.

8. **He's going up Fool's Hill.**
When asked how old an adolescent is, his or her parents may use this reply. Around Shelburne, Nova Scotia, it means he or she is between fifteen and eighteen years old.

9. **You're so sweet, you make my teeth ache.**
Said to any child being too smarmy. Contributed by Chris Retterath, Moorefield, Ontario.

18. CHUTZPAH

Chutzpah is a word in Hebrew, then in Yiddish, for gall, insolence, or overweening impudence. The classic instance is the man who murders his parents, and then throws himself on the mercy of the court because he is an orphan.

1. **She's got more nerve than a canal horse.**
   Horses that towed barges along towpaths were notoriously aggressive about not letting other horses or humans near the bank of a canal along which they were towing a barge.

2. **He's got more nerve than a sore tooth.**

19. CRAFTINESS

1. **Slicker than hen poop on a pump handle.**

2. **Slicker than vaseline on a door knob.**

3. **Smooth as a stucco bathtub** (that is, not so crafty as one might think oneself).

4. *Malin comme un pichou*
   'Sly as a lynx.'

5. **He's as slippery as snot on a rooster's lip.**
   Heard in Whitehorse, Yukon, by Jon Schmidt and contributed by Gordon Schmidt.

20. CRAZINESS

1. **Crazy as a bag of hammers.**
   Presumably because the hammers would point in different directions, like a crazy person's train of thought. This is a variation of a British catch-phrase recorded as early as 1750 that describes someone who is wall-eyed: "He has a squint like a bag of nails."

2. **Nutty as a fruit cake with the fruit left out.**

3. *Avoir des bébites dans la tête.*
   'To have bugs in your head', to be a little crazy.

4. **Crazy as a shithouse rat.**

5. **Crazy as an outhouse mouse.**

6. **Crazy as Joe Blow's dog—jumped in the river to get out of the rain.**
Contributed by J. H. Toop.

21. CROWDING

1. **Living in each other's pockets.**
Said of neighbouring families that are too friendly and too close together.

2. **There were thousands and thousands from Tyne Valley alone.**
This localism, belonging solely to Prince Edward Island, is comic exaggeration to describe a very small crowd.

22. DEATH

1. **Gone to the Sand Hills.**
A southern Alberta euphemism for death. The Sand Hills are the Happy Hunting Grounds for the Blood people of the sandy hill country south of Lethbridge.

2. **Heavier than a dead minister.**
When a local reverend passed on, everyone in the parish wanted to be a pallbearer (?).

3. *Pèter au fret*
'To fart in the cold' = to die, in lively Québecois folk speech.

23. DISMISSAL

1. **Shove it up the highest rafter of your ass!**

2. **I'd know your hide in a tannery.**

3. **He just went around the corner with a rat in his mouth.**
When asked where someone worth dismissing is.

4. **She'd give a dog's arse heartburn.**

5. **Useless as casters on a crutch.**

6. **Useless as tits on a boar** (or a bull).

7. **Useless as a whip-socket on a car.**
    The whip-socket was a metal or wooden cylinder attached to the dashboard of any horse-drawn carriage to hold the handle of the whip.

8. **Useless as a spare prick at a wedding.**

9. **Useless as a fart in a thunderstorm.**

10. *Va pèter dans le trèfle*
    'Go fart in the clover,' *c'est-à-dire*, piss off.

11. **As small as a dimple on a pimple on a sand flea's arse.**

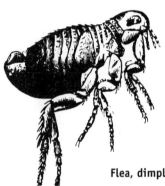

Flea, dimple not shown.

12. **That's hail on a tin roof.**
    Said to dismiss what someone has said as meaningless noise. E. C. and G. I. Lougheed contributed 11 and 12.

13. **He's lower than a snake's belly in a wagon rut.**
    From Three Hills, Alberta.

14. **Go to hell and pump thunder!**
    A dismissal that suggests the hearer does not believe the speaker.

15. **He's not fit to carry guts to a bear.**

16. **Go to Halifax!**
    Canadian and British naval curse. A minced oath for "go to hell!" But British use recalls the Elizabethan beggars' prayer: "From Hull, hell, and Halifax, Good Lord deliver us"(in print by A.D. 1586). "Go to Halifax" could mean "go and be hanged." This refers to an actual bit of historical legislation in the Yorkshire cloth-making town of

To die of a hempen fever.

Halifax. On this side of the Atlantic briny, our Nova Scotian capital was named in 1749 after George Montagu Dunk, Earl of Halifax, a prominent merchant of eighteenth-century Nova Scotia. Back in Merry Old England, the Halifax Gibbet Law provided severe penalty for anyone caught stealing goods worth more than 13 1/2 pennies, namely beheading on the Halifax gibbet. Now this gibbet, a renowned and lethal piece of municipal ordnance, was unique in England in that it resembled closely a French guillotine. The law, repealed in 1650, originated as a local attempt to thwart theft of cloth left drying on open racks at Halifax. Vagabonds targeted Halifax when in need of "a nice bi' o' stuff." The severe law gave rise to the myth that at Halifax the captured miscreant was hanged first, and then after the necktie party, a brief inquiry was held to determine what precisely he had done wrong. "From Hull, hell, and Halifax, Good Lord deliver us" indeed. Thieves and wanderers shunned the British town of Hull because citizens there made beggars do manual labour in order to earn food. The rope of choice for the gallows was braided of sturdy strands of neck-cracking hemp, hence the origin of a grisly old English phrase: to die of a hempen fever = to be hanged.

24. DISTANCE

1. **Just a hen's race from here.**
   A short distance, because chickens can only run a short distance at high speed.

2. **Far as ever a puffin flew.**

25. DISTRUST

1. **He's so sneaky I wouldn't trust him in a shit house with a knife and fork.**

2. **Fine words butter no parsnips.**
This is distrust of high-flown promises that turn out to have meant nothing. The saying is British and recorded as early as 1750.

1. **They're out today in their figures.**
That is, folks have taken off their bulky winter clothes and now in fair weather one can see what their bodies look like.

2. **All dressed up like a spare bedroom.**

3. **It's snowing down south.**
Said when a lady's slip is showing.

4. **All dolled up like a barber's cat.**
This is a late nineteenth-century Canadianism. Never saw such a fancy feline, myself.

5. **Neat but not gaudy, as the devil said when he painted his arse pink, and tied up his tail with pea-green ribbon.**
Nineteenth-century British.

26. DRESS

"It's snowing down south."

27. DRINKING ALCOHOL

1. **Strong enough to grow hair on a wooden leg in three days.**
Said of potent home brew and collected from Campbell's Bay, Québec.

2. **That hootch would raise a blood blister on a leather boot.**
Heard in Whitehorse, Yukon.

3. **He's got Brewer's Droop.**
Said of a man who has drunk too much and cannot perform sexually.

4. **He's got his snowsuit on and he's heading north.**
From northern Manitoba.

5. *Avoir mal aux cheveux*
    To be so hung-over that you are having a 'hair ache.'

6. **Your eyes look like two cherries in a bowl of buttermilk.**

7. **Wine's in, wit's out.**

8. **I'm so dry, I'm fartin' dust.**

9. **I feel like a cat had kittens in my mouth.**
    This describes the disagreeable symptom of a hangover when one's tongue feels "furry."

10. **She has a brick in her hat.**
    She's a little top-heavy with hootch and staggering. British, from 1870 onward.

28. EASE

1. **Easy as driving a herd of bees through a snowstorm with a cow switch.**

2. **Easy as opening an oyster with a bus ticket.**

3. **Just remember, you can't get manure from a rocking horse.**

29. EMBARRASSMENT

1. **Redder than a turkey's ass at cranberry time.**

2. **Blush like a black dog.**

30. EQUANIMITY

1. **It's better than a poke in the eye with a sharp stick.**
    Contributed by Ron Bronson, Waterloo, Ontario.

2. **It's better than a kick in the head with a frozen boot.**

3. **It's better than a slap on the belly with a dead fish.**

4. **Don't go getting your knickers in a twist.**

5. **It's not as green as it's cabbagey-looking.**

6. *Mange-toi du pain blanc.*
'Eat your white bread.' Sometimes said in Québec French when a situation is only going to get worse. Enjoy what you have before you.

"Don't go getting your knickers in a twist."

7. **It's down cellar behind the axe.**
Said when asked where something is. The answer implies equanimity: I don't know where it is, and I don't much care. Find it yourself.

31. EVIL

1. **He has a heart as black as the Earl of Hell's riding boots.**
Contributed by Gale Woodall of Elmira, Ontario. Irish settlers first brought this saying to Nova Scotia in the eighteenth century. But it is recorded in England in the seventeenth century. Sometimes it's the Earl of Hell's vest. And it refers to any object, deed, or feeling of Satanic hue which grabs the speaker's attention.

32. EXCREMENT

1. **He went for a dump and the gophers got him.**
Said of anyone lost on the prairies.

2. **Common as cat shit—and twice as nasty.**

3. **If bullshit were bullets, he'd be an arsenal.**
Contributed by Lew Gloin.

4. **He's as fine a fellow as ever shit over the heel of a boot.**
Heard in the Ottawa Valley.

33. EXCUSES

1. **Excuse me for livin'. I musta fell out of a hearse.**
   This was the favourite expression of an Ursuline nun who taught at Tecumseh, Ontario, and it was sent in by several of her former students.

34. FAKERY

1. **Phony as a three-dollar bill.**

2. **Fake as Canadian diamonds** or *aussi faux que les diamants Canadiens.*
   When Jacques Cartier returned to France in 1542 after a third voyage to the New World, he sailed home with barrels of rocks that he thought contained diamonds and gold. For he was merely the first European to be fooled by those twinkling tricksters of geology: quartz and iron pyrite (fool's gold). Continental French still has the expression.

35. FATNESS

1. **He's got a gut on him like a poisoned pup.**
   Contributed by Marjorie Andrews quoting "Old Jack," her late neighbour in the Coboconk-Burnt River area of Ontario.

2. **He's as fat as mud.**
   That is, healthy. The simile is cited as early as 1864 by John Geikie in his *George Stanley; or, Life in the Woods*, in a part of the pioneer memoir where the speech of early Canadian settlers is discussed.

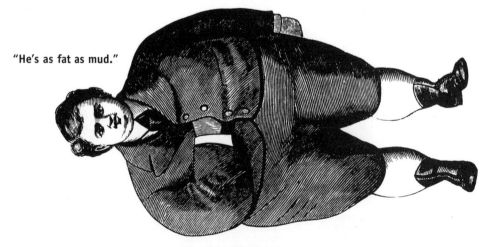

"He's as fat as mud."

1. ***Ich wunsch' ich wäre daheim, und der Hund wär da*** 'I wish I were at home and the dog was here.' Joan Gerber of Cambridge, Ontario, submitted this German expression from the Amish and Mennonite community of Waterloo County. It means: I fear what I have to do and what is plainly before me and is my duty to do.

36. FEAR

37. FLATULENCE

1. **Funny as a fart in a space suit.**

2. **The fox smells his own hole.**
   Said to the accuser when one is accused of just breaking wind.

3. **Not bad for a half-inch woofer.**
   Said when an audiophile breaks wind.

4. **Speak, O toothless one!**
   Said when someone breaks wind.

5. **An empty house is better than a bad tenant.**

6. **Disappeared faster than a fart in a dancehall.**

7. **He could outfart the Old Fart himself.**

8. **He was all over the place like a fart in a glove.**

9. **Se pèter les bretelles** 'to fart off your suspenders,' that is, to burst with pride.

10. **The fartin' horse will never tire.**
    The fartin' man's the one to hire.

11. **Small boy: My bum is asleep.**
    Grandfather: Yep. I hear it snoring.

Awww.

12. **Better to fart and bear the shame than not to fart and bear the pain.**
The folk myth claims that this was the instantaneous retort of a courtier accused of breaking wind in the presence of Queen Victoria who was, naturally and by regal prerogative, not entirely amused.

13. **"Book!" he says, and can't read a paper yet.**
Said after a child or an illiterate has loudly farted. British.

38. FOOD

1. **This food is so bad it would hare-lip a dog.**

2. **Her cookin' is so bad the flies are taking up a collection to mend the hole in the screen door.**

3. **She's awful clever with a bite.**
Said of a good cook in Chipman, New Brunswick. Contributed by Lauchlan Fulton.

4. **I'm so full I feel like I'm going to have a batch of dead 'uns.**

5. **What's for dessert? Wait-and-see pudding!**
Said by the cook to inquiring children.

6. **What's for supper? Bread and pull-it.**
   A pun on pullet or chicken?

7. **Two tall Swedes couldn't shake hands over that plate.**
   Said of a big helping of food on farms around
   Irma, Alberta.

8. **Gone over a goodish piece of grass.**
   Said of tough mutton, implying it's meat from a
   very elderly sheep.

39. FRECKLES

1. **Freckles? Looks like she swallowed a dollar and broke out in pennies.**

2. **You must have gotten your tan through a screen door.**

3. **He was christened by a baker.**
   Big freckles resemble bran splotched on the face
   of one baking.

40. FUN

1. **We're gonna raise hell and block it up with a chip.**
   Contributed by Marjorie Andrews.

41. GINGERLINESS

1. **Grinnin' like a mule eatin' cockleburrs.**

2. **Smiling like a fox chewing bumblebees.**

42. GOSSIP

1. **His tongue is so long, he can lick his own asshole like a cat.**

43. HASTE & SLOWNESS

1. **Faster than you can say, "Jack Miner's geese."**
   Karen Watson heard this one in southwestern
   Ontario near Jack Miner's bird sanctuary at
   Kingsville, Ontario.

"Going like Torchy Peden."

2. **They're off like the bride's undies.**

3. **Faster than the mill-tails of Hell.**
From Nova Scotia and many other locales in Canada. E. C. Lougheed who was born in the Georgian Bay area town of Thornbury, Ontario, writes that there was a dam with a mill there and later a hydro-electric power plant and much use of the "mill-tails of Hades" expression. Lougheed also contributes the next Canadian saying.

4. **Going like Torchy Peden.**
That is, riding very fast on a bicycle. Peden was a champion Canadian cyclist.

5. **Schlau wie die Hille** 'Slow as the hills.'
A German-Canadian expression from Waterloo County, Ontario, this is probably a Mennonite dialect transformation, with attendant alteration of meaning, of the standard German *schlau wie die Hülle* 'sly as the veil.'

6. **He could step dance faster than a cat could lick its ass.**

44. HATRED

1. **I hope you get lockjaw and have to vomit.**

2. **I hate you so much that, when you pass my gate, I wish you'd run.**
From Gay Kurtz, Woodrow, Saskatchewan.

45. HELP REQUESTED

1. **I wouldn't piss in his ear if his brains were on fire.**
Contributed by genial former *Toronto Star* word columnist Lew Gloin, who states that it was heard circa 1961 in the composing room of the *Hamilton Spectator* when a supervisor asked a favour of an inferior.

1. **He's so crooked he has to sleep on a warped board.**

2. **He's so low he'd have to climb a ladder to kiss a snake's belly.**

3. **Straight as a loon's leg.**
   Or, honest, in Nova Scotia.

4. **Twisted as a ram's horn.**
   Not quite so honest in Nova Scotia.

5. **Honest as the day is long.**

46. HONESTY & DISHONESTY

1. **Hungry? I could grab the slack of my belly and wipe my eyes with it.**
   This is a nautical catchphrase from the British merchant marine of the late nineteenth century.

2. **I'm so hungry I could eat a dead skunk through a screen door with a toothpick.**
   Attributed to John E. Potter, a farmer near Woodstock, Ontario, submitted by his son John of Ridgeville, Ontario.

3. **It's been a pig's picnic.**
   Contributed by Father Keith Whittingham, St. Barnabas Church, St. Catharines, Ontario.

4. **They eat like gannets.**
   On Cape Sable Island, Nova Scotia, folks so describe greedy eaters, people who bolt their food whole, as gannets swallow fish whole.

47. HUNGER

"They eat like gannets."

48. KNOW-IT-ALLS

1. **He's the type who would try to teach his grandmother how to suck eggs.**

49. LONELINESS

1. **Lonely as a gander at settin' time.**
   When female geese are incubating their eggs, they have no time for anserine hanky-panky.

50. LIARS

1. **Your butt is suckin' wind!**
   Said of a liar in Alberta.

2. **If bull shit were a whistle, he'd be a brass band.**

3. **Crookeder than a pan of guts.**

4. **It's a cake of lies with bullshit icing.**

51. MACHISMO

1. **You'll be a man among geese when the gander's gone.**
   Said to any bragging male.

2. **He'll be a man before his mother.**

52. MENSTRUATION

1. **The dam's up on the Red River.**

2. **Rosie's visiting.**

3. **The captain is at home.**
   This euphemism for menses is first recorded in Britain in the eighteenth century, so it may be a pun on an early and obsolescent medical term for one's period, catamenia. It is worth noting how many synonyms for menstrual flow used by women refer to masculine names. I have heard the following: "Fred's here" and "This is Ben's week."

4. **O.T.R.**
   Acronym for "on the rag."

5. **Riding the cotton bicycle.**

6. **To have the D.A.s**
Domestic afflictions.

7. **Padlock's on the pleasure-garden.**

8. **The manhole cover's on.**

9. **To have** (an attack of) **the vapours.**
This Victorian euphemism for "the monthlies" was
heard all across Canada until well into the late
1940s.

53. MESSINESS

1. **It's a shithouse in distress.**
This Nova Scotian saying describes a very messy
place.

54. NERVOUSNESS

1. **Wired up like a Christmas tree.**

55. NITPICKING

1. **A blind man on a galloping horse would never
notice it.**

2. **She'd look for a knot in a bulrush.**
She looks for problems where none exist.

56. OLD AGE

1. **So old he could have been a waiter at the Last
Supper.**

2. **They'll never comb grey hair together.**
Said of a newly married couple who fight on their
wedding day.

3. **There's many a good tune played on an old fiddle.**

57. OLD JOKES

1. **First time I heard that one I laughed so hard, I
kicked a slat off my crib.**

58. PATIENCE

1. **Patience is a virtue. With the aid of vaseline, you can bugger a fly.**

2. **Patience is trying to take a pin out of your butt with a boxing glove.**

59. PHYSICAL IMPERFECTIONS

1. **You have friendly eyes; they always look at each other.**

2. **She puts her bra on backwards, and it fits.**
   Said of a female hunchback.

3. **Tough as leather lightning.**

4. **You're on your beam ends.**
   Said to anyone in poor condition, like a ship wrecked at sea that sits on the ends of her beams.

60. POVERTY

1. **Poor? Listen, we were so poor that if you didn't wake up in the morning with a hard-on, you had nothing to play with all day.**
   Said by a well-known Canadian hockey star, speaking of his childhood in western Canada.

2. **I'm so poor I couldn't buy a louse a shootin' jacket.**
   Paul Bell of Ontario writes, "When as a small child I asked for a penny for candy, my grandmother in Owen Sound used to say this."

3. **His shoes were so thin, he could step on a dime and tell whether it was heads or tails.**
   This is Depression-era humour from 1930s Saskatchewan.

4. **I'm so poor, I couldn't buy a ticket to a free lunch.**
   Contributed by Karen Watson.

5. **Poor as Job's turkey. Couldn't raise more 'n three feathers, and had to lean against the barn to gobble.**

6. **They were so poor there was nothing on the table but elbows, and the mice in the cellar had tears in their eyes.**

7. **He's poor because he invested all his money in houses and lots—whorehouses and lots of booze.**
Contributed by J. H. Toop of Windsor, Ontario.

8. **You'll find it mighty dry chewing.**
Advice to poor youngsters planning to get married and live on love.

9. *Arm wie a Kirchemaus*
'Poor as a church mouse.' From the German of Mennonite and Amish farmers near Kitchener, Ontario (in standard German *arm wie eine Kirchenmaus*).

61. QUIET

1. **It was so quiet you could hear a fish fart.**
From Newfoundland, contributed by John McGrath.

62. REPUTATION

1. **Earn the name of early riser, and you can sleep 'til noon.**

63. RESPONSIBILITY

1. **If you burn your bum, you bear the blister.**
With its more widespread variant: "if you dance, you gotta pay the fiddler," itself an alteration of "who pays the fiddler, calls the tune" with its "money talks" echo.

2. **He paddles his own canoe.**
He is responsible for himself, an independent type.

3. **She could sleep on a clothesline.**
Said of one who can rough it, or looks after herself responsibly.

64. RUNS IN THE FAMILY

1. **You didn't lick that off the ground.**

2. **It wasn't from the grass he licked it.**

3. **She didn't get that from anybody strange.**
All these expressions mean the person referred to is displaying a familial trait. The sayings came from Ireland.

4. **Descended from a bull, a bitch, or a pine stump.**
Said of a person of uncertain lineage. Contributed by E. C. Lougheed.

65. SADNESS

1. **Sad enough to bring a tear to a glass eye.**

66. SEX

None of these sayings is politically correct, and many are revolting. All are nevertheless part of our Canadian sexual history.

1. **Noisier than inbreeding on a cornhusk mattress.**

2. **With him, every night was like hormone day at a mink ranch.**

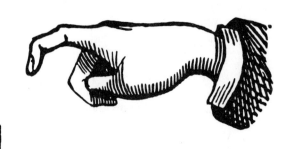

3. **When your cock stands up, your brain sits down.**
   This paternal advice to a young man is a direct
   translation from Yiddish.

4. **He's about as handy as a bear cub with its dick.**
   Said of a sexually clumsy man

5. **Hotter than a flicker's nest.**

6. **She's been around, like a ring in a bath tub.**

7. **She's an all-weather gal. In the winter, use her
   to cuddle; in the summer, use her for shade.**

8. **He was all over her like white on rice.**

9. **That fellow's loose as a pan of soot.**

10. **Sincere as a chorus girl's kiss.**

11. **Whatever turns your crank.**

12. **If she had as many sticking out of her as she'd
    had stuck in her, she'd look like a porcupine.**

13. *Grosse Corvette, p'tite quéquette* 'Big car, little
    dick.'
    Said of an automotive braggart.

"Sincere as a chorus girl's kiss."

14. **Devenir orignal** 'to get horny,' literally 'to
    become the moose.'

15. **She was pure as the snow, but she drifted.**

16. **She's so butch, she kick-starts her vibrator.**

17. In the eastern townships of Ontario, a woman of
    loose morals was "**the village mattress**" and a
    similar man was "**the town pump**."

67. SEXISM

1. **A woman, a dog, and a walnut tree:**
   The more you beat 'em, the better they be.
   An old Scottish rhyme brought over in the nineteenth century when abuse of women was wrongly celebrated in cheap verse.

2. **A woman drives like a goose shits, in bunches.**
   Janice McConnell of Marlbank, Ontario, writes that she was for a time the only woman school-bus driver on a rural route between Madoc and Marlbank, Ontario. The male drivers used to say this, meaning women speed up, then slow down, then speed up again. A totally false and sexist generalization, and one that overlooks women's superior safety record as school-bus drivers.

3. **Every pot finds its own cover.**
   This is a direct translation from Dutch of a sexist thought sometimes expressed as "a girl for every boy."

68. SHYNESS

1. **Wouldn't say boo to a goose.**
   Old British expression, in print by A.D. 1580.

2. **He wouldn't say baff to the shadow of a wolf.**

69. SINGING

1. **She's a diva alright. She has a beautiful voice for diving.**

70. SKEPTICISM

1. **I'll tow that alongside awhile, before I bring it aboard.**
   From Nova Scotia.

71. SLEEPING-IN

1. **If you don't get up soon, the sun is going to burn an extra hole in your ass.**
   Said by a parent to slugabed children.

1. Margaret Reid of Dundas, Ontario, writes: "My grandmother used to say that a snooty or conceited person was '**smelling thunder**' (walking around with their nose in the air)."

2. *È s'mouche pas avec des pelures d'oignons.*
In Québec slang, to indicate an uppity woman, one might say, "She wouldn't blow her nose on an onion peel."

3. **He couldn't say shit if his mouth was full of it.**

4. **The higher the monkey climbs, the more he shows his arse.**

5. **He was wearing Full Nanaimo.**
Are B.C. recreational boaters and yachtsmen a trifle snooty? They seem to pay finicky attention to how their fellow mariners dress. Full Nanaimo is an insult that applies to a chintzy outfit worn by a boating parvenu. Whitebuck shoes, white belt, polyester pants, and a blue blazer with a spurious yachting crest brand the wearer as a floating yutz of the first water. In Ontario, it is heard as a Full Oakville. A similar chop is FDAM, pronounced to rhyme with ram. The acronym stands for **F**irst **D**ay **at** the **M**arina.

6. **She goes with her head up and her tail over the dashboard.**
That is, too proud by half.

7. **You come of good blood and so does a black pudding.**
This is said to deflate one boasting of high birth. A black pudding was also called a blood pudding because of one ingredient.

72. SNOBBERY

8. **They're very haw-haw.**
Said early in this century by Canadians about newly arrived immigrants from Britain who were putting on airs or pretending to be terribly upper class, don't you know. During World War II, a Nazi sympathizer named William Joyce did radio broadcasts of anti-British propaganda from Germany. His plummy accent caused Fleet Street to dub him "Lord Haw-Haw." But Joyce wasn't laughing when he was hanged for treason in 1946.

73. STINGINESS

1. **He would fart on a stone to save the grease.**
Contributed by John A. D. McLean, Belleville, Ontario.

2. **Tighter than a frog's ass, and that's watertight.**
Contributed by John McGrath.

3. **He'd give you the sleeves off his vest.**

4. **Tighter than a wet boot.**

5. **She's so cheap she avoids cold showers, because goosebumps are hard on soap.**

6. **Money? Stuck to him like snot to a suede jacket.**

7. **He was so tight you couldn't drive a flax seed up his ass with a mallet.**

8. **So cheap he'd pick the pennies off a dead man's eyes, and then kick the corpse because they weren't quarters.**

9. **Tighter than a bull's arse in fly time.**

10. **She's so cheap she'd skin a louse for the tallow.**

11. **He's so tight, when he farts, his ankles swell.**

12. **He's so stingy he wouldn't pay a nickel to see Jesus go over Niagara Falls on water skis.**

13. Variant: **She's so cheap she wouldn't give ten cents to watch Christ ride an ATV** (all-terrain vehicle).

14. **She's so tight, she'd squeeze a cent until the Queen cried.**

15. **He's so cheap he skims the lard off his farts.**

16. **She's so cheap when she opens her purse, the Queen squints.**

17. **He's so cheap he wouldn't give you the droppings of his nose.**

18. **She squeezes a nickel until the beaver shits.**

19. **He's tighter than a crofter's lease.**
    This bitter line, almost always uttered in full earnest, was brought to Canada from the Scottish Highlands in the days of skinflint lairds and massive eviction of crofters, when it proved more profitable for absentee landlords to raise sheep than to let human beings eke out a miserable subsistence.

20. **He's so tight if you shoved a piece of coal up his ass, it would come out a diamond.**

74. STUPIDITY

1. **Hang crepe on your nose; your brains are dead.**

2. **You were born ignorant and you've been losing ground ever since.**

3. **He doesn't know which finger to scratch his nuts with.**

4. **It'll never get well if you pick it.**

"He's about two sandwiches short of a picnic."

5. **His elevator doesn't go all the way to the top.**
Contributed by Donald Smith, North Bay, Ontario.

6. **He's not the sharpest knife in the drawer.**

7. **He's about two sandwiches short of a picnic.**

8. **If brains were lard, he wouldn't grease much of a pan.**

9. **Two bricks short of a pallet.** Variant of "a few bricks short of a load."

10. **He doesn't know "Sic him" from "Get out."**
Said of a dumb person or dog.

11. **Stupid as the day is long.**

12. **He doesn't know enough to suck alum and drool.**
From the days of patent medicines, when alum powder was used as an expectorant.

13. **One wall in his attic isn't plastered.**

14. **He couldn't pour piss out of a boot if the instructions were printed on the heel.**
This Canadian folk saying, widespread after World War I, indicated lack of intelligence. The expression originated in 1915 when Canadian soldiers were issued new army boots made of stiff leather. Oddly enough, a legitimate method of softening the leather was to urinate in the boots and leave it in overnight. Of course, it helped if one did empty and wash the footwear in the morning before attending to one's military duties.

15. **He's stunned as Tom's dog—put his arse in the water to get a drink.**

16. **If brains were leather, you wouldn't have enough to make spats for a louse.**

17. **I've seen more brains in a sucked egg.**

18. **No use keepin' a dog and barkin' yourself.**

19. **He's got his solar panels on the north side.**
Contributed by Ron Bronson, Waterloo, Ontario.

20. **Number than a hake.**
Presumably a caught hake is quite numb.

21. **Bright as a two-watt bulb.**

22. **Dull as a box of dirt.**

23. **He has a one-track mind, and that's narrow gauge!**
An old Canadian railroader's insult. Contributed
by J. H. Toop.

24. **She's nine parts damn fool.**

25. **He's so stupid he thinks Medicine Hat is a cure
for head lice.**
From Red Deer, Alberta.

26. **He's got rooms for rent upstairs.**
This saying has a British equivalent: "He's an
apartment to let."

27. **I see eggshells; I can guess eggs.**
This implies the speaker is not stupid. From Prince
Edward Island.

28. **Talking to him is like pissing in the wind and
trying not to get wet.**
That is, he's stupid, and so are you for trying to
talk to him.

29. **That explains the milk in the coconut.**
Said upon hearing an explanation of something
complicated. This is a sly pretence of stupidity on
the part of the one who speaks this line.

30. **Were you born in a barn?**
Said to someone who foolishly leaves a door open.

31. **Green as duckweed.**
Foolish, but approaching stupidity.

32. **His driveway doesn't go all the way to the road.**

75. SURPRISE

1. **There he stood, winkin' and blinkin' like a toad under a spike-toothed harrow.**
From Aylesford, Nova Scotia.

2. **If that don't bang all!**

3. **I've been around the Horn.**
That is, nothing surprises me; I've had plenty of experience in life, the equivalent of sailing around Cape Horn. E. C. Lougheed contributed 2 and 3.

76. TEA

1. **The tea is strong enough to trot a mouse on.**
This phrase indicates the point at which certain English persons think tea has been brewed to sufficient potency and is fit to drink. Contributed by Peter Polley, a teacher at York Mills Collegiate Institute, and picked up from his English grandmother.

77. TEETH

1. **Whole family's got buck teeth. Great grandfather musta jumped a beaver.**

2. **Buck teeth! She could eat an apple through a tennis racket.**

3. **Buck teeth? Only man I ever met could eat grass through a picket fence.**

4. **Buck teeth? Only guy I ever saw could eat a tomato through a tennis racquet.**
Contributed by Lew Gloin.

5. **He had a set of teeth, would make a bucksaw sing with envy.**

1. **Holding on like a puppy to a root.**

78. TENACITY

1. **I had one but the wheels fell off.**
Said when asked about an object of which one is ignorant.

79. THINGAMAJIGS

2. **A silver know-nothing with a whistle on top.**

3. **Handy as a pocket on a shirt.**
Said of a clever, new device.

"I had one but the wheels fell off."

80. THINKING

1. **That girl's bright as a head of cabbage in a pumpkin field.**

2. *Être une tête à Papineau* literally 'to be a Papineau head.'
   A Québécois folk saying that means to be smart as a whip, very clever indeed, recalls one of the heroes of French Canadian history. Joseph Louis Papineau (1786–1871) led a group of radical reformers in Lower Canada. Their grievances against the government of the day came to a head in the Rebellion of 1837, fomented by Papineau in Lower Canada and William Lyon Mackenzie in Upper Canada.

3. *Vous vous faites aller la marde de tête.*
   You are concentrating really hard, literally 'you are going to pass a "brain" turd.'

81. THINNESS

1. **She hasn't enough ass on her to keep your balls out of the sand.**

2. **He's so thin his pyjamas only got one stripe.**

3. **He's so thin if he took a dose of salts, why, we could watch it work.**

4. **She's so thin, she has to run around the shower to get wet.**

5. **He's so thin, he has to stand in the same place twice, just to make a good shadow.**

6. Of a very thin bride: **Poor dear, she's so thin he'll have to shake the sheets to find her tonight.**

7. **He's so skinny, if he turned sideways holding a glass of tomato juice, he'd look like a thermometer.**

8. **Thin? I've seen more meat on a hockey stick.**

9. **He's finer than frog hair.**

1. **Cruisin' for a bruisin'.**
   Once in high school gym class I asked the instructor, whom I shall call Lou Gronk, about the value to my intellectual development of vaulting repeatedly over a gym horse. Puzzled, Gronk stared at me. So I acted out my question with sock puppets and soon understanding spread across the lunar surface of puck dents that comprised Gronk's face. Finally his steroidal foghorn of a voice boomed in the gym, "Casselman, you're cruisin' for a bruisin'." Herewith some alternate bullyings that yahoos may wish to caterwaul at underlings:

82. THREATS

"I'll hit you so hard you'll starve to death bouncin'."

2. **Achin' for a breakin'.**

3. **Aimin' for a maimin'.**

4. **Hurtin' for certain.**

5. **Do it again, and I'll slap you bald-headed.**

6. **I'll hit you so hard you'll starve to death bouncin'.**

7. **I'll pull a leg off you and spank you with it.**

8. **I'll give you what Paddy gave the drum.**
   Namely, a damn good beating. Possibly of Irish origin.

1. **Ugly? Looks like a dog's arse sewn up with a logging chain.**
   Contributed by Teresa Sinkowski, Waterford, Ontario.

83. UGLINESS

2. **Ugly as a bouquet of smashed assholes.**

3. Variant of 2: **Homely as a cartload of fannies.**

4. **Uglier than 40 acres of burning stumps.**
From Northumberland County, Ontario.

5. **She fell out of the ugly tree, and on the way down hit every branch.**

6. **Homely as a hedge fence.**
Contributed by Carol Aubé, Barrie, Ontario.

7. **Got a face like a ripple in a swill bucket.**

8. **He's so ugly that, when he was born, the doctor slapped his mother.**

9. *Laid comme un pichou.*
Pichou 'lynx' in Québec French also means the soft grey moccasins used with snowshoes. A face looking like a blackened, oft-wetted and dried *pichou* would qualify as ugly. Contributed by Jean Paré, Outremont, Québec.

"If I had a face like that, I'd shave my ass and walk backwards."

10. **If I had a face like that, I'd shave my ass and walk backwards.**

11. **She looked like a professional blind date.**

12. **She was ugly when I met her in the beverage room, but I drunk her pretty.**

13. **He's so ugly, when he looks in a mirror, it fogs itself over.**

14. **He looks like the back of a hack.**
The backboards of a hackney coach were often mud-spattered from the unpaved streets of the nineteenth century and frequently bedaubed with horse manure.

15. **He's so ugly he has to slap his feet to make them go to bed with him.**

16. **I could shave my dog's arse and teach it to walk backwards, and still look better than you.**
Variant of 10.

17. **Ugly? Looks like he came third in an axe fight.**
From Red Deer, Alberta.

84. UNPLEASANTNESS

1. **Don't change. I want to forget you as you are.**

2. **She's a hurricane on a ten-cent piece.**

3. **Livin' with him's about as much fun as having a shit hemorrhage in a hurricane.**
Medical literature is silent about the dread malady here christened "shit hemorrhage" which I first heard in my native Ontario county of Haldimand. But folk descriptions of infectious mishaps often have their own humour. Doreen Andreson writes to tell me about the old fellow in rural Manitoba who didn't have much education, but was just as concerned as you or I would be after a visit to his physician: "Doc says I got the diarrhea in my teeth, and it went all down through my cistern."

4. **Meaner than a junkyard dog with 14 suckin' pups.**

85. UNTIDINESS

1. **He looks like he threw his clothes in the air, and ran under 'em.**

2. **She looks like she just spent a month in her 18-hour bra.**

3. **She dresses like a sow with side pockets.**

4. **Dressed up like a sore finger.**

5. Looks like he's been chewin' tobacco and spittin' down wind.

86. UTILITY

1. That's about as much use as a white bean in a black cat's ass.

87. VARIOUS CONDITIONS

1. **Long as a sleigh track.**
    This Canadian simile has regional variants such as one from Prince Edward Island: "as straight as a sleigh track on the Western Road" quoted in Pratt's *Dictionary of Prince Edward Island English.*

2. **Jealous as two undertakers in a one-hearse town.**

3. *Rare comme d'la marde de pape.*
    Quite rare, literally 'costly as it might be to purchase the pope's excrement.'

4. **Subtle as hollyhocks around an outhouse.**

5. **Smooth as a butterfly's belly.**

6. **Rough as a corduroy road.**
    Pretty bumpy, like some Canadian pioneer roads made of logs laid transversely across a roadbed.

7. **As out of place as a brass doorknob on a pig pen.**
    Heard around Irma, Alberta.

8. **Don't look down; you'd find the hole soon enough if there was hair around it!**
    A Canadian (originally British) army drill-instructor's command to recruits learning to fix their bayonets without casting a downward glance.

88. VOMITING

1. **To make a call on the porcelain telephone.**
   This is a synonym for vomiting into the toilet bowl.

2. **To reconsider breakfast.**
   An Ontario summer camp euphemism for the verb "to vomit."

3. **To York.**
   This has been playfully suggested as the perfect Toronto synonym for the verb to vomit. Many of the synonyms for vomit arise from imitating the sound of vomition, e.g., barf, cack, puke, ralph, and retch.

4. **To defood.**
   A bit of euphemistic gobbledygook that avoids the unpleasant sound of vomit.

89. WEAKNESS

1. **He's so weak he couldn't put a dent in a pound of butter.**

2. **Poor dear was so weak she couldn't pull the skin off a rice pudding.**

3. **He's so weak he couldn't pull his finger out of a lard pail.**

90. WEATHER

1. **That wind is strong enough to blow the nuts off a gang plough.**
   Said of a Saskatchewan storm.

2. **The wind is blowin' and it's too lazy to go around you.**

3. **It's storming so bad, the birds are walkin'.**

4. **It was so windy, my hen laid the same egg twice.**

5. **It's a cold wind to calf your ass up against.**

6. **Colder than a well-digger's knee.**

7. **The old woman is pluckin' her geese today.**
Said of a fluffy snowfall. R. M. Lawson was told this one by a great grandmother who owned a general store in Burford, Ontario. She had heard it first in 1889. But, interestingly, this is a direct translation of a Ukrainian folk saying that also shows up in Manitoba earlier in the century.

8. **It's colder than a witch's tit in a cast iron bra.**

9. **Snappin' cold.** This refers to the way trees snap in subzero temperatures. Contributed by Marjorie Andrews, Bethany, Ontario.

10. **It's damper than duck dung.**
Said of Vancouver weather.

11. **It's drier than a popcorn fart.**
Said of a hot summer in Alberta.

Canadian weather

12. **Water's flatter 'n a plate of puppy pee.**
British Columbia boaters' slang. Newfoundland slang has the zippier variant 'flatter 'n a plate of piss.'

13. *Le diable est aux vaches.*
'The devil's in the cows.' In Québec, it means the weather will change soon.

14. **There's a circus around the moon.**
Said of a lunar halo.

15. **Hot as a June bride in a feather bed.**

16. **It's hotter than the hubs of Hades.**

17. *Le temps a viré comme une anse de cruche* 'the weather's turned like the handle on a jug.'

18. **Cold as the icicle on a polar bear's dick.**

19. **Blowin' a gagger.**
Ontario expression to describe a north wind
blowing south off Georgian Bay. Contributed by
E. C. Lougheed.

20. **The sun is splitting trees.**
That is, it's hot! From Prince Edward Island.

21. **It's a poor day to set a hen.**
Said humorously during a violent storm. From
Prince Edward Island.

91. WELCOME

1. **Welcome as a turd in a punch bowl.**

2. *Reçu comme un chien dans un jeu de quilles*
'welcome as a dog in a bowling alley.'

92. WORK

1. **She's so lazy you'd have to put a stake beside
her to see if she's moving.**
Contributed by Marjorie Andrews.

2. **The best fertilizer for the soil is the farmer's
footprints.**

3. **You can't live on the wind and roost on the
clothesline all of the time.**
Collected by Martha Jackson of Toronto. It was
said in rebuke to children who complained of
doing chores on the farm.

4. **He works harder than a dog under a covered
wagon.**
During the settling of the prairies, homesteading
drylanders drove covered wagons along trails. The
wiser dogs raced alongside in the shadow cast by
the brown tarp covering the wagon. It was cooler

there than in full sun, and dogs could run farther without tiring.

5.   **He's always puttin' things off. Why, he didn't get a birthmark until he was seven.**

6.   **I could jump down any shaft you ever dug, and not even break my ankle.**
From gold mining slang in Timmins, Ontario, when a shaftman is bragging how well he digs.

7.   **Tired? If my arsehole drags any lower, I'll have to stick it in the cuff of my pants.**

8.   **I'm sweating like a hen drawing rails.**

9.   Variant of 8: **Hotter than a hen drawing rails in July.**

10.   **Harder than pushing your truck uphill with a rope.**
8, 9, &10 were submitted by Don Shanahan of Brighton, Ontario.

11.   **A new broom sweeps clean, but it takes an old one to get in the corners.**

12.   **I was picking shit in the hen house with a wooden beak.**
Said of any messy chore. 11 & 12 from Teresa & Jerry Sinkowski of Waterford, Ontario. E. C. Lougheed of Guelph, Ontario sent this variant to describe tedious labour: **Might as well get a tin beak and pick corn with the hens.**

13.   **He could put a wooden arse on a cat.**
Said of someone who is handy.

14.   **Busy as a hound covering turds in long grass.**

15.   **As busy as a one-armed paperhanger with hives.**

Western work.

16. **Who will lift the cat's tail, if the cat won't?**
This is a direct translation from Finnish, and is still heard among descendants of immigrants from Finland in northern Ontario.

17. **A man who watches the clock remains one of the hands.**

18. **He could work all day in a bushel basket and still have room to move.**

19. **Advice to the lazy: donkeys go best loaded.**

20. *Avoir le trou de cul en dessus du bras* 'to have your ass under your arm,' that is, to be dead-tired.

21. *Être comme une queue de veau* 'to be as busy as a calf's tail.'

22. **That's as easy as stuffing soft shit up a wild cat's ass with the narrow end of a toothpick.**

23. **He doesn't ride the day he saddles.**
A translation from Danish, this is said of one who procrastinates.

24. *Avoir les deux pieds dans la même bottine* 'to have both feet in one boot,' that is, to be lazy, to have no get-up-and-go.

25. **Busier than a bee in a vacuum cleaner.**

26. **Come a horny onto her!**
From Nova Scotia's South Shore, this saying means 'to give something your best effort.' Contributed by Catherine Hiltz of Bridgewater, Nova Scotia.

Office work.

27. **I can't piss and fart, and draw the cart, all at once!**
This reply is given when a person already busy is asked to do something more. It was heard in the Star City area of Saskatchewan among homesteaders who had come north from Nebraska, and was contributed by Margarita Hill of Prince Albert, Saskatchewan.

28. **Even if it's only the breath of your arse, do it well.**
Advice to a young man starting his first job.

29. **Never say "whoa" in a bad spot.**

30. **She's busier than a two-headed cat in a creamery.**
From Three Hills, Alberta.

31. **You'll soon see the rabbit.**
This Prince Edward Island folk saying implies that work is almost completed. When you cut hay beginning at the perimeter of a field, a rabbit in that field will run toward the centre. When there is no cover left, the rabbit bolts. This is T. K. Pratt's explanation in his *Dictionary of Prince Edward Island English*.

32. **You could ride to Halifax on that blade.**
This workaday saying is said in eastern Canada of a dull knife, a scythe, or any other bladed farm implement.

93. THE END

1. **It's just like wiping your ass with a hoop. There's no end to it.**

2. Marjorie Andrews recalls a neighbour named Old Jack who always said, when the final whistle had ended a Saturday night hockey game on radio or TV, **"It's all over, Mary; pull down your dress."**

CHAPTER FOUR

NEIGHBOURHOOD WORDS ACROSS CANADA

n 1860, the Colony of Vancouver Island opened the second session of its Assembly amid a cluster of new public buildings erected the year before on the south side of Victoria harbour. The edifices featured fancy brickwork and pagoda-like roofs whose shape reminded residents of a then popular cage of pet birds. For the next thirty years, the nickname of the government buildings was The Birdcages. The soubriquet lasted until 1893 when construction began on a new government complex that in its turn was nicknamed The Marble Palace.

In the final fifteen years of the last century, Vancouver's Richards Street and Georgia Street were lined with the mansions of plutocrats who had grown rich in the Vancouver boom. In 1893 a U.S. financial crisis spread north. Capital for new investments dried up. So many loggers were out of work that the next year, 1894, Canada's first Labour party was launched on the coast. Mortgages on the palatial residences along Richards and Georgia were foreclosed, and the formerly ritzy section of the town slumped into a five-year recession, earning a new nickname, Blue-Blood Alley.

VICTORIA
THE BIRDCAGES & THE MARBLE PALACE

VANCOUVER
BLUE-BLOOD ALLEY

BROLLYWOOD .

American film crews love Vancouver for the excellent local movie-making facilities, good crews, and the Canadian film union rates, cheap compared to Hollywood. Some U.S. movie types call British Columbia and Vancouver "Mexico North." Of course, these wanderers from the Californian deserts do sometimes bitch about rain and changeable weather in the Lower Mainland of British Columbia. A comic place name thereto appertaining was coined in 1994 by Jim Sutherland, editor of *Vancouver* magazine: Brollywood. Come up and film; just bring your umbrella, or, as some Brits say, your brolly.

HALLELUJAH POINT

This spot near the collection of totem poles in Vancouver's Stanley Park was named after Salvation Army revival meetings held in this pleasant setting for many years. Stanley Park, named after an early Governor-General of British Columbia, Lord Stanley, actually began long before B.C. entered Confederation, when bigwigs in the Royal British Navy, fretful about the possibility of any future dust-ups with pesky Yankees from the south who had been complaining about the manifest destiny of Oregon and Washington territory to be part of the United States (it was manifest, was it not?) looked at the 1,000 acres of land on Burrard Inlet and reserved it for military use. In 1886, the first meeting of Vancouver City Council passed a resolution to open the land as a public park.

KITSCHILANO

The Kitsilano area of Vancouver starts roughly near Kits Beach and runs along the south shore of English Bay out towards the campus of the University of British Columbia on Point Grey. Kits extends up to 16th Avenue. Kitsilano was home during the early 1970s to a rainbow of countercultural activities along 4th Avenue: a Greenpeace office, the Divine Light Mission, the Soft Rock Café, and happy hippies, students, and young British Columbians just starting in the work force. John Gray's Kitsilano novel, *Dazzled*, records the flower-power giddiness of those days: 4th Avenue incense shops, love beads, psychedelic posters, a Doors LP

wailing like a stoned banshee from every back porch.
Between 1971 and 1976 more than fifteen hundred
condominium apartments were built in Kitsilano, many
of them handsome low-rise buildings in natural B.C.
wood. During the eighties and nineties, yuppies brought
their Porsches, designer jeans, designer water (Perrier),
and designer lives to Kitsilano to dwell in the most
expensive small bungalows known to Canadian real
estate—but over the years, head shops, health food
stores, used bookstores, and trinket emporia remained
to peddle kitschy ephemera. This may be the origin of a
snobbish and punning nickname for the Kitsilano area:
Kitschilano. Vancouver's somewhat gentrified
Ambleside Park, at the north side of the Lions' Gate
Bridge, is similarly often called Amblesnide. And newspaper cartoonist Len Norris dubbed a pseudo-British
part of West Vancouver Tiddlycove.

The name Kitsilano belonged first to a Squamish
chief *Khahtsahlanogh* who settled in Stanley Park, east
of Prospect Point, around 1860. In the Coast Salish of
his Squamish band, his name means 'spirit man,'
although other experts claim it is 'chief man of our
band.' When around 1913 the Canadian Pacific
Railway decided to make a new housing subdivision of
some land nearby, the chief's name was Englished so it
would rhyme with Capilano across the inlet. In 1913 the
government of British Columbia bought 80 acres near
the mouth of False Creek that had become known as the
Kitsilano Indian Reserve. They intended to make a great
new harbour at False Creek. As for the comic tag,
remember that *Kitschilano* is a pun. As someone who
lived two blocks from Kits Beach for one happy year
(1976), I do not think it is in any way a valid comment
on a wonderfully diverse neighbourhood. But the word
kitsch is worth a comment.

KITSCH

Kitsch began as a simple German noun for shoddy
goods, trash, junk, or flashy gewgaws. One German
verb meaning 'to cheapen' is *verkitschen*. *Kitsch* is also
used in Yiddish with the same meaning. The word *kitsch*
had appeared in English early in the twentieth century,

Nineteenth-century porno-kitsch, in which the visual simile of "fairy wings" pretends to be the topic of a Victorian woodcut.

but it really entered the vocabulary of North American English after becoming a buzz word in art criticism. Its spread in academic discourse can be traced directly to American art critic Clement Greenberg's accurate prophecy in his famous essay "Avant-Garde and Kitsch" printed in the *Partisan Review* in 1939. Greenberg had sensitive antennae, finely tuned to pick up alterations in the artistic Zeitgeist, and he early recognized that, in the twentieth century, high art (e.g., Mondrian's experiments in space and colour) and mass art (the labels on food, plastic toys, advertisements) were distinct but—the wily prediction—destined to influence each other profoundly.

Mass art is trashy but has vulgar *élan*. One thinks of Noel Coward's remark about "the potency of cheap music." The artist can make the art objects he creates partake of this kitschy street energy by borrowing it. The artist picks up a used egg carton, sprays it orange, and glues it to his latest construction, which also contains a plastic birdcage, a Dinky toy, a doorbell that does not ring, and a whalebone corset with most of the stays missing. Kitsch is sometimes defined by this separation of form from original function. The egg carton has its dull, daily usefulness as an object that holds and protects eggs and then is tossed into the paper-recycling bin. But now, glued to an art work, the piece—as kitsch—gives off new visual and semantic vibrations as part of a campy construction. "It's good because it's awful," wrote Susan Sontag in "Notes on 'Camp'" in her book *Against Interpretation*. We admit the garish or sentimental crappiness of the original object; at the same time we enjoy its very kitschiness. In less formal criticism of popular art, kitsch is still used in its original German sense to mean 'low-brow junk of poor quality': for example, "That painting of a bullfighter on black velvet is pure kitsch."

SKIDROAD

Skidroad and its later variant skid row come from west coast lumbering slang. The first Skid Road in Canada was in Vancouver in an area presently bounded by Carrall and Cordova Streets. From there the term spread across Canada as the designation of any slummy part of a city or town populated by rubbies and winos. In Vancouver's early days, the area was the terminus of an actual skidroad, a slideway used to drag logs to water or to railway track for transport to a lumber mill.

A skidroad was a specialized kind of corduroy road. Skids were peeled and greased logs, laid transversely across a cleared pathway, so that teams of oxen, horses, or mules could haul rough timber down them. In the first B.C. lumber camps the grease used was frequently dogfish oil. The men who built such logging trails were called skidders and so were the teamsters who drove the horses. Later on, when motorized vehicles replaced horses and mules, the phrase "skidder tractor" appeared.

How was skidroad altered to Skid Row? Unemployed loggers often gathered at the end of these trails to ask a boss for work. When no jobs were available, it was time for a little logging R & R. In Vancouver and in Seattle, this involved booze, broads, and brothels to which gambling was soon added. Then came cheap lodging houses for the out-of-work loggers, rough hiring halls, beer parlours, mission soup kitchens, and an influx of transients, derelicts, and petty criminals. The apex for a time in Vancouver was Water Street with its rows of saloons and flophouses. Canada can stake a claim to this second Skid Road, but not the first one. That was a street called Yesler's Way in Seattle, Washington, constructed in 1852. When coastal stands of lumber were depleted and logging operations moved inland, the name Skid Road stuck, and was soon altered by folk etymology to Skid Row. "On skid row" became synonymous with down-and-out.

From Canadian lumbering slang sprang several verb phrases:

- to hit the skids   'to be broke or unemployed, to fail utterly'
- to grease the skids   'to make things easier'
- to pull the skids out from under   'to cause to decline, to abandon support for'
- to put the skids under 'to topple, to cause to fail'

Skid is one of the words borrowed into Old English during the Viking raids and settlements toward the end of the first millennium. Old Norse, now also called Old Scandinavian, had *skith* 'stick of wood.' The same root gave us 'ski,' a specialized stick of wood.

CALGARY
EAU CLAIRE

This part of Calgary, with many high rises and condos, lies between the Bow River and the big buildings of commerce. Its name derives from a turn-of-the-century Eau Claire Lumber Company, which milled logs at the site.

ROULEAUVILLE

This was a French part of Calgary, annexed by the city in 1907, and rechristened with the spiffy name Cliff Bungalo! The city is currently building a park in the district which will be named Rouleauville Park in memory of the city's small but proud French heritage.

SCOTCHMAN'S HILL

From this Calgary lookout at Salisbury and 6th Street, one gets a superb vista of foothills, Calgary's city core, the Saddledome, and the Calgary Stampede grounds. Scotchman's Hill is one of the best spots to view the fireworks set off during Stampede celebrations. The name arose because cheapskates can watch many of the Stampede activities from the hill for free, instead of paying admission. Och, it's a wee libel against the inherent generosity of the true Scot, would you not say then?

EDMONTON

Bruce Ibsen at the city archives in Edmonton offered us these neighbourhood words, all except Edmonchuk, which we heard ourselves as a politically incorrect reminder of the great contribution that Canadians of Ukrainian origin have made to the city and to the province of Alberta. Edmonchuk can be used as a racist sneer, true; but I have heard it playfully tossed back into a smug, waspy face by a Ukrainian-Canadian with a big laugh. Sometimes the knife wielded in a verbal chop can nick the speaker too! The city, once centre of the western fur trade, was named Fort Edmonton by a clerk in the local Hudson's Bay Company post, who dubbed it so in memory of his birthplace, Edmonton (Edmond's town), now part of London, England.

DOG PATCH

Now known as Riverdale from its site in the valley of the North Saskatchewan River, Dog Patch is an older community of small, gentrified houses. Once, however, as heart of the downtown it received poor newcomers who may have reminded luckier residents of the mythical community of Dog Patch where cartoonist Al Capp's L'il Abner dwelt—a hamlet composed of hicks, rubes, and rural innocents. Dog Patch's small homes were subject to flood damage in early days. Also in the river valley area is Rossdale, known as The Flats.

PACKINGTOWN

This district once had four meat-packing plants. The nickname is passing out of existence as the neighbourhood improves, even to a Spanish rechristening as Santa Rosa.

The stylish, yuppie area of Edmonton now called Lavine used to be called Skunk Hollow, presumably because it is near the river and was therefore attractive to skunks. Edmonton too has a Knob Hill in the residential neighbourhood of Rutherford on the east side of Mill Creek overlooking the downtown. The park area of Cannard Ravine is Rat Creek. An underground tunnel on 109th Street is universally dubbed The Rat Hole.

WINNIPEG

The sometimes cold centre of this windy city is Portage and Main and is often nicknamed Portage and Pain. At the corner of Corydon and Osbourne in "the Peg" several roads intersect causing great confusion for bus drivers and pedestrians, and earning the crossroads the moniker "Crazy Corners." The Granola Belt of Winnipeg along Wolseley and in Osbourne Village was home to hippies and vagrants in the sixties and early seventies, but now it is yuppified and waspy. The Forks of the Red and Assiniboine Rivers where local settlement began are a must-see part of Winnipeg with museums and markets and pleasant walkways along the riverbanks.

TORONTO

The rest of Canada loves to loathe T.O. Was it dubbed Hogtown due to a slather of piggeries and meat packing plants makin' bacon, or—as invidious non-Torontonians claim—because Toronto hogs everything for itself? No one knows. Due to pioneer bad roads, it certainly was Muddy York when Upper Canada's first Governor-General, John Graves Simcoe, laid out a little hamlet in 1793 by the harbour and called it York. The city was incorporated as Toronto in 1834. Now some residents say *Trawnuh*. As early as 1898 its Methodist piety and Anglican reserve earned it the nickname Toronto the Good. A vast block of the original site, some 251,000 acres from the Scarborough Bluffs west, had been purchased from the Mississauga people for 10 shillings, giving early credence to its reputation as a community of sharp dealers. The Wendat (Huron) place name Toronto was first applied to what is today Port Hope. Toronto probably means 'meeting place' in Wendat, because it was the trail-head for a land-and-canoe route that aboriginal peoples used to get from Lake Ontario up to Lake Huron. Explorer Étienne Brûlé knew this trail as *Le passage de Terounto* in 1615. The first buildings were called Fort Rouillé, burned down in 1759. Its ruins were excavated on the present site of the Canadian National Exhibition on Toronto's lakeshore.

AGINCOURT

This suburban sprawl of what was once farmland north of Toronto was named after the place of a famous battle in northern France. In 1415 Henry V's longbowmen trounced a French army, allowing Henry to lay claim to the French throne. The French town bears an early Teutonic warrior name, probably *Hakenkurz* 'Short Blade' modified by French folk etymology, helped by the fact that the German adjective for 'short' *kurz* is related to the French court, and both derive from the Latin *cohors, cohortis* whose ultimate meaning is something enclosed like a garden, Latin *hortus*. That was the original meaning of court in English, and all the many related words we now use like courtesy, courtesan, and curtsy. The Roman army divided a camp up into areas, named after farm enclosures, *cohortes*. A fellow soldier sharing the same enclosure was your cohort.

Agincourt may also be a pure place name in early French like *Agincortis* 'feudal estate whose symbol is the blade of a sword' with the medieval Latin *cortis* 'estate, domain, town' and *agin*, a French diminutive of *ac* 'sharp edge.'

The Agincourt near Toronto now has an influx of Oriental Canadians and sometimes gets the ugly label Asiancourt. But racist putdowns often lose their taint and take on new, purged meanings—as Toronto's Cabbagetown has done.

BLOOR STREET

Trendy, toney, and expensive shops line Bloor Street west of Yonge in Toronto. It's called the Mink Mile. A few blocks west is my favourite Toronto place nickname: a block of Hungarian restaurants that students from the nearby University of Toronto dubbed The Goulash Archipelago in the late eighties. An older tag was the Schnitzel Strip. Not to be confused with The Strip, which is Yonge Street's sleazy pin-ball haven between Gerrard and Dundas Streets. And don't confuse Toronto's Mink Mile with the Miracle Mile, which is cabbies' slang for a stretch of Danforth Avenue from Victoria Park to Coxwell, so named because, if cab drivers time their speed just right, they can get green lights for many blocks.

CABBAGETOWN

From 1860 to 1880 poor immigrants from Ireland and England lived in small garden lots in central Toronto. They grew cabbages and boiled them to eat, giving the area an aroma and a nickname. A perusal of old deeds makes clear that there were far more British newcomers than Irish ones in the first Cabbagetown. The greatest concentration of poor Irish was further south in an area of Toronto once but no longer called Corktown.

Between the two world wars, Cabbagetown became a slum. One native who wrote about working-class lives there was Hugh Garner—his novel *Cabbagetown* was published in 1950. Canadian painter Albert Franck put on canvas many scenes from Cabbagetown backyards and alleys during his career. Then, in the 1960s and 1970s, yuppie white-painters moved in and renovated with a passion, boosting real estate prices in the neighbourhood and changing forever the aura of the word *Cabbagetown*. Some urban professionals who work in the high-rise canyons of Bay Street live here and chuckle at their cohorts who must endure long traffic jams every morning as they drive in from the suburbs. Cabbagetowners can stroll to the office, hop a bus, or take a subway to work.

THE GAY GHETTO

Toronto's most visible gay community is centred at the intersection of Church and Wellesley Streets. Even gay residents call it The Fruit Basket. There is a schmoozing and cruising zone outside the nearby Second Cup café called The Steps. Just east is the Track, where prostitutes of all sexes ply their trade. Just southwest is Trac II or Boys' Town where the johns and their pickups are gay males.

OTHER T.O. NICKNAMES

Ryerson Polytechnic University in central Toronto is widely ribbed as Rye High. York University's chilly setting further north is The Tundra, while the University of Toronto's controversial Robarts Library building looks to many students like the place where Arnold Schwarzenegger's *Terminator* would live, had he been a medieval prince. The library has accumulated labels like Fort Book, The John, and Robo-Monster.

Parkdale in Toronto's west end has been christened Perkdale, because the prostitution and street drug trade once made Percodan pills a common medium of exchange.

A few streetcorners in T.O. have playful, alternative names. Young business people thronging Yonge and Eglinton earn this yuppie crossroads the title of Yonge and Eligible. Queen and Roncesvalles in Parkdale is a hangout for prostitutes, so it's Queen and Raunchy. The most notorious road in Toronto for motorists is the D.V.P., the Don Valley Parkway, but widely known as the Death Valley Parkway, due to traffic fatalities and many serious vehicle accidents.

SCARBOROUGH

Now a city, once Toronto's largest borough, Scarborough was dubbed Scarberia in the late 1950s because snobbish downtowners thought of it as a distant barrenland of new housing divisions and no class. Like some other neighbourhood names, its latest nicknames are racist. New Canadians of Caribbean origin in some numbers are moving out of the inner city and into the suburbs of the Torontonian megalopolis, thus one hears anti-Black nicknames like Scarbados and Scarlem, punning on Barbados and Harlem. But the original name was no lovely moniker either. Scarborough means *Harelip's Fort*, a fact no doubt unknown to Elizabeth Simcoe, wife of Upper Canada's first Governor-General, John Graves Simcoe, when she named the village because the local bluffs reminded her of cliffs near the town of Scarborough in Yorkshire. Scarborough in England was a Viking settlement. A Norse saga recorded that one Thorgils Skarthi founded the North Yorkshire settlement around 965 A.D. Viking warriors liked frightening and repellant names. *Skarthi* meant 'harelip' in Old Norse. In Old English the settlement became *Skaresborg* 'Harelip's Fort.'

OTTAWA

Minor fur-trading spots, at which French trappers exchanged goods with Algonkian peoples were the first settlements at our capital, Ottawa. In 1800, a small farming community, Wrightsville, was established on the site of the present-day Hull. The first unofficial name in English of the settlement was Rideau Canal. In 1826, Lt. Col. John By of the Royal Engineers, a town planner and administrator, having supervised the construction of the canal, established and managed Bytown, which later took the Englished version of the name of the Odawa 'traders' people.

GLADSTONE STREET

Some Ottawa bus drivers call it Happy Rock. The street was named for William Ewart Gladstone, a Prime Minister of England.

MECHANICSVILLE

The name of this area in northwest Ottawa derives from railroad maintenance crews who first formed the community. It was based around a CP Rail roundhouse in which mechanics repaired locomotives. Later the city of Ottawa operated an industrial garage there to fix heavy road-making machines. In the early 1960s and 1970s Mechanicsville was rezoned for apartments and government buildings. This rezoning was part of an urban renewal scheme that saw the replacement of small, older houses with high-rises and office towers. A group of concerned residents, "Action Mechanicsville," formed to try to preserve the neighbuorhood's character. It is now known as Hintonburg.

ROCKCLIFFE

Rockcliffe Park, where the highest-paid civil servants, deputy ministers, and assorted upper crust of Ottawa dwell in splendour, received its name from one early house built in 1835 by Duncan Rynier MacNab who called it Rockcliffe after a beloved childhood haunt in Scotland. The original edifice was a Regency-style freestone cottage with verandahs, to which many additions were later made. In 1928 the building was completely rebuilt in the French Directoire style. One of Ottawa's humorous neighbourhood nicknames belongs to Manor Park in the northeast of the city. *Rookie Rockcliffe* supposedly describes the aspirations of its upper-middle-class residents.

FREDERICTON

The Green is a spacious scroll of lawn stretching along the Saint John River where residents of Fredericton have ambled, taken the air, and lolled on the grass to sunbathe for more than a hundred years. In days of yore, band concerts and riverboat excursions began here as well. Spritzing happily in front of City Hall, and a common meeting spot, is Freddie the Fountain, more recently dubbed Little Nude Dude.

FICKLE FINGER OF FATE

This is one nickname for a well-known former landmark of the city, a 4-metres-long hand pointing straight up to heaven, which once adorned the steeple-tip of Wilmot United Church. It had to be taken down for safety reasons, but is on display inside the church. Members of the early British garrison in Fredericton called it Thumbs Up and many residents made appointments to meet one another in the shadow of The Finger.

HALIFAX

Known in the argot of the Royal Canadian Navy as Slackers, Halifax was so dubbed because of slack time during shore-leave granted when ships are in port. The area around Brunswick and Gottingen Streets is Dutchtown, because of early German immigrants. In the mid-eighteenth century it was the German Mission. Dutch is an illiterate clerk's misspelling of *Deutsch*. One neighbourhood nickname that remains in use is Dutch Village, on the outskirts of Halifax. Haligonians colourfully nickname local buildings as well. The site of the old Churchfield barracks on Brunswick Street near the corner of Cogswell is the Twelve Apostles. They are twelve attached barracks for married soldiers built on the old army cantonment model. Still standing, they are now privately owned. Summit Place next to Sackville Landing is a squat, green-glass edifice waggishly known as The Green Toad. It was the Kodak building until leaders of the G-7 Summit held meetings there one weekend. And there is the notorious Liquordome where five loud pick-up bars are all connected together so the bleary searcher after sex can wander from one pie-eyed emporium of plonk to another, getting only his whistle wet. Still controversial is the obliteration of Africville, once home to a small community of African Nova Scotians. Africville was expropriated and the residents removed by force to create SeaView Park and the McKay Bridge and its overpasses and underpasses. My thanks for these notes go to Lou Collins, the honorary civic historian of Halifax.

CHARLOTTETOWN

The central block of downtown Charlottetown, bounded by Grafton Street, University Avenue, Kent, and Queen Street has been called the Dizzie Block for many years. Is it because it was once the only block of buildings in town worth circumambulating, and hence the walker-around became dizzy after repeated circlings? Or, is it because the block is so small that walking around it even once very fast would make one dizzy? Charlottetown now has many pleasant venues and vistas, and is still the friendliest capital in Canada, whether one is strolling, zipping about in one's Bimmer, or being borne high in a gold-lamé litter by six giant Nubians. Actually, I wouldn't try that last one in Charlottetown if I were you, especially if you "come from away."

ST. JOHN'S

We could speak of many colourful neighbourhood names, both current and historical, like The Cribbies, Maggoty Cove, and Tarahan's Town, but we shall quit this little tour at an appropriate place, the highest point of Signal Hill, in fact, the highest point of St. John's, called Ladies' Lookout, either because sailors' wives climbed to the spot to look out anxiously for their husbands' ships making home for the harbour, or because sailors and soldiers liked to "walk out" with their ladies fair to take the breeze of a gentle evening long ago.

CHAPTER FIVE

THE CANADIAN NATIONAL MUSEUM OF BAFFLEGAB & GOBBLEDY-GOOK

elcome! Or, as one might say in pure gobbledygook: interface with me in an optimally prioritized, decisional residuum encompassing positively impacted, person-focused cognition and collaborative integration. Now shake my hand and come in.

What is gobbledygook? It is language expressed to deceive, not to communicate. The Pacific Seafood Processors Association told the *Vancouver Sun* (Dec. 7, 1988) about their "bycatch." It looks and sounds like a fisherman's honest and sturdy term. It refers to thousands of seabirds, seals, dolphins, whales, and sea lions who die strangled in ocean driftnets set to catch surface-swimming squid.

A medical services coordinator for a fire department in Canada reported that emergency personnel had found a victim "in a non-viable condition—he had no pulse and was not breathing." Well now, Mr. Coordinator—can I call you Lem?—that'd be—what?— dang near ready fer a white nightie and little wings? Leastways, tuggin' at the Grim Reaper's hem, eh? I mean, you git a citizen up there in the higher realms of non-viability, you're talkin'—the buzzards are circlin',

Two worthies attend a non-viability demo.

right? I think what you're sayin', Lem, is this dude was rapidly approaching non-dudedom. Bone-yardwise, ready to be planted. Would I be close? Lem, seriously now and all kiddin' towards one side, could this guy be—dead?

Gobbledygook is language spoken or written to evade responsibility, not to answer a question but to defuse it by coating the answer in a syrup of verbal glop. Acid rain in Canada becomes "atmospheric deposition of anthropogenetically-derived acidic substances." Such language means to suffocate stark fact in a muffling blanket of mumbo-jumbo.

Gobbledygook can be euphemism for the lowest motive. A Canadian funeral parlour is now a "Bereavement Resource Centre." As someone driving by their tasteful, glow-in-the-dark plastic sign wondered, "Gee, do they still take the dead?" A CBC TV interviewer asks a surgeon about the source of a transplanted kidney. "From a cadaveric donor," says the pussyfooting sawbones. If he had not used euphemistic gobbledygook, think how influential this doctor (who had just benefited along with his patient from the process) could have been, by reminding people to sign the donor card on the back of their driver's licence and by stating that spare parts of the newly dead can keep some people alive. But no, he chose not to offend viewers and fudged the source with the rare adjective "cadaveric." Such misdirected gentility makes some want to jump up and yell, "You mean you cut it out of a stiff, eh, Doc?"

MEDICAL TERMS

But gobbledygook in medicine is—one might say—a two-edged scalpel. Most doctors want patients to know as much as the patient can know about a disease the patient may be suffering. With wider access than ever before to on-line medical literature, current and historical, via the Internet and other computer networks, it is not unusual for a patient to present initially in the doctor's office with print-outs of a few journal articles about a suspected malady. Even if the patient has not understood all the technical language in the medical journal or report, the doctor has a basis for corrections to the diagnosis and explanations in everyday language. But that said, a doctor's effective bedside manner is now part of "patient management," which might include hiding distressing terminology from a patient and hovering relatives. This is never done as a matter of course.

CANCER JARGON

Suppose a bedridden person has just been told he has cancer. In the initial days of his adjustment to this fact, his attending physician may have to refer to the cancer and may judge the blunt word too unbearable to repeat in front of his patient. Years ago, a doctor could have used the word "carcinoma" and been reasonably sure most patients would not have known this synonym for cancer. That is not always true today, when public awareness of the major diseases and the vocabulary used to describe them has grown. But medical jargon provides a long list of euphemistic alternatives. Doctors can and do refer to cancer as "the mitosis," "a neoplasm," or "a neoplastic figure." If a cancer has spread to form new foci of disease distant from the original site, they might say "the mitotic incident has metastasized." But plenty of patients know and fear the word "metastasis." So more obscure levels of technical language and circumlocution may have to be plumbed, when the doctor refers to one specific cancer site as a "melanosarcomatous excrescence." In general, however, such technical jargon is not necessary during doctor-patient interchanges. Even in medical literature, one seldom needs to call a black eye "a circumorbital hematoma." On the other hand, as I have shown, there are compassionate reasons for employing gobbledygook now and then in the practice of medicine. See page 109 for a discussion of the legitimacy of specialized medical vocabulary items like cholecystostomy.

ORIGIN OF CANCER

This is a brief detour to explain how English got the words "cancer" and "carcinoma." Both early Greek and Roman physicians used their nouns for *crab* to refer to the disease. *Cancer* means 'crab' in Latin. English

Cancer is the Latin word
for crab.

"canker" and "chancre" derive from that root. Cancer as a crab is one of the signs of the zodiac. The Greek word for crab is *karkinos*. The Roman doctor Galen (A.D. 131–201) like many of the best physicians of the Roman empire was a Greek who wrote in Greek. His writings summarize ancient anatomy and medical procedure, adding new observations based on his own practice. For fourteen hundred years Galen's writings were the authority on medicine in the Christian world. Galen wrote that cancerous veins [sic] extend out from the disease site like the claws of a crab. Another early medical writer claimed that, like a crab, cancer reaches out when it metastasizes and seizes many different parts of the body.

Much earlier than Galen, in the Hippocratic school of ancient medicine, *karkinos* meant 'a non-healing ulcer,' and *karkinoma* was 'a malignant tumour' (a cancer). Carcinoma is the Greek word for crab with the common suffix *-oma* added, which has the medical meaning of benign or malignant tumor or swelling. A few paragraphs back was the medical word "hematoma" from the Greek stem *hemat* 'blood' + the suffix *-oma* to name a swelling composed of clotted blood that has escaped from its vessels and collected in an organ, tissue, or space. Most medical words ending with *-oma* indicate benign tumour or neoplasm.

Hippocrates, often called the father of medicine, was a Greek physician born around 460 B.C. He was famous in his lifetime as a doctor and teacher of medicine at an academy he founded on the Greek island of Cos. His medical writings survive in part, along with papers written later by his own students and by physicians who lived many centuries after him.

The famous Hippocratic oath begins, "I swear by Apollo the physician..." Its most famous principle for the student doctor is now usually quoted in Latin: *primum non nocere*. First, do no harm.

Gobbledygook is language wrapped in twaddling clothes and dying in a manger. It is twaddle because it often does not make sense. It's in a manger of the same straw that packs the heads and hearts of those who use it. And it is dying because it is language drained of vital reference. By obscuring common referents to which the listener or reader can attach everyday meaning, bafflegab hopes to slither off into the underbrush of unmeaning before one realizes what has been said. A bureaucrat from the British Columbia Ministry of Education comes to a school with bad news for its teachers, but never once uses the now context-sensitive word "teacher." Instead, throughout his speech, this evader speaks of "on-site facilitators of pupil learning."

On-site facilitator of pupil learning investigates fisticuffs.

GOOBLEDYGOOK

No surprise is it to learn that this term sprang to the lips of a man who had to listen to politicians blabbing. During World War II, Congressman Maury Maverick of Texas made the word up one day in Washington, D.C., after listening to more verbal bamboozlement than he could abide. In May of 1944 Maverick told the *New York Times* magazine: "Perhaps I was thinking of the old bearded turkey gobbler back in Texas who was always gobbledygobbling and strutting with ludicrous pomposity. At the end of this gobble there was a sort of gook." The new word was so echoic and fitting that it passed immediately into popular speech. The congressman has an interesting last name. Could it be the origin of the word "maverick" to name anyone unorthodox and not part of a group? Yes, the congressman's grandfather was Samuel E. Maverick (1803-1870) who was a Texas rancher and state politician who refused for certain practical reasons to ever brand his stock, vast herds of longhorn cattle. He then playfully claimed that all unbranded range stock might belong to him, following an agricultural precedent of pioneer America that unbranded animals on the open range, not rustled and unclaimed, belonged to whoever first branded them. Texas ranchers took to calling any unbranded cattle that wandered from a herd "mavericks." Then use in Texas politics followed, and a maverick became any politician who would not follow his party's policy line.

THE MUSEUM

Now, pardner, round up them little dogies; keep them varmints away; you got a hard day's writhing ahead, fer it's time to leave the herd behind yuh. Enter now my museum. Forget the "Silence, Please" sign. Loud jeering and catcalls are encouraged.

EXHIBIT 1

A REAL CANADIAN JOB SUBCATEGORY: SNOW

In August, 1987, the Health Sciences Center in Winnipeg placed a Help Wanted ad for a "Co-ordinator, Occurence [sic] Screening, Quality Assurance Department." Uh-huh. Not too assuring a start. The word "occurrence" is misspelled, not once but four times more in the explanation that followed. Help is indeed wanted. But here is the real meat and potatoes of the advertisement, or should I say, the veridical carnal comestibles and solanaceous tuberosities thereof.

The ad reads: "Occurence [sic] screening is an objective, criteria-based review of medical records conducted concurrently and retrospectively to identify and flag, confirm, analyze, trend, and report instances of suboptimal care attributable to health care disciplines. Under the general direction of the Director, Quality Assurance, the incumbent will co-ordinate the development, implementation and maintenance of multidisciplinary and integrated systems of occurence [sic] screening; will assess and review adverse patient occurence [sic] data; will assist with the identification of existing and/or new resources required to conduct occurence [sic] screening."

Now I am a mere medical layman in a state of mystification, but it appears all they want is a clerk to tote up procedural mistakes. But is that the job offered? I will never know, due to the ad's muzzy verbiage. By the way, would death be an adverse patient occurrence? I do want to say something positive. It is assuring to be "under the general direction of the Director"—as long as he's not directing their spelling.

This example and several others in this chapter are drawn from Rick Coe's excellent and unfortunately discontinued "Doublespeak Update" which appeared twice a year (1987–1990) in the academic journal *English*

Quarterly, published by the Canadian Council of
Teachers of English. Mr. Coe is a professor of English
at Simon Fraser University in Burnaby, B.C.

Must gobbledygook always consist of many-syllabled
senselessness? No, often it appears in language plain
and bare. In 1996, Prime Minister Chrétien's Liberal
government brightened hopes of school-leavers with a
"First Jobs" program. Canadian corporations will help
young people get into the work force by hiring them for
one year. As I write this in late April of 1996, final
details are yet to be announced. "First Jobs" emerged
from a brain-storming session with federal Treasury
Board chairman Art Eggleton and the Boston
Consulting Group which then canvassed corporations
for their ideas. Many of these same corporations are in
the process of massive layoffs designed to increase
profit at the expense of Canadian workers. The young
people—really temporary help who can be let go after
one year—are going to be paid near-minimum wages.
What "First Jobs" amounts to is the Liberal government, elected on a promise to create jobs, now giving
sanction and perhaps financial assistance to corporations to fire older, full-time employees working for
higher salaries and replace them with minimum-wage
internships by temporary workers. "First Jobs" is a
weasel term. A more accurate title is "Short,
Meaningless Jobs Designed by the Liberals to Woo
Corporate Canada."

EXHIBIT 2
"FIRST JOBS"
SUBCATEGORY: SNOW

Here is a list of sneaky phrases and wheedling
euphemisms that Canadian public school and high
school teachers use to design computer macros to print
out "personalized" report cards, and to reduce quarrels
on parent interview days. This list or a variation circu-
lates among teachers in Ontario and British Columbia,
and probably by now in other provinces.

EXHIBIT 3
SCHOOL DAYS,
SCHOOL DAYS,
DEAR OLD GOLDEN
FOOL DAYS

Young Nigel depends on others to do his work.

DON'T USE	USE
lazy	can do more when he tries
cheats	depends on others to do his work
below average	working at his own level
steals	borrows without permission
insolent	outspoken
lies	tends to stretch the truth
mean	has difficulty getting along with others
selfish	seldom shares with others
will fail	has a chance of passing if. . .

Remember this sickening list of lies is to be used by teachers who are charged with showing our children the proper use of English. To its credit, the Ontario Ministry of Education included this chart in its 1988 publication *Explorations in Language* and the author, Peter Evans, suggested another use for this list: give it to students for classroom use in learning about euphemism and dishonest language. Good for him! Parents shocked at this bafflegab might consider what they said the last time a teacher offered criticisms of their child.

EXHIBIT 4
PEDAGOGICAL POPPYCOCK

"Little Rupert falls on his head a lot."

Another way to gloss over unpleasant facts in the parent-teacher interview is use by the teacher of the jargon of educational psychology, or the semi-literate tatters of such jargon which have become clichés. Suppose an impertinent mother comes to school and actually is bold enough to want to find out how her child, young Rupert, is really doing, no matter how upsetting a valid assessment may be. If the teacher were versed in educational doublespeak, and spoke in the same language he uses to write report cards, this little scene might ensue:

Mother: How's Rupert doing?

Teacher: The student in question is performing minimally for his peer group and is an emerging underachiever.

Mother: But Rupert's at the bottom of his class. He's a lazy klutz at home. Does he do anything well in school?

Teacher: The student exhibits prowess in manual plastic conception.

Mother: He knocks them dead in clay class? Makes bunnies from Plasticene?

Teacher: Well, I wouldn't put it quite that way. Rupert is also late in group integration and reacts negatively to aggression stimuli.

Mother: Yep, he's always been a loner and a crybaby.

Teacher: And he seems to have developed tardily in magno-muscle control facility.

Mother: Little Rupert falls on his head a lot. But then, so does his father.

There is no body part called a "magno-muscle" in anatomical literature. Utterly unknown to physiology is the concept of magno-muscle control facility. The teacher's English is that of the obfuscator and the liar, afraid to speak plainly because giving offence will upset the parent and take up too much of the teacher's already scarce time, hours that might be spent profitably reviewing more articles in educational journals.

EXHIBIT 5

"WHEN CONSTABULARY DUTY'S TO BE DONE, TO BE DONE"

In 1995, a knife-wielding intruder slipped past those guarding our Prime Minister's residence and penetrated the mansion as far as the Chrétiens' bedroom. Although the trespasser was caught before physical harm came to the Prime Minister and his wife, the RCMP sentinels were lax. This sloppy guarding called forth a paper blizzard of departmental studies. Here is part of one public RCMP document, *Security Breach—24 Sussex Drive. Final Report, 1995-11-17*. One section of this report entitled "Shift Scheduling" begins with basic information: "The members attached to the Prime Minister's/Governor-General's Uniformed Security Detachment work on 12-hour shift rotations consisting of 2 days, 2 nights and 4 days off.... A member rotates from post to post with commensurate breaks depending on resource numbers." Then comes a review of whether or not a 12-hour shift is too long for an individual RCMP guard. Here the reader asks himself how attentive anyone is after doing anything for twelve hours straight. The report continues: "Schedules impact morale and health, as well as operational efficiency. Often the greatest levels of efficiency improvement will result in unacceptable attenuation of 'quality of life' considerations. Hence a schedule that is acceptable to both the workers and the managers will likely consist of a negotiated trade-off and will often be less than maximally efficient. The demarkation of reasonable efficiency ranges that are also consistent with psychological, social and physical health is important. Quality of life [sic] considerations...translate into such issues as minimizing the number of consecutive duty tours in nights, maximizing the number of complete or partial weekends off during the year, and maximizing the predictability of working tours."

In plain English: Do cops get careless, tired, and sick after too many consecutive night shifts? Yes. Just like all the rest of us other human beings who have evolved as day-active mammals designed to sleep at night. But the report's author cannot bring himself to utter such clarity. It might sound like the RCMP was whining. Clear statements about too few guards getting dopey from too long, poorly designed shifts would not be stern, police-like, and mature. But that is the excuse offered in this report for the bad police work.

In order not to make the RCMP sound like a bunch of complaining sucks then, the report puffs itself up with deceptive language: semi-sociological jargon mixed with a stuffy bluster of pseudo-psychological bureaucratese. A gobbet of gobbledygook like "unacceptable attenuation of 'quality of life' considerations" might read on the surface as brisk and concerned, until one pauses to ask what it means. In the context of the paragraph quoted above, it means: put guards on long shifts and they'll get clumsy, inattentive, maybe injured or shot by intruders. Scientific reports in correct English don't make formal mistakes like "unacceptable attenuation of 'quality of life' considerations." When a noun phrase is used as an adjective before another noun, one does not surround it with single quotation marks; one hyphenates the phrase so that it appears like this: quality-of-life considerations. The very act of putting 'quality of life' in single quotations is also a macho dismissal of the phrase—as if to say: I'm putting this in quotes because I'm a big, brave policeman and quality of life is only for weaklings. Yes, it's a tiny point. But little mistake after little mistake sticks in the alert reader's mind, until very early in perusal of the report, the reader sniffs the reek of prose sweat, the stench of English sentences straining to be what they are not.

This prose wants to appear scientific. But it is only a cheap imitation of the general sound of scientific prose, the best of which communicates ideas, reports facts, clearly labels suppositions and hypotheses. This prose's little choo-choo ride towards respect runs off its rails in almost every paragraph. In the passage quoted, notice "demarkation" instead of the much more common Canadian and British and American spelling "demarcation." A quibble? Perhaps, but demarkation is already marked rare in many dictionaries.

Such copy also loves itself. There is a self-congratulatory smugness in the repetition of clichés borrowed from business reports and scientific abstracts—words like "commensurate," "impact" as a verb, "maximally efficient," "predictability." This is not English clear and simple and eager to tell you something. This is a ready-to-burst colostomy bag of words. It's full of shit, and the person who wrote it knows that. But the report had to be written. Orders descended from Ottawa politicians, from the PMO, from RCMP HQ as faces reddened and leaders became vulnerable to bad press about the break-in. Yes, after the break-in and after this report, some changes occurred in the way the RCMP guards our Prime Minister. But better prose, more clearly expressed, in an earlier report, might have prevented the frightening duration of the trespass.

An Ottawa civil servant once said that it had taken years to learn to write in a style such that his government department could not be held accountable for any error.

EXHIBIT 6
RELEASE ME

Here's another light sprinkle of federal flapdoodle, as found in *Budget Impact, National Defence* published in February, 1994, by the authority of the Hon. David Collenette, Minister of National Defence. The paper concerns firing 8,100 military personnel and 8,400 civilian workers in the Defence Department by 1998. "The military reductions will be accomplished through attrition, restrictions on recruiting, occupational reassignment and encouraged release through the Force Reduction Program. The directed release of military personnel will only be used as a last resort." Isn't that noble? "Encouraged release" means if you quit when the Department of Defence asks you to, there will be a bonus of "additional leave entitlements and special annuity provisions." Sure, and what about an exit door prize, sergeant? How about pillows in a cheerful maple leaf pattern and pleasantly plump with shredded Somalia inquiry documents? If you stick around and make the department fire you, or necessitate "directed release," well, the budget impact statement does not say, but it bodes ill for you. Maybe directed release involves being propelled off-base one midnight from the barrel of the regimental cannon, or a funsy going-away party where members of the disbanded Airborne Regiment perform colourful blood tests to see if you are Aryan? It's bad enough to fire people; but it is lower than pond scum to deny them any final dignity by trying to worm out of the firing by calling it directed release. Shame on the verbal charlatans who came up with this evasive claptrap. Perhaps all those with "release dates" can join in a plaintive chorus of "Release me, and let me go"?

EXHIBIT 7
SMALL PRINT ALERT

Be suspicious of small print. Use a magnifying glass. Copy is not set in teeny type to save space, but to discourage people from reading the gobbledygooked message. Here is part of an application for a joint chequing account once used by a Canadian chartered bank. By signing it, you agreed:

> that the Bank is hereby authorized to credit the said
> account with all monies paid to the Bank (i) at the

branch of account or (ii) at any branch other than the branch of account for the credit of any one or more of us, the proceeds of any orders or promises for the payment of money, of bonds, debentures, coupons or other securities, signed to be drawn by or payable to or the property of, or received by the said Bank (i) at the branch of account or (ii) at any branch other than the branch of account for the credit of us or any one or more of us, and to endorse any of such instruments on behalf of us of any one or more of them.

Whew! Any reader of that would wave the olive branch and sue for semantic peace. That is the worst English I've ever seen in small print. Would you entrust financial responsibility to an organization that approved such incomprehensible bank-speak? I would not. It could be rewritten in clear English using lists, clarifying punctuation, and nixing the not-legally-necessary repetitions. This is old-fashioned, pompous legalese, imitating the clotted English of Victorian contracts, and even as such it is an amateur's botched attempt at contractual precision.

Nor is there a cogent reason for ingredient lists and nutritional information printed on product labels to be set in small type. The manufacturer merely wants its brand-name to be large at the expense of the purchaser's knowledge of what the product contains. If consumers simply refuse to buy things with unreadable labels, the sleazoids who make such packages will be forced to set content lists in legible type. For a playful take on small print, check out my ad for eyedrops.

EXHIBIT 8

THE CALIBRATION OF PERSONAL NORDICITY

or, freezing your Canuck butt off, but taking comfort from the fact that you know precisely how far north your goose-bumped patootie is

Since everywhere else in this book I take unusual Canadian words seriously and do not indulge in fantasy, I can only beg brief pardon for what happened when I encountered the word "nordicity" in 1996. It was new to me and unlisted in any dictionary I possessed. A pestering of learned friends drew blank stares. "Not in my vocabulary, old boy," sniffed a pear-shaped polymath from his table at a trendy Toronto eatery, The Donner Party Deli (Today's special: Mom's Leg of Dad). Now I pride myself on being as pompous as the next man. Well, alright, the next man happens to be Louis XIV. Folks, I tried humbleness, but I couldn't drop my *h*'s like Uriah Heep. Although I know a number of obscure Canadian words, nordicity flummoxed me—*moi*, fount of all earthly Canadiana, hard drive of compacted verbal wisdom, magneto-optical storage device of gigabytic capaciousness. A brisk riffle through tomes of etymological lore did bring to light the unrelated word "nordicism" with its spooky image of some blond, blue-eyed psychopath worshipping spruce trees while accompanied by a dirndled milkmaid who pauses under the sprucey boughs to whisper, "Lars, I would rather do it with a walrus than put on that helmet again, just so you can get it up."

Do you sense that, in my quest for nordicity, scholarly resolve was melting away?

No, I pressed on. I consulted by e-mail the great lexicographer Fred de Gaspy Azmatov, who has not stopped talking since 1961. Okay, once he stopped: May 17, 1973, when a house wren built its nest in his mouth. A last-minute wrenectomy saved him. Fred could offer no definition.

CAUTION: DENDRASTS AHEAD!

So I put an ad in a newspaper, only to receive one lone reply from a Fritz Pfropf who wanted me to meet him at the bus station in North Bay, Ontario—whence we would travel deep into the woods to join a coven of dendrasts. Although not found in any dictionary, dendrast is a word derived from two Greek roots, *dendron* 'tree' and *erastes* 'lover.' Dendrasts are persons whose sexual predilections are chiefly arboreal.

Fritz put it bluntly: "They whine for the pine; they screech for the beech; they mount the olive." No, dendrasty was not for me. I declined the invitation with a postcard: "Sorry, Fritz. Bark would tend to abrade the penile epidermis. And, as a gentleman, I do not propose to play hide-the-sausage with a knothole."

Then, at last, reality! Lexical pay dirt! In *The Canadian Encyclopedia* under the head word "nordicity" was a coloured map and a very long entry by Louis-Edmond Hamelin, author of *Nordicité canadienne* (1975, revised 1980, translated in 1979 as *Canadian Nordicity: It's Your North Too*).

Now I was getting somewhere—namely, smack dab into a cat's cradle of Canadian geographical gobbledygook. Nordicity is an index of northern-ness that calculates and quantifies certain polar values, criteria acronymed as VAPO. True, I have always longed to quantify, but the closest I ever came was to Qantasfly— on that trip to Australia. VAPO is an acronym of French origin, from the initial letters of ***valeur polaire*** 'polar value.'

DISEMBOGUEMENT

With chagrin I discovered that, according to nordicity quantification, I dwell below the dread isonord (a line on a map joining points that have equal VAPO) that is the limit of "Base Canada." I live where I was born in the pleasant town of Dunnville, Ontario. A few miles hence, the Grand River disembogues its modest billows into Lake Erie. Disembogue? Of a river or lake, to empty itself into, to flow out of the mouth of a river. Isn't that gobbledygook, Bill? No way! Disembogue is, I admit, a now obsolete verb borrowed into Elizabethan English (A.D. 1595) from Spanish *desembocar* 'to come out of the mouth of a river.' According to the *Oxford English Dictionary*, it's last appearance in print was in 1862. But the verb merits revival because it so aptly suggests the discharge of a sluggish liquid into a receptacle large (Lake Erie) or small (a spoon). Doesn't cough syrup disembogue into a spoon? Doesn't clotted jargon disembogue from the mouth of someone using words like nordicity? My Dunnville home, therefore, has a VAPO index of nil. Zero. *Nada. Rien. Nichts*. Do I therefore repine? Do I mope like a wilted begonia? Well, sometimes—you know, when tickets to some Toronto alternate theatre production get lost in the mail? Just last week I missed the premiere of "Poodles in Bondage." You've heard of Theatre Under the Stars? "Poodles" was opening on Queen Street at Theatre Under the Stairs. But no, I do not sulk. I will bear my town's VAPO index of zero like a man—a bedraggled, broken homunculus, yes—after delving into nordicity—but still, a man.

NORDICITY EXPLAINED

King Winter attempts to assign VAPO rating to gentleman standing in ice water. Assignment is abandonned after gentleman is consumed by polar bear.

Please, class, sit up straight. Here comes the heavy-duty McCoy. The Polar Value (VAPO) criteria (geographical and human) are ten in number: variables like latitude, summer heat, annual cold, types of ice, accessibility by land, air service, resident population, economic activities, and availability of licorice all-sorts by arctic rescue helicopter. Yeah, yeah, I made the last one up. Sorry. Now pay attention. Each VAPO criterion is expressed on a scale of 0–100. The north pole has VAPO to the max, dude. Its index is 10 x 100 = 1,000. Churchill, Manitoba, in the Middle North has a VAPO of 450; Yellowknife, 390 VAPO; the centre of Hudson Bay, 622 VAPO; Alert, NWT, 878 VAPO; Red Lake, Ontario, 220 VAPO.

    Right. And Jack Frost's dick has a VAPO of 6.

    Turning aside from the vertiginous contemplation of nordicity, we look now at the language in which this "science" is couched. In his engrossing article in *The Canadian Encyclopedia*, Mr. Hamelin writes sentences like these:

• "Nordicity does increase abruptly above isonord 200."
• "A quantitative denordification of approximately 25% has occurred" [in the last century].
• "At least 2 categories of nordicities of exploitation must be identified: nordicity of use and normative nordicity."
• "Many activities in the North seem to have been determined by…the inadequate appreciation of Amerindian ethnicity." Could he mean, *by screwing the natives*?

Class, do not confuse such writing with clear expression.

By using nordicity criteria, writes the author, "nordic space occupies about 70% of Canada's territory. This seems a more exact estimate than the official 39%." Here we reach a crux of the presentation and perhaps the true reason for the creation of nordicity. By using the nordicity system, geographers interested in the North can claim they are devoting their attentions to much more than half of Canada. This comes in handy at government-handout time, when geographers go begging for federal grants. Even in the dankest pits of obfuscatory gibberish, always look for the buck.

Nordicity can be quite fairly viewed as a cool tool to assist in the economic exploitation of the North. Mr. Hamelin himself points out that it has already been used to make up a wage scale for certain workers in our North (sorry, in our norddom), in predicting tourist traffic (of a nordoid direction), and in a study by the Fisheries Board of Canada. His Nordship then adds: "This index would provide a more realistic basis for determining royalty zones in the development of northern petroleum than does the simple division by latitude now used." I think northern residents can detect the possible devastation in that remark.

USES OF JARGON

The making of new words is a sign that a language is vital. But never be under the illusion that because a new label has been plastered on something, because it has been dubbed with a scrap of pseudo-scientific jargon, we—somehow—will know it more deeply.

On the other hand, all sciences need a private vocabulary. Some jargon is necessary. In one sense, all professional terminology is jargon, including that of medicine, law, education, business, sports, theology, etc., because the unique word-hoards of these fields contain terms not familiar to the general population. Linguists estimate that one-half of the vocabulary of all major world languages consists of scientific and technical terms. In Modern English, with more items of vocabulary than any other language that has existed, technical vocabulary makes up closer to 80 percent of all words.

NORDICITY

These private technical vocabularies often contain words composed of roots from classical Latin and Greek. Nordicity appears to have been coined in French first, so it has a suffix that forms many abstract nouns in French, namely *-icité*. *Nordicité* apes French nouns like *publicité*. English borrowed *publicité* as publicity, and it acquired a new meaning. *Publicité* was formed as if from a Latin noun *publicitas* 'public-ness.' As it happens, the abstract noun stems from the French adjective *publique*, but the noun was formed to imitate noun-making precedents derived from Latin. This particular suffix was much used in Latin to form feminine abstract nouns ending in *-tas, -tatis*. Examples still in English include vanity from *uanitas* and liberty from *libertas*.

WHY USE LATIN & GREEK?

As one expects, science requires a large number of new nouns naming various abstractions, objects, and processes. To tag these verbal concepts, science goes back to classical Latin and Greek when making the new words it needs. And that suggests a question: Why use those 'dead' languages to form scientific and technical terms? First, there is historical precedent. We have borrowed such words into English since the birth of the language. Second, in a dead language the meaning of a word does not change. It is semantically frozen. It is crystallized in obsolescence. But in a living language, words acquire new meanings. In 1930, acid meant a chemical like the acetic acid in vinegar. By the middle of the 1960s, acid had added yet another meaning: it could refer in English slang to LSD, a dangerous hallucinogenic drug. That new meaning spawned other new terms, like "acidhead" and "bad acid trip." Like healthy tissue, language is organic; it grows, it sheds old word cells, and creates new ones.

Because precise meaning and precise use of words is crucial in all forms of scientific communication, it helps to be able to make new words from Latin and Greek roots which themselves always mean the same thing. The Greek root *acro-* will always mean 'high' and *phobos* will always mean 'fear,' so acrophobia will always mean 'morbid fear of heights.' Makers of new scientific words don't have to worry about *acro-* acquiring a new meaning. Classical Greek is a dead language. The root meanings cannot change, as they can in English. We ought to note here that Modern Greek is a vibrant tongue, still very much alive in Greece and wherever in the world Greek people gather. By the way, knowing *acro-* helps in ordinary English word origins too. An acrobat was first a high-wire walker, a walker on ropes strung across a room or a street. The high, defended part of an ancient Greek city was an acropolis from Greek *polis* 'city.' Athens had the most famous one. Can you guess what and where the Acrocorinth was?

One final reason we use Latin and Greek roots to form scientific words is—believe it or not—they make terms that are shorter and more convenient than long descriptions in English. Let's take one example from medicine. Yes, medical words are daunting, even frightening, if you've never encountered them. Big, polysyllabic jawbreakers like cholecystostomy are not part of everyday English. However, cholecystostomy is much quicker and easier to write than its definition in English: namely, the surgical making of a mouth-like opening (Greek *stoma*) in the wall of the gall (Greek *chole*) bladder (Greek *cysto-*) to introduce a catheter for the purpose of draining excess fluid accumulation. Greek and Latin terms provide a kind of shorthand for the description of complex objects and procedures in medicine and many other sciences. Personally, I'll take cholecystostomy any day. Now that I know the simple Greek roots, I can even remember more easily how to spell the word.

NORDICITY, MY FELICITY!

Finally, to return to exhibit # 8 in our Canadian National Museum of Bafflegab & Gobbledygook, nordicity is similar to other new concepts. It too will have its fate in the verbal marketplace. Nordicity has already been lollygagging in the foyers of geographic academe since the 1960s. It may be here to stay. New terms are minted and then must brave circulation. Some will endure, some fracture, some fall into disuse and oblivion.

But long, technical words do not always spring from practical or noble motives. Sometimes they pepper academic writing because the author is insecure and needs to impress the reader. Sometimes the very science is new. Elsewhere in this museum you can see exhibits from educational sociology. When that science was in verbal diapers, it spewed forth silly, polysyllabic jargon at a dictionary-boggling rate—still does, from time to time.

In the end, of course, one does want to be fair-minded. By all means, give nordicity every chance. Even I am trying to adopt the right norditude. Let's see now. I'll conserve strength by not taking part in communal northern sex (a nordgy). I'll try to express this in language worthy of those who write about nordicity. By extrapolation from the conjecturally applicable variables is manifest the incontrovertible substantiation of one further, pertinent—er—um—guess: Perhaps nordicity does herald an advance in techniques of biogeographical measurement? With thumping heart I await fresh vistas of insight with the advent of concepts like westment, eastacy, and southizationmentarianistalismness.

And, while waiting here in my fur booties and parka, I certainly plan at all costs to avoid hypernordosis of the buttocks.

As for the scourge of multinorditiveness in the common geographical article, well, that's a whole other kettle of—ichthyonordic entities.

CLOSING HOURS

Strange flowers unfold in the garden of Canadian gobbledygook. It is an ever-burgeoning patch in the pasturelands of our Dominion, and no one gardener can find every verbal weed. If you pluck a bouquet of bibble-babble someday, and think it deserves a future exhibit here in the museum, do send it to me. My address is at the end of the preface

CHAPTER SIX

THE MEANING OF FAMOUS CANADIAN SURNAMES

"You all have such funny names."
"But aren't all names funny until you get used to them?"
"Think of Shakespeare and Churchill. Think of Pillsbury."

John Updike, *Couples* (1968)

ovie star and Canadian Keanu Reeves has a given name that is Hawaiian and means 'cool breeze.' *Ke-ahe-anu* is literally 'the breeze cool.' There are many books about family names, but only this chapter of this book explains how some first and many last names work by using surnames important to Canadians. There's a fascinating surprise behind almost every surname borne by Canadians. And our last names, like ourselves and our ancestors, have come to Canada from every major linguistic family in the world.

To begin with, a human needed only one name. But eventually, even one named Ugh spewed forth spawn whose existence had to be differentiated from his father. Ugh, Jr.? Possibly. Ugh Ughson? Sure. Ugh McUgh? Is there not an alternative to tacking *-son* on the father's name? Yes, indeed, and this chapter displays the inventive ploys humans have used to confect surnames in many languages.

Take English as an example, where few surnames existed at all until the twelfth century. At first there were bynames—tags added to distinguish among, say,

Several Canadians have legally changed their name to *Shakespeare*.

SURNAME HISTORY

three or four Johns. Rich people with land to bequeath in wills soon needed something more than Long John and Short John. So surnames began first among the wealthy. Sometimes the tag showed the father's name: John Donaldson, Jock MacDonald; sometimes the added epithet identified a person's job: John the fowler, John the smith, John the fisher; sometimes the tag indicated where the founding ancestor of a family lived: John Atwood, John Greenfield. Other early surnames sprang from physical description of the person: John Long, John Lang, John Laing, John Talman; or the surname might highlight his character: John Fox, John Goodfellow, John Mudd. Mudd? A black-hearted rogue? No. Remember, only a few monks and learned sages could read. Many clerks and priests who recorded names in baptismal registers were only semi-literate. Mudd might be an early mangling of Maude (a surname too) or, more likely, of Old English Mod 'heart, courage.' The noblest-sounding surname may begin in the barnyard, while the lowly Mudd is suddenly elevated by its origin to become the proud label of a warrior ancestor's pluck.

British novelist Henry Fielding (1707–1754) whose masterpiece was *Tom Jones*, was once visiting the Earl of Denbigh. The earl's family name was Feilding, and naturally, one rook-streaked twilight, over goblets of finest malmsey, the two men discussed Fielding's belonging to the same family line. The earl wondered why the names were spelled differently. Fielding replied that he could give no reason, "except perhaps that my branch of the family was the first to know how to spell."

CAUTION: MEANING BUMP

Although the original meanings of surnames fascinate most of us, let's bong one gong of caution here. Names don't mean in the same way most words mean. A word can represent an actual thing or feeling or sense perception like colour. A name may have started lexical life that way, but as it became specialized—some might say fossilized—as a name, and joined the select word-hoard

of surnames (about 100,000 in English) the word as surname loses its referential quality. Even if we know
Arabic, no one nowadays expects a person named
Haddad to be a blacksmith. Yet *haddad* is one Arabic
term for such a craftsman.

In his short piece, *A Toast to Ava Gardne*r, the poet
and anthologist Robert Graves wrote: *In Spain, a married woman keeps her maiden name, but tacks on her
husband's after a* de. *Thus, on marrying Wifredo Las
Rocas, our Majorcan friend Rosa, born an Espinosa,
became Señora Rosa Espinosa de Las Rocas—a very
happy combination. It means 'Lady Thorny Rose from
the Rocks.' Rosa was luckier than her maternal cousin
Dolores Fuertes, who thoughtlessly married a lawyer
named Tomás Barriga, and is now Dolores Fuertes de
Barriga, or 'Violent Pains of the Stomach.'*

YOUR NAME'S ORIGIN

If, after feasting on the banquet of surname origins
spread before you here, you hanker to discover what
your own last name means, be aware that I prepare individual origins of surnames, not genealogy only etymology. Write for a brochure at the address given at the end
of the preface.

What we may call somewhat grandly the principles of inclusion are simple. How did we pick the surnames found here? Being famous helped. So did having
a surname with an interesting word history. So, if you
are renowned and were left out, don't phone.

NOT GENEALOGY

Each entry details the etymology (word roots) of a
name. This is NOT genealogy—although many bearers
of these names will like to include the information in
their family records. And frequently nuggets of genealogical lore will be found embedded in the motherlode
of a surname's etymology.

The presentation of the word roots of a surname is
self-explanatory, except perhaps for the use of an asterisk placed before a word root, for example, *baroz*. The
asterisk means this Old Teutonic word-form meaning

'barley' is a hypothetical root, with no printed evidence of its existence. The asterisk means the root suggested is a guess, a presumed form, but a guess based on the best available contemporary linguistic theory.

As you read the entries, you also get a discursive capsule history of English, and of other languages from which we have borrowed name words. English has been well called "the great thief of tongues", for our language brims with loanwords from every country on earth. Therefore, spur your cognominal curiosity to the charging point, and set forth, with the words Shakespeare gave King Henry V, as he exhorted his troops on the eve of the Battle of Agincourt:

> *"Then shall our names,*
> *Familiar in his mouth as household words,...*
> *Be in their flowing cups, freshly remembered."*

A ABBOTT

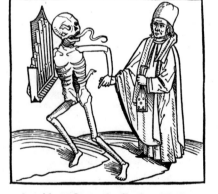

An abbott faces the final music in this medieval woodcut.

Sir John Joseph Caldwell Abbott 1821–1893
The lawyer and politician became the third Prime Minister of Canada (1891–1892) and was the first Canadian-born Prime Minister.

Abbott is of course from abbot, the head of a monastery or convent. Now—as we all know, class—abbots were priests and were celibate, so they could not found families. And even if they did enjoy a quick tryst under a moonlit table in the refectory with a scullery wench, it would have been unwise to advertise the fact by labelling one's bastard spawn in public registries. Therefore Abbot as a surname usually meant the founding ancestor of the family was the lay servant of an abbot. The word entered English from ecclesiastical Latin *abbas*, from Koine Greek *abbas*, from Hebrew *abba* 'father, abbot,' from Aramaic *abbá* 'father.' In modern Hebrew *abba* with the first syllable stressed means 'father, daddy, papa, and abbot.' The ancient Hebrew root *ab* could refer to God the Father and begins many Hebrew personal names:

- Abigail   'father rejoiced'
- Abner   'God the father is light'
- Abraham   'father of many'

• Absalom   'God the father is peace.'

Compare *shalom* in Hebrew and *salaam* in Arabic, the beautiful greeting of peace common to both these members of the Semitic language family.

The Scots Gaelic surname MacNab does mean '**son of** the abbot.' The official MacNab clan excuse is that the ancient chiefs of this clan were only *lay* abbots of Glendochart. Och, laddie, then it's nay but a wee misunderstanding of the old terms, is it not?

Bryan Adams 1959–
The Canadian rock singer and composer was born in Kingston, Ontario.

The majority of English surnames are based on the first name of the founding male ancestor of the family. Yes, it was oinky and chauvinistic of those frowsy Saxons to deprecate female names, but, shall we revise history? No, *herstory* won't work as one peruses the rise of surnames.

As we might expect, Adams was in medieval English a genitive form, *Adames* 'of Adam.' This could be appended in a parish registry to a first name like John, so that John Adames would mean John, son of a man named Adam. But note that it could also commonly refer to anyone of the household of a man named Adam. If that Adam had servants, his underlings' newborn children could be baptized with their master's name. So Adams can also mean 'servant of Adam.' If a family wished to make clear that the child being baptized was a legitimate heir of the founding ancestor, the relationship was stated plainly by putting "Adam's son" after the first name, so that John, Adam's son would become in time John Adamson.

In Scotland, MacAdam was the form, and one of that name, a surveyor, John Loudon McAdam (1756–1836) helped pave the way for better roads by suggesting many layers of broken stone as a roadbed. He also gave us a verb, "to macadamize." Another illustrious bearer of the name was John Macadam, an Australian chemist, after whom is named the Australian tree whose fruit we eat as macadamia nuts.

ADAMS

Adam and Eve expelled from Eden. Gustav Doré's engraving to illustrate Milton's *Paradise Lost*.

Spelling did not become standardized in England until the spread of dictionaries and general literacy. So variant forms of the surname appear as Addams, Adems, and Adhams.

Sometimes the founding ancestor's pet name, often a diminutive form, was the origin of the surname. Pet names for Adam in medieval English included Addy, Ade, Adcock, Adekin, and Adnett. These pet names produced a profusion of Adam-based surnames that include Adcocks, Addey, Addis, Haddy, Addison, Addyman, Ades, Adey, Adkins, Atkins, Adnitt, and so forth. There is an Irish-Gaelic diminutive form too that appears in the name of the eighth-century Irish St. Adamnan, 'Little Adam.'

The majority of first names in all countries of Christendom were taken from the names of Christian saints, often by legal enforcement. For example, in 1563 the Council of Trent decreed that children baptized in the Roman Catholic Church must be given names that appear in the Catholic calendar of saints' names. This stricture was made to combat the then-growing Protestant habit of using Old Testament names. What the anti-Semitic Council of Trent was actually in a racist tizzy about, of course, was the fact that most Old Testament names were Hebrew, and Rome did not want the entire population of Europe tagged with Jewish names. Well, this may be a *goyishe welt*, but that ploy didn't work. A very large percentage of all first and last names in every language of Europe can be traced back to Hebrew originals in the Old and New Testament. Thus failed one bit of papal anti-Semitism.

And so it behooves any bearer of the name Adam or Adams to know just what the name of the first man means in Hebrew. One striking feature of the Adam and Eve creation myth in Genesis is the pottery metaphor: a god formed humans from clay. This is a worldwide element in creation stories. Compare the Hebrew and Christian version in Genesis 2:6,7 as translated in the King James version of 1611: "There went up a mist from the earth, and watered the whole face of the ground. And the Lord God formed man of the dust of the ground..." So, even today, in brickyards of the Middle East, does the brickmaker sprinkle water on the clay before he kneads it into shape. The Bible's name for the first man reflects this too. Adam means 'human being, person.' With only a slightly different voicing, *adom* means 'red.' Both may be related to Hebrew *adamah* 'clay' or 'red earth of Israel.' In Old Testament Hebrew it is usually *ha adam* and the definite article makes some scholars suspect that the name, like some others in Hebrew, was very early borrowed from neighbouring Assyrians. If so, it might stem from Assyrian *adamu* 'to make or produce.' Thus Adam would mean 'the made one, the created one.'

The ultimately Latin word 'human' also reflects this pottery myth in creation stories. The prime meaning of Latin *humanus* is 'clayey' or made of *humus* 'earth, soil, clay.' The Roman word for human being or man, *homo*, as in our species *Homo sapiens*, also stems from the same root. In Old Latin it was *hemo* 'the earthen one' or 'the person of clay.' The idea must have occurred early in human history, when primitive humans first dug up an interred body to discover bones and dust. Dust thou art; to dust shalt thou return.

Adario

ADARIO

The early seventeenth-century Huron chief was the prototype of the 'noble savage.'

Adario was chief of a tribe of the people whom the French called Huron. A French explorer's report about Adario's life inspired the French writer Jean-Jacques Rousseau to write about the 'noble savage,' the shining example of natural goodness, dignity, and nobility untainted by the evil of civilization. Rousseau propounded this Romantic stereotype particularly in *Émile*, his 1762 novel about the education of children. Adario's name in his native Wendat language means 'muskrat.'

John Black Aird 1923–1995

AIRD

He was a lawyer, senator, Lieutenant-Governor of Ontario, chancellor at Wilfrid Laurier University and University of Toronto.

An aird above a valley.

Aird is a place name in the former Scottish county of Ayrshire and also in the former Wigtownshire. In Scots Gaelic *aird* means 'peak, direction, or point of the compass,' and so would be used to name an elevation of land that helped indicate direction to early settlers or travellers along a path or trail. It is not, as several amateur books about Scottish surnames suggest, derived from the name of the River Aire. Aire is a very old river name and probably means 'river.' Aire might stem from Old Norse *eyjar* 'islands' or possibly Aire is Celtic or pre-Celtic for 'flowing strongly.' There is no instance of a terminal *d* suddenly and mysteriously being tacked on to the end of a river name to make a Gaelic surname.

ALAN
ALLAN
ALLEN

Andrew Edward Fairbairn Allan 1907–1974
He was a leading director of CBC radio drama during the golden age of Canadian radio drama in the forties and fifties.

Sir Hugh Allan 1810–1882
From Montréal, he was during the 1830s one of the world pioneers in transatlantic steamship service.

Ted Allen 1916–
This is the pseudonym of Alan Herman, writer of radio, TV, and screenplays, and biographer of Norman Bethune.

Ralph Allen 1913–1966
One of Canada's great journalists, he was the best-loved editor of Maclean's *magazine (1946–1960), at the* Toronto Star *briefly, and author of a popular history of Canada,* Ordeal by Fire, *and of a 1954 satirical novel about the CBC,* The Chartered Libertine.

Allan became a popular name for men right after the Norman Conquest of Britain in A.D.1066 for this very good reason: Two of William the Conqueror's French generals were Alain, Count of Brittany, and Alain, 1st Earl of Richmond. To be in favour with the French who controlled Britain, parents rushed to give their children French names. Earlier, Alain was also the name of the Bishop of Quimper who became a popular Breton saint. And many Bretons came to England after the Norman Conquest, settling particularly in Lincolnshire where Alain was among the ten most popular names in the twelfth century.

There is much dispute about what the word means, but three contending theories have emerged. One posits a direct borrowing from the name of an ancient Scythian nomadic tribe named The Alan who dwelt near the Caspian Sea two millennia ago and spoke an Iranian language. Although no direct record of the Scythian tongue exists, related roots suggest that *alan* meant 'the people' in their language. The second theory suggests that Alan derives from what the earliest speakers of French would have called Germans, namely, *Alemanni.* This meant 'all the men' or 'the people' in Proto-Germanic, and gives rise to the present French word for Germany which is *Allemagne.* The third theory about the source of *Alan* suggests the saint's name in Old Breton Alan may be related to the Gaelic root *ail* 'rock.' Some of the Scottish surnames spelled Allan in English certainly derive from the Gaelic names *Ailene* and *Ailin.*

Norman Z. Alcock 1918–

He was a Canadian peace researcher and author of books such as The Bridge of Reason *(1961),* The War Disease *(1972), and* The Logic of Love *(1976).*

ALCOCK

No, this name does not have its origin in the common fantasy of adolescent males. Alcock was an affectionate nickname for someone named Alan. First the founding ancestor may have been known by the shortened form, Al; then, as Basil Cottle puts it succinctly in *The Penguin Dictionary of Surnames,* cock, "the strutting barnyard fowl, became a generic term for pert lads, and was attached as a suffix to diminutive forms."

In Elizabethan English a mother could call her son "my little cock robin." Cock as a noun was applied to servant boys and apprentices. It gives rise to several common English surnames: Adcock, Simcock, Wilcock, Wilcox, Wilcoxson, and the matronymic Babcock 'son

Cockerel and hen.

of Bab.' Bab and Babs were/are pet forms of Barbara. Simcock is from Sim, pet name for a Simon.

Although the cockerel was a domestic fowl, the phallic meaning of cock distressed certain English gentry, especially it seems after any Simcock family acquired wealth, and so, to remove even a hint of low, anatomical taint such as might bring a blush to a dowager's dewlap, Simcock was altered by some families to Simcoe, including the one that produced Lord Simcoe, the first Lieutenant-Governor of Upper Canada, whom Ontario celebrates by calling August civic holiday, Simcoe Day.

Note also Silcox for Silcocks, Sil being a pet form of Sylvester or the Norman *Sylvein*. Pocock, on the other hand, is an attempt to disguise Peacock, a surname from a nickname, probably not based on fine dress, but on the strutting arrogance of the ancestor.

ALMIGHTY VOICE

Kakeesay-manitou-wayo 1874–1897
A Cree man turned outlaw by Whites' policies toward First Peoples

In 1895, he was arrested for killing and butchering a farmer's cow. He escaped and evaded capture for almost two years, murdering four men including a Northwest Mounted Police officer. He and two companions were run to ground and blown up by NWMP cannons in 1897. *Kakeesaymanitouwayo* means 'voice of the Great Manitou' in Cree. Manitou is a spirit, and the Great Manitou may be translated as 'God.'

ALMOND

Paul Almond 1931–
The Montréal-born director of CBC television dramas went on to direct an important trilogy of Canadian feature films starring his wife, actress Geneviève Bujold: Isabel *(1968),* Act of the Heart *(1970), and* Journey *(1972).*

Almond only looks like a nut. It has nothing to do with almond which is *amande* in French. The French surname derives from an ancestor's first name, *Alamond*, which was a French version of the compound Germanic warrior name *Adalmund*, whose elements are *adal* 'noble' and *mund* 'protection.'

FRÈRE ANDRÉ

André (né Alfred Bessette) 1845–1937

The Roman Catholic healer, a brother of the Congregation of the Holy Cross founded St. Joseph's Oratory on Mount Royal in Montréal which became the most visited Catholic shrine in Canada, and Brother André the most revered religious figure of twentieth-century Québec. As usual, the leaders of the Catholic Church in Québec were at first appalled by the tawdry miracles attributed to the intervention of Frère André's patron Saint Joseph, but soon they were persuaded by the immense popularity of the illiterate brother to spend the years 1924 to 1955 erecting a vast basilica and oratory beside the humble little chapel he began.

André (Andrew) is one of the most popular first names in the Christian world. Andrew was the first disciple. In the Koine Greek of the New Testament, Luke (6:14) calls him 'Andreas' based on the adjective *andreios* 'manly, bold.' But it is unlikely the first apostle had a Greek name at all. Andreas is probably a translation of a Hebrew name indicating maleness or boldness, like Adam 'first man, earthly one, created one' or Gabriel 'strong man of God.' Saint Andrew is the patron saint of Scotland, Russia, and fishermen.

HOW ONE CHRISTIAN NAME, ANDREW, LEADS TO DOZENS OF SURNAMES

ENGLISH	FRENCH	SLAVIC	SCANDINAVIAN	SCOTS GAELIC
Andrew	André	Andreivitch	Andersen	Gillanders
Andrewes	Andras	Andreiov	Andersson	McAndrew
Andrews	Andreix	Ondruchuk	Andersholm	
Andrewson	Andrisse	Andrushky		
Anderson	Andriu	Andreev	SPANISH	
Enderson	Drieux	Andric	Andrez	
Anderby	Landrieux		Andrillos	
Anderton	Andrivet	ITALIAN	Andros	
Andree	Andriveaux	Andretti		
Andrey	Drivet	Andreotti	CORSICAN	
Andress	Andreaut	Andrucci	Andreolli	
Andriss	Andréol	Androletti	Andreoly	
Andison	Andreault		Andreani	

ANDREW IN SEVERAL LANGUAGES

Dutch	Andreas
French	André(e)
German	Andreas
Italian	Andrea
Hawaiian	Anederea
Latin	Andreas
Polish	Andrej
Swedish	Anders
Russian	Andrei

ANHALT

István Anhalt 1919–
Hungarian-born Canadian composer of avant-garde music

But Anhalt is a German name. The founding ancestor came from Anhalt, a former duchy in central Germany north of Saxony. In 1848 Anhalt comprised some 898 square miles of territory. As a noun in medieval German, *Anhalt* suggested a place at which a rider or a coach might make a temporary stop, and this sense is likely to be the origin of the duchy and the surname, the founding ancestor living at or operating an important inn or imperial stopping place on a major route. It occurred frequently as a local place name throughout German-speaking Europe.

István is the Hungarian form of Stephen from the common Greek personal name *Stephanas* 'wearer of a laurel crown for some achievement' from *stephanos* 'crown.' Its widespread use in Christian Europe is due to the popularity of Saint Stephen, the first Christian martyr. English surnames derived from Stephen include Stevens, Stevenson, Stinson, Stimpson, Stenson, and Steenson.

APPLEBAUM

Louis Applebaum 1918–
He composes music in a broad range of musical styles including Hollywood film scores, and has been associated with the Stratford Festival, CBC, National Film Board, CAPAC, and has played many gigs as musical administrator.

Applebaum is a partial Englishing of the Jewish surname Apfelbaum 'apple tree.' Variant spellings may indicate the origin of the founder. Among Polish, Hungarian, and Russian Jews, those speaking western Yiddish, it can be Apelboim or Appelboym. Eastern Yiddish speakers, like some Lithuanian Jewish families, may spell it as Apelbeym.

In certain German Jewish families, their surname is traceable directly to the medieval Frankfurt ghetto called the *Judengasse* 'The Street of Jews.' House numbers and street names were not common until the end of the eighteenth century, simply because most ordinary

Europeans were illiterate. Houses and shops bore signs
to identify their owners. More than two hundred Jewish
surnames based on signs arose and have come down to
us from the Frankfurt ghetto alone. Animal signs could
represent many German Jewish first names like Baer
'bear,' Loeb 'lion,' Wolf, Fisch 'fish,' Lachs 'salmon,'
Hecht 'pike.' This happened in Poland and Russia too,
e.g., Polish Karash 'carp,' and Slavic Karassick 'little
fish.' Among the tree signs identifying houses and
owners were Apfelbaum 'apple tree,' Birnbaum 'pear
tree,' Buxbaum 'box tree,' Grünbaum 'green tree,' and
Nussbaum 'nut tree.' These house signs sometimes also
served to identify a shop or place of business.

But Apfelbaum might also have been pleasing to
the pious because of its mention in the Torah and other
ancient Hebrew religious texts. Now this is not the fruit
in Genesis, not the apple of temptation in the garden of
Eden, a piece of which, folklore says, lodged in Adam's
throat to give us the English phrase *Adam's apple*, referring to the little swelling in the front of the neck caused
by the projection of the thyroid cartilage of the larynx.
No, the pious took note of the apple and apple tree in
Proverbs and, for example, in the Song of Solomon
2:3–5: "As the apple tree among the trees of the world,
so is my beloved among the sons. I sat down under his
shadow with great delight, and his fruit was sweet to my
taste....Stay me with flagons, comfort me with apples,
for I am sick with love."

Red-faced generations of skittish Talmudic revi-
sionists have rushed to convince readers that the Song
of Solomon is not what it plainly is: a luscious passage
of ancient Hebrew erotic poetry, composed to be chant-
ed at a wedding feast as a celebration of sexual desire
and love. In feats of allegorical exegesis that would
cross a rabbi's eyes, commentators have insisted that the
apple tree here symbolizes the love between God and
his people, Israel. Well, read the Song of Solomon for
yourself. The apple tree is a symbol alright, a symbol of
a big, healthy, potent bridegroom, full of seed and ready
for his wedding night. Later Christian writers also
blushed to find such piquant sensuality enshrined in

Holy Writ, so Roman Catholic dogma states it's all about the love between Christ and the Church. Not to be outpurged by mere papists, Protestant divines swoon in the moist deeps of the Song of Solomon as well, assuring all sex-hating sects that the poem concerns the love between God and man's soul. Not in the apple of my eye.

Biblical apples harbour a few other worms of contention. The modern Hebrew word meaning apple, pronounced 'tapPU'ach', could never have referred to the fruit of the genus *Malus* that we know today, made big and juicy by hybridizers only in the last two hundred years. The species of the *Malus* genus that throve in the hot places of the ancient Middle East were miserable shrubs, stingy with fruit that was tiny, hard, acidic, unpalatable and virtually inedible, and resembled crab apples the size of marbles! Now listen to how the Bible describes its 'apple': Joel 1:12 says it was a tree of the field like the vine, fig, and pomegranate. The Song of Solomon 2:3 and 7:8 says the apple had a sweet perfume and taste. Other passages say it hung in a tree that offered much shade.

I don't want to upset your apple-cart but Biblical scholars believe the fruit referred to by the word *tappuach* was an orange, a quince, or, most likely, an apricot. Ancient Palestinian folk wisdom said the apricot possessed aphrodisiac qualities, so its use as a sexual metaphor in the Song of Solomon is most apt. And apricot trees grew throughout ancient Palestine.

So ends our traipse around the orchard. None of this takes away a whit of the delight its bearers may take in the surname Applebaum. For my little excursus is only a side path that I hope you have dawdled along with some etymological pleasure.

APPLEYARD

Peter Appleyard 1928–
The British-born musician has been in Canada from 1951 as a jazz vibraphonist with much concert, night-club, and studio work.

Appleyard was a place in the West Riding of

Yorkshire and a country synonym for orchard. Old English *geard* 'enclosure' (pronounced *yard*) is related to garden, and an Old Norse cognate *garthr* gives English "garth," an open space within a cloister or a yard, garden, or paddock. Apple trees were a method of identifying fields and houses of founding ancestors, and thus contributed to several English surnames:

- Apperley   'clearing with apple trees'
- Applin   '(among) the apples' from the Old English dative plural *aepplum*
- Appleby   'apple farm' with Old English *by* 'a farmhouse' then 'a village,' with cognates in Swedish and Danish *by*, all akin to Viking word *byr* 'a farm'
- Appleford   from one of several place names describing the shallows of a river where livestock could cross easily and where apple trees grew beside the ford
- Applegarth   'apple enclosure'
- Applegate   ultimately from Old Scandinavian *apaldrsgardr* 'apple-orchard'
- Appleton   'apple farm' with Old English *tun*, a common suffix on English place names. The meaning of *tun* expanded through history. Its initial sense was a hedge, a fence, an enclosure, a homestead, then a farm, a manor, a settlement, a hamlet, and finally a village. Our modern form of the word is town.
- Applewhite   from Applethwaite 'a clearing with apple trees' where *thwaite* is Old Norse for 'meadow, enclosed land'

Fresh from the appleyard.

Charles Joseph Sylvanus "Syl" Apps 1915–
The athletic all-rounder (British Empire Games, 1936 Berlin Olympics) was famous as centre for the Toronto Maple Leafs from 1936 to 1948, where he was one of professional hockey's best team players.

    Apps locates the ancestor as living at or near aspen trees. Another form of the same surname is Asp.

APPS

The *p* and the *s* have been transposed in a natural linguistic process called metathesis. A good modern example is the non-standard English for ask, as in "Don't **aks** me no questions."

Some consonant clusters give speakers trouble, so the brain makes our speaking apparatus interchange the offending consonants. Some young English-speaking children say *pesghetti* instead of spaghetti because children cannot always immediately utter all the consonant sequences in a language. Some clusters remain tricky even for adults who may say *perscribe* for prescribe. Historical examples of this reordering in English are wasp from Old English *waeps*, bird for Old English *bridd*, Manx for Middle English *Manisk*, and third for Old English *thridda* (compare the modern German *dritte*).

AQUIN

Hubert Aquin 1929–1977

The important twentieth century avant-garde Québec novelist and influential political activist has an œuvre that includes Prochain épisode, Trou de mémoire, L'Antiphonaire, *and* Neige noire.

Aquin also appears in the forms Achin, Achain, and Acquin, a French surname from an ancestor who bore the Germanic warrior name *Acwin*, a compound of *ac* 'blade of a sword' and *win* 'friend.'

ARCAND

Denys Arcand 1941–

He is a leading Québec film director, screenwriter, sometime actor, and movie producer whose films include Réjeanne Padovani *(1973),* Le déclin de l'empire americain *(1986),* Jésus de Montréal *(1989), and* Love and Human Remains *(1994).*

Arcand is probably from an Old Germanic adjective used as a first name, *Ercan* 'genuine, sincere, excellent.' It may even be a shortened form of the common Old German name *Ercanbald* 'sincere-bold' which gives Archibald in English, and French surnames like Archambaud. A much remoter possibility would be an origin from Latin *arca* 'box, chest,' as a nickname or signifying one who made and sold wooden chests.

Gilles Archambault 1933–

Montréal-born novelist whose works include La Fleur aux dents *(1971),* À Voix basse *(1983), and* Le Regard oblique *(1984).*

Joseph-Papin Archambault 1880–1966

The Montréal-born Jesuit priest, an early militant French-Canadian antisocialist and nationalist, worked with Abbé Groulx at the periodical L'Action française.

Louis Archambault 1915–

The Montréal-born sculptor has been called the "greatest Canadian sculptor of his generation."

Archambault is one of the earliest French surnames to become established in Québec. In France the founding ancestor of the family bore the Old Germanic warrior name *Arcanbald*, a French variant of *Ercanbald*, a compound first name containing the Germanic elements *ercan* 'genuine, sincere' and *bald* which is cognate with English 'bold.' There are several variants: Archambault, Archaimbaud, Arcambal, and Arquimbau.

Dick Assman 1934–

A service station attendant who pumps gas at a Petro-Canada station in Regina, Saskatchewan, he became famous after his name was ridiculed on The David Letterman Show. *Good-naturedly he agreed to appear on the show, obtained the services of an agent, and made a few bucks from his unusual surname.*

Assman is an Englishing of the not uncommon German surname *Assmann* whose variants include *Asmann*, *Assmus*, and *Asmus*. We don't wish any Assman to be the butt of a joke, and thus we happily point out that all variants have a most noble origin. They derive from Saint Erasmus, a fourth-century Christian martyr who, pious legend states, was dispatched by having his intestines wound out of his body on a windlass. Now a windlass resembles a ship's capstan, and so Erasmus became the patron saint of sailors—so says another coincidence-crammed legend that stretches resemblance and credulity to the snapping

ARCHAMBAULT

ASSMAN

Erasmus 1469–1536

point. One nickname of Erasmus is Elmo. St. Elmo's fire of nautical note refers to Erasmus. St. Elmo's fire is a luminous electrical discharge sometimes seen by seafarers sparking off the masthead of a ship during a storm. To further ennoble the surname Assman, let us report that the saint's name derives from the Greek adjective *erasmios* 'lovable, pleasant, desired, beloved.' Note, however, that the German names *Assmann, Asmann, Assmus*, and *Asmus* do not derive from the Erasmus who lived from A.D. 1469 to 1536. That Dutch humanist and most famous scholar of his day was born after the German names first appeared in print during the thirteenth and fourteenth centuries. The humanist Erasmus was named after the saint, too. I hope, David Letterman, this will teach you not to make ignorant fun of Canadian names of such noble lineage, you hoser! Perhaps, Dave, you might better reflect on the origin of Letterman, which is an Americanization of Ledermann 'leather-man,' a medieval German surname from an ancestor who was an itinerant huckster of cheap leather goods on the dusty roads of fourteenth-century Europe. Touché, eh?

ATWOOD

Margaret Eleanor Atwood 1939–
The poet and critic is one of Canada's most popular novelists whose works include Bluebeard's Egg, Cat's Eye, The Edible Woman, The Handmaid's Tale, Lady Oracle, Life Before Man, *and* Alias Grace.

Atwood is a reduced spelling of Attwood 'at the wood.' The earliest person of the name in English records is one Thomas Attewode listed in the Assize Rolls of Somerset for 1243 A.D.

A number of English surnames kept the preposition in little phrases added after an ancestor's first name to specify where he dwelt and to differentiate him from others with the same first name. This class of surnames includes:

• Atberry   for Atbury 'at the manor-house,' in Old English *burh*

• Atbridge

• Atbrook

- Atcliff   or Attercliff
- Atcot   'at the cottage'
- Atford
- Atherfold   'at the fold' (perhaps a shepherd?)
- Athoke   'at the bend in the road or river' from Old English *hoc* 'hook'
- Atholl   for atte Hole 'at the hollow'
- Atkey   'at the quay' hence a dock worker
- Atlow   'at the hill' Old English *hlaw*
- Attenborough   'at the hill, grove, or fort'
- Attlee   'at the lea' that is, at the wood or clearing
- Attwater
- Attwell
- Attwick   'at the dairy-farm'
- Atty   'at the enclosure or common pasture' Old English *teag*
- Atyeo   'at the river'

AUGUSTYN

Frank Augustyn 1953–

The Hamilton-born ballet dancer was a frequent partner of Karen Kain in the National Ballet of Canada, and is now a choreographer and teacher.

    Augustyn is a Ukrainian surname, based on the name of Saint Augustine, whom the Russian Orthodox Church, like the Roman Catholic one, holds in pious regard as one of the fathers of the Christian religion. Aurelius Augustinus (A.D. 354–430), author of *The Confessions* and *The City of God*, had a second name based on the Latin adjective *augustus* 'venerable, consecrated' but literally 'increased in human regard,' which was of course made popular by the very first emperor of the Romans who himself chose the name Caesar Augustus.

BAILLAIRGÉ   B

Jean Baillairgé 1726–1805

Carpenter, joiner, architect in Québec from 1741, he founded a dynasty of architects, painters, and sculptors in the province.

François Baillairgé 1759–1830
Sculptor, architect, painter

Thomas Baillairgé 1791–1859
Architect, sculptor, painter

Charles Baillairgé 1826–1906
Architect, civil engineer, surveyor, inventor, writer

William-Duval Baillairgé
Son of Charles, twentieth-century city engineer of Québec City

Baillairgé is a variant of the occupational surname Baillarger, common in history along the Atlantic coast of France. *Un baillarger* was a farmer who grew *baillarge*, a kind of barley with double columns of seeds. This genetic sport of the common cereal was well-known in antiquity. The French word stems from the Latin term for this barley *balearicus*, which seems to have originated in the Balearic Islands off the coast of Spain. However, some French etymologists dismiss that as mere folk etymology and prefer the source as a French borrowing from Old English *bœrlic* or Middle English *barleche*, both of which seem related to Old Teutonic * *baroz* 'barley.'

BAIN

George Bain 1920–
The witty, Toronto-born, former Ottawa columnist and oenophile for the Globe and Mail *taught journalism and was director of journalism until 1985 at King's College in Halifax. He has published the humorous* Letters From Lilac, *and several other books.*

Several languages supply possible origins for this surname:

- If the family was of Norman-French provenance, *bain* 'public bath' identified an ancestor who owned, operated, or worked at an ancient spa such as Bath.
- The Scottish Bain is Gaelic *bàn* to describe a person 'of fair complexion.'
- The Bain deriving from Old Norse *beinn* singled out a Viking settler 'straightforward or ready to oblige.'

- The form Baines sometimes stands for the Northern English and Scottish pronunciation of the nickname based surname, "Bones," given to someone unusually thin, gaunt, or gangly. Retired pirates also favoured the moniker and enjoyed stumping into a gin-damp tavern to be hailed by a phlegmy chorus as "Bones!"

Charles Marius Barbeau 1883–1969

The father of Canadian folklore studies, collector of French-Canadian and aboriginal songs and texts at the National Museum of Canada, he was also the founder of the Archives de folklore *at Laval University.*

Jean Barbeau 1945–

The Québec playwright makes clever, playful use of joual in popular dramas like Manon Lastcall *(1972) and* Joualez-moi d'amour *(1972).*

Marcel Barbeau 1925–

Painter, sculptor, filmmaker, performance artist

Barbeau was the nickname of the founding ancestor who probably had a sparse beard. Barbeau is in Old French as early as A.D. 1175 as the name of a large European freshwater fish of the carp and minnow family (Cyprinidae). It has a few fleshy, antennae-like filaments hanging from its mouth, hence the French name derived from Latin *barbellus* 'little beard' diminutive of *barba* 'beard.' In English the fish is a barbel, and the fleshy protuberances around the mouth of most members of the carp family are barbels. Five hundred years later the common blue cornflower of France was named *barbeau* as well, describing the little 'beard' of ray-like petals that encircle the ovary of cornflowers. But the French surname predates the flower name, so we can be reasonably sure the last name is of whiskery provenance.

Dave Barrett 1930–

Feisty NDP premier of British Columbia 1972–1975

In all its many spellings (Barrat, Barratt, Barrett, Barritt, Barrott), the surname begins as a scurrilous

BARBEAU

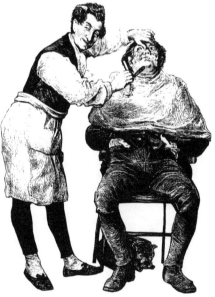

Pas de barbeau.

BARRETT

nickname in Middle English where *barrat* had a range of meanings that encompassed 'trouble, distress, fraud, deception, or strife.' The vexatious noun did not survive into modern English, but two related and mildly obscure legal terms did. A barrator is a person who causes public discord. In marine law, barratry is gross negligence aboard a ship by the captain or crew, or it is fraud at sea committed against owners of a vessel.

BASSETT

John White Hughes Bassett 1930–
The one-time owner of the defunct Toronto Telegram *and of CFTO-TV was a founder of CTV. His son Douglas is now CEO and president of Baton Broadcasting Inc., which owns CFTO-TV in Toronto. His granddaughter Carling Bassett was a championship tennis player.*

The family is not named after the stubby-legged basset-hound first bred to run badgers and foxes to ground. The earliest printed reference to the dog is in 1616, while a Ralph Basset is listed in the Domesday Book of Hertfordshire in A.D. 1086. In Old French *basset* meant 'of low stature,' a diminutive of *bas* 'low,' perhaps even referring to a dwarf. One ancient commentator said Ralph Basset was elevated by King Henry II *de ignobili stirpe ac de pulvere* 'from low-born stock and from the dust of the ground.' However, this might have been a little pun on the part of a scribe who knew French, or merely the snottiness of some envious, low-born clerk.

BASSO

Guido Basso 1937–
One of the world's great jazz trumpet players. The mellow brass of his fluegel-horn adorns jazz cuts on many albums by the Boss Brass, of which band he was a charter member.

Basso means 'low' in Italian. As an Italian adjectival surname it can refer to a low and melodious voice, to the low land where the ancestor lived or to his physical shortness. The very ancient surname can also derive from a cognomen of Republican Rome, *Bassus*, itself borrowed from one of Latin's Italian sister-languages,

Oscan, where *bassus* meant 'stout, fat.'

Guido as a given name is a Romanized form of the Teutonic warrior name **Wido* from the Old High German root *witu* 'wood, forest.' Many cheap dictionaries of first names will tell you that Guido is related to the English word 'guide.' It is not. Guide stems ultimately from the Old Provençal verb *guidar*, itself from Frankish **witan* 'to direct, to show the way to' and thus 'guide' is a distant kin to the modern German *weisen* 'to point out, to show' and to all those German adverbs in *-weise*.

Norma Beecroft 1934–

A Canadian composer of serious avant-garde music herself, and a tireless promoter of Canadian composers, she worked often for CBC Radio as a producer and host. Her own works were heard frequently on the national radio service for many years.

BEECROFT

Beecroft, like Beeman, is a surname based on the ancestor's occupation. In Old English a croft was a fenced field next to a house in which crops were grown, and where, sometimes, as here, beehives were set.

Jean Beliveau 1931–

BELIVEAU

He joined the Montreal Canadiens in 1953 and led the most powerful team in hockey history through eighteen smash seasons.

Beliveau is from a medieval nickname, *beli, beslif,* an adjective in Old French where it meant 'on a slant' or 'the wrong way' or of some bodily part:'crooked.' It would be equivalent to *de travers* in the modern French sentence *Il a la jambe de travers* 'he has a crooked leg.' For example it might have been the nickname of an ancestor who limped, or one who tottered because he tippled too much of the fermented grape.

Dr. Leslie Richard Bell 1906–1962

BELL

He founded the Leslie Bell Singers, a popular Canadian choral group of the 1940s and 1950s.

Marilyn Bell 1937–

The swimmer crossed Lake Ontario in twenty-one hours in 1954 to become a Canadian sports heroine.

Bell is among the one hundred most widespread English surnames due to its manifold sources. As a matronymic, where the family name derives from the mother's first name, Bel was a frequent affectionate diminutive for Isabel.

It was also one of the rare sign names in English; compare John atte Belle listed in a document of 1332 A.D. This may have been a merchant who did business at the sign of the Bell, or one who lived near a church or town belltower or bellhouse. As an occupational surname, it denoted a bellman or bellringer, while Beller was one who cast bells in a foundry. As an ancestor's nickname, Old French has *Bel* 'handsome, beautiful.'

BENGOUGH

John Wilson Bengough 1851–1923

He was the most renowned Canadian political cartoonist of the nineteenth century. His work appeared frequently in George Brown's Globe, *in* The Canadian Illustrated News, *and in* Grip *(1873–94), the comic weekly founded by Bengough.*

Bengough is a Welsh surname based on an ancestor's nickname. In Welsh it's *pencoch* or *bengoch* 'red-haired.'

BENNETT

W.A.C. Bennett 1900–1979
William Richards Bennett 1932–

Both father and son were popular and controversial Premiers of British Columbia.

Richard Bedford Bennett 1870–1947

He was the Prime Minister of Canada from 1930 to 1935. Born in New Brunswick, the stuffy, unsympathetic lawyer led Canada through the worst years of the Depression. Massively defeated in 1935, Bennett retired in bitterness to England in 1937.

Bennett is among the most common surnames in the English-speaking world. It was the customary pet form of Benedict in Middle English, and was far more frequent a first name in England than Benedict ever was. *Benedictus* meant 'blessed' in Latin (literally and originally 'spoken well of'), and was made especially popular by Saint Benedict, founder of the Benedictine Order and writer of the Holy Rule, still used by some Christian monks. He was born in Umbria around 480 A.D. and died in 547 at Monte Cassino, the majestically perched Italian monastery which he founded in the Apennine foothills midway between Rome and Naples.

Jehane Benoît, née Patenaude 1904–1987

BENOÎT

Madame Benoît was a Cordon Bleu authority on Canadian and Québecois food, made famous through radio and TV appearances and her many cookbooks.

Benoît is the early French form of the Latin name *Benedictus* 'blessed' made popular by Saint Benoît de Nurcie (480–547 A.D.) founder of the Benedictine Order, and patriarch of Western monks.

Pierre Berton 1920–

BERTON

Canada's popular historian, journalist, and TV and radio personality

The surname Berton stems from a French ancestor who bore the Germanic pet name of *Berhto* or *Berhta*, both from *berht*, the Old High German adjective meaning 'shining, famous.' The English word 'bright' has the same root. *Berhto* was similar to a nickname for bearers of compound Germanic names beginning with this root, for example, *Berhthraben* 'bright raven,' *Berthold*, and *Bertlinde*.

Allan Emrys Blakeney 1925–

BLAKENEY

Rhodes scholar, lawyer, civil servant, politician, and NDP Premier of Saskatchewan (1971–1982)

Blakeney is a surname based on where the founding ancestor of the family lived. Two places in England are named Blakeney, one in Norfolk, one in Gloucestershire. In Old English the place name was *blacan-eg* 'black island' which referred to the dark soil of a small island or to dry ground in a marshy area.

BOBAK

Bronislaw Josephus Bobak 1923–
"Bruno" Bobak is an artist and administrator long associated with the University of New Brunswick where he and his wife, artist Molly Joan Bobak, née Lamb, have taught and painted.

Bobak is a Polish occupational or sign surname. *Bób* 'bean' suggests a farmer who grows beans or one who sells them. The other possibility is a surname based on an ancestor's shop sign depicting a bay-tree or laurel from Polish *bobek* 'laurel.'

BOGGS

Jean Sutherland Boggs 1922–
Art historian, director, National Gallery of Canada (1966–1976)

Boggs is either Irish or English. If Irish, it refers to an ancestral dweller beside a bog from Irish Gaelic *bog* 'damp, miry.' Consider also the local word in our Canadian maritimes 'bogan,' a small creek or branch of a stream, perhaps from Gaelic *bogainn* 'marsh' but influenced by 'pokelogan,' a marshy place or stagnant pool connected with a river, a backwater. This word is aboriginal, and related to a word in a local language of New Brunswick and Nova Scotia, Malecite, in which *pekelaygan* means 'stopping place' (for a canoe). When Boggs is of British provenance, the surname stems from an ancestor nicknamed with the Middle English adjective *bogeys* 'bragging, saucy, stuck-up, bold.'

BONDAR

Roberta Lynn Bondar 1945–
The Sault-Ste.-Marie-born scientist and astronaut was the first Canadian woman in space on January 22, 1992, for which she has received many honorary awards. For a time she did research under the auspices of the faculty of kinesiology at the University of Western Ontario.

Bondar is the general Slavic word for a cooper, that is, a maker of barrels and casks. In Ukrainian, it's *Bondar*. In Russian, it appears as *Bondare*. In another Slavic language, Polish, it's *bednarz*, giving rise to surnames like Bednarski 'son of the cooper.'

Phillip Borsos 1953–1995

The gifted Canadian film director was born in Tasmania of Greek stock. His work included an Academy Award nomination for an early short, Nails, *and feature films like* The Grey Fox *(1983) and* One Magic Christmas *(1985), and his one disaster,* Bethune:The Making of a Hero *(1988).*

Borsos is a word in the ancient Greek dialect of the city state of Elis which was located in the western part of the Peloponnesus. *Borsos* is an Elean word for crucifix, specifically the cross of Christ. A pious ancestor would take it as a surname. It is equivalent to the standard Greek word for cross or crucifix, *stavros* which gives a male first name in Modern Greek, *Stavros.* The holiness of the word is saved from profanation, so Greeks believed, by shifting the accent from the final syllable to the first. Modern Greek does the same accent-shifting with the word for Christ. The Saviour is *Christós* while the first name for male children is *Christos.*

BORSOS

Borsos or Byzantine cross.

Henri Bourassa 1868–1952

From a long prominent Québec family, he founded Le Devoir, *one of Canada's most influential newspapers in 1910, and, as an important Québec politician, advanced French-Canadian nationalism in what Laurier and others thought was an extreme manner. He was the grandson of Papineau.*

Robert Bourassa 1933–

Premier of Québec (1970–1976 and 1985–1994) he helped draft the Meech Lake Accord and supported the Free Trade Agreement.

Bourassa is a regional variant of the French occupational surname *Bourrassier,* one who makes and sells *bourre de laine* 'homespun cloth of brown wool.' *Bourre* also came to mean the flocking or wadding with which furniture was stuffed. In the spelling *bure,* it was the material from which poor monks' robes were made. The word came into Old French from the popular street Latin of the Romans who conquered ancient Gaul

BOURASSA

Bure was the homespun wool cloth from which monks' robes were made, like the monk here, carving a gargoyle during the completion of *Notre-Dame de Paris.*

where *burra* meant 'rough wool' or 'a shaggy garment.' *Burrus* was an old Latin adjective for brownish-red, the colour of such clothing. Incidentally, it was also the colour of a small donkey used as pack animal, and Roman soldiers posted to the Iberian peninsula called the animal *burrus*, thus planting the verbal seed for one of the earliest words in the Spanish language, *burro*. In Mexico, a tortilla wrapped around a filling of spiced beef and other yummies looked to eaters like a little donkey loaded down with a colorful pack, and so the diminutive form *burrito* meaning 'little donkey' came to be applied to the food as well. *Burrus* was borrowed from or was akin to the Greek colour adjective *pyrros* 'fiery red' whose root is cognate with English 'fire.' Compare these English words: pyre, Pyrex™, and pyromaniac.

BRAITHWAITE

Max Braithwaite 1911–
Novelist, humorist, and author of children's books

Braithwaite is a surname taken from the place of residence of the founding ancestor. Several places in England bear the name, derived from a Viking field name, *Breidrthveiti* in Old Scandinavian, from *breidr / breithr* 'broad' and *thveit* 'thwaite, clearing, meadow, paddock.' A subclass of British surnames like Bassingthwaite and Linthwaite 'clearing where flax (to make linen) is grown' bear similar endings. The prime meaning of thveita in Old Scandinavian was 'hew.' Akin to this root was Old English *thwitan* which gives a dialect form *thwittle*, and our modern English verb for cutting or paring with a knife, whittle. A thwaite was a piece of land cut out for a special purpose, like woodland with trees cleared so it could be arable land. This sense gives English place names and surnames like Applethwaite, Crossthwaithe, Ormthwaite, and Seathwaite.

BRONFMAN

Samuel Bronfman 1889–1971
He built a family liquor business into the largest distilling company in the world. Relatives now control huge real estate, entertainment, and financial institutions.

Bronfman is a particularly apt occupational surname in Yiddish where *bronfn* 'spirits, whisky' gives the
original form *Bronfenman* for one who made and sold
whisky. *Bronfn* is a dialectic condensing of the German
Branntwein where the letter *t* drops out, the German *w*
becomes a Yiddish *f*, and the final vowel is shortened.
By the way, *Branntwein* is literally 'burned' wine, wine
that has been distilled over a fire. A similar form in
early Dutch *brantwijn* led to *brandewijn* which was borrowed into English as brandywine, and by the middle of
the seventeenth century Englishmen were shortening it
to brandy, a liquor distilled from wine or fruit juices
then reduced over a fire.

Horst Bulau 1962–

*The Ottawa-born champion ski jumper won more than a
dozen World Cups.*

BULAU

Bulau is a German surname derived from a place
name, Bülau in the northeastern state of Mecklenberg-
West Pomerania on the Baltic coast of Germany. The
town dates back before 1000 A.D. and may have been
founded by Slavic-speaking people. Some topographic
feature near the place may have resembled a breadroll
which is *bula* in early Slavic. Compare a Russian
diminutive form like *boolachka* 'small French breadroll.'

German *Horst* is a shortened form of several compound Germanic names like *Horstmar* 'famous in the
little wood' or *Horstwin* 'friend of the copse,' both of
which suggest Teutonic first names that might have
been medieval occupational nicknames for a forester, a
guardian of certain woods. In Middle Low German
horst meant 'coppice.' In modern German *Horst* means
'eyrie,' something high in a wood or on a hill, namely
the nest of a bird of prey who builds high up. The
German word is akin to the Old English West Saxon
noun *hyrst* 'wooded hill' which appears in numerous
British and Canadian place names like Crowhurst,
Gravenhurst, Longhirst, Pinehurst, and Whitehurst, not
to mention plain Hurst, which is the source of the
English surname in all its spellings: Herst, Hirst, Hurst.

C

CADILLAC

Antoine Laumet de Lamothe Cadillac 1658–1730
*In Québec by 1691 he was a commandant and fur trad-
er. A few years later he founded a fur-trading fort at
Detroit, hence the name of General Motors' luxury car.
Charges of empire building sent him down to Louisiana
as Governor from 1710 to 1717. Further charges of
sharp dealing sent him with great wealth home to
France in 1718.*

Cadillac is the name of a place near Bordeaux and
of a little town in the Dordogne that springs from the
name of a Gallo-Roman territory of ancient Gaul,
Catiliacum, itself composed from a Latin cognomen
mentioned by Cicero and Pliny *Catilius* and the Latin
locative suffix *-acum*. *Catus*, an adjective in street
Latin, meant 'smart, intelligent' and the noun *catus* was
a tomcat. The diminutive of that noun *catulus* meant the
young of any animal, especially puppy or kitten, and
was the nickname of an ancestor of the greatest lyric
poet of ancient Rome, Catullus.

CAMERON

William Cameron 1943–
*Vancouver-born Bill is a writer, journalist, television
reporter, and CBC TV host, interviewer and newsreader.*

Cameron, one of the fifty most common names in
Scotland, is a Scots Gaelic surname arising from an
ancestor's nickname, many of which were typically
dour. In Scots Gaelic *cameron* means 'crooked nose,
hook-nose.' There are several places in Scotland from
the same root, but there 'crooked nose' refers to some
local feature of topography, e.g., a peculiar bend in a
river or perhaps a rocky outcropping of nasal shape.
Both Irish and Scots Gaelic have male names of less
than good omen. This mode of naming is sometimes
called apotropaic, that is, names chosen to drive away
(Greek verb *apotrepein*) either evil spirits or enemies in
battle.

CAMP

Dalton Kingsley Camp 1920–
*Progressive Conservative politician, witty writer, news-
paper columnist, and CBC Radio commentator whose
political memoirs include* Gentlemen, Players and

Politicians *(1970)*, Points of Departure *(1979)*, *and* Eclectic Eel *(1981)*

Camp began as an occupational nickname in Old English *cempa* 'warrior.' In Middle English, spelled Kempe, it could mean 'athlete' or 'wrestler.' Old English also had *camp* 'battle' and *campian* 'to fight' both akin to the German *Kampf* 'battle' as in the deranged blatherings of Hitler's *Mein Kampf* 'my struggle.'

Early Teutonic mercenaries working for the Romans on the edges of their empire may have borrowed the word *Kampf* into Proto-Germanic from the Latin *campus* 'level field' on which one could train soldiers, do battle, or pursue studies. In Italian it became *campo* and one who won on the field of battle was a *campione* which French, then English, borrowed as "champion" and "champ." Little mushrooms growing in a French field were *champignons*. A conflict restricted to one field of battle, even a political contest, was a *campagne* 'campaign.' If one were a cowardly rogue, one might run away from a battle and be branded a scamp in its original Italian sense of 'an escape' (Italian *scampare* from Latin *ex* 'away from' + *campare* 'to be in a field'). Now let's scamper away from camp.

Edibles of the countryside were *champignons*.

Iona Campagnolo, née Hardy 1932–

Born on Galiano Island in B.C., she worked as a broadcaster and local politician in Prince Rupert, rising through posts such as Liberal MP for Skeena to become the first female president of the Liberal Party of Canada (1982–1986).

Campagnolo is an Italian surname indicating where an ancestor lived, or in this case, perhaps what he owned, a little group of flat fields. *Campagna* is 'a plain' and *-olo* a diminutive suffix. The surname can also indicate an ancestor who came from the fertile plains of ancient Campania south of and inland from Naples, and in that case the *-olo* is sometimes called an affectionate diminutive, equivalent to some English phrase like "that great person from Campania."

CAMPAGNOLO

CAMPBELL

Rt. Hon. A. Kim Campbell 1947–
Nineteenth and first female Prime Minister of Canada (June–November 1993)

Campbell is another of those Gaelic surnames based on a salty nickname, in this case the Scots Gaelic means 'crooked mouth.' It could apply to a harelip, wry-mouth, any disfiguring facial tic, or, topographically, to some local feature of the landscape beside which the founder of the family lived. Campbell is a common name in Irish Gaelic as well. It is the family name of the dukes of Argyll and of six other members of the Scottish peerage. In 1958 Campbell was the seventh most frequent name in Scotland.

CARDINAL

Douglas Joseph Cardinal 1934–
He is a Métis architect born in Red Deer, Alberta, whose great works include St. Mary's Church in Red Deer and the Canadian Museum of Civilization in Ottawa. His mother was a nurse, his father a provincial wildlife officer of half-Siksika (Blackfoot) heritage. Cardinal has stayed involved in Métis and aboriginal issues, all the while growing as an architect.

Harold Cardinal 1945–
Assembly of First Nations vice-chief, he is a political activist, for a time chief of his natal band at the Sucker Creek Reserve in Alberta, and author of two important books critical of Canada's policies toward first peoples: The Unjust Society *(1969) and* The Rebirth of Canada's Indians *(1977).*

Tantoo Cardinal 1950–
Born in Fort McMurray, Alberta, this Genie Award-winning actress has starred in TV films like Loyalties *(1987) and been featured in blockbusters like* Dances With Wolves, *as well as many educational films in Alberta and other parts of Canada.*

The startlingly coloured cardinal is often a totemic bird of our founding peoples, important in native ritual, myth, and consequently part of the naming vocabulary of first peoples. Thus the English word for the red bird is usually a translation of an aboriginal name.

Emily Carr 1871–1945

She was a Canadian painter of pacific forests and beaches, of vanished villages and totem poles, and later in life, after a heart attack made painting difficult, writer of books like Klee Wyck, *which won the Governor-General's Award in 1941. After her death, four volumes of her journals were published.*

Shirley Carr

She is a union activist who rose to become president of the Canadian Labour Congress (1986–1992) and as such the first Canadian woman to lead a national labour organization.

Carr is a common root in British place names in the Danelaw and then a surname in northern Britain indicating where an ancestor lived. Its root is Old Norse *kjarr* 'marsh, boggy thicket.' Other spellings are Kerr and Ker.

James "Jim" Carrey 1962–

Born in Jackson's Point, Ontario, the rubber-faced Canadian actor, comedian, and writer began in comedy clubs, moved on to the Fox network TV satire In Living Color, *then to colossal success in slapstick films like* The Mask *(1994),* Ace Ventura: Pet Detective *(1994, sequel 1995),* Dumb and Dumber *(1995), and* Batman Forever *(1995) where he played The Riddler.*

Carrey is an orthographical variant of Carey and Cary, the latter a British surname taken from the River Cary in Somerset. If Celtic, it is possibly from the Indo-European root **kar* 'hard' or 'stony' in reference to the bed of the stream. If pre-Celtic, you could mug a druid and still be in the etymological dark, for the names of many rivers are of such immemorial antiquity that their true meanings are forever lost. However, of the old river names whose roots we can trace, the great majority mean 'river,' 'wet,' or 'flowing.' Take your pick.

Brent Carver 1952–

The Canadian actor and singer won plaudits for his roles in Broadway megamusicals like Kiss of the Spider

Woman *(1992). Born in Cranbrook, B.C., Carver played Robert Ross in the film version of Timothy Findley's* The Wars, *and at Ontario's Stratford Shakespearean Festival he starred in* Hamlet, The Pirates of Penzance, *and* Cabaret.

If of Norman provenance, Carver is Old French *charvier* 'ploughman'; if of English stock, the occupational surname suggests wood-carver or stone mason.

CASSELMAN

Barbie Casselman 1956–

Nutritionist, author, TV cooking expert whose books include Barbie Casselman's Good-For-You Cooking: A Healthy Eating Guide *(1993)*

Leah Casselman

She is a union leader, president of OPSEU, the Ontario Public Servants' Employment Union, who led a strike in 1996 against the union-bashing tactics of Ontario Premier Mike Harris.

Karen Leigh Casselman 1942–

A writer, broadcaster, lecturer, and fabric artist living in Cheverie, Nova Scotia, she is author of the internationally published Craft of the Dyer *(1980).*

William Gordon Casselman 1942–

Your humble deponent has flogged his wares in Canadian newspapers, magazines, radio broadcasting, television production, and in 1995 was the author of the bestselling Casselman's Canadian Words.

My Lutheran Kasselmanns fled religious persecution in eighteenth-century Hesse. Many walked from Germany through the Netherlands, and then by boat reached London at the dawn of the eighteenth century. There, to afford passage to the New World, they signed indentures to work with the British navy. By 1712 my ancestors lived in the small towns of Schoharie and Stone Arabia in the Mohawk Valley, west of the Hudson River in present-day New York State. Earlier they had worked caulking ships in a British navy yard on the Hudson.

During the War of American Independence, most

Casselmans remained loyal to King George III, their loyalty buoyed up by the offer of free land along the St. Lawrence River, to which haven they removed themselves with due alacrity as the New York air grew thick with musket shot. But some Casselmans remained in America, enough to make a character named Suffrenus Casselman one of the villains in Walter Edmond's 1936 novel *Drums Along the Mohawk*. And Sophrenus was a real given name in the Casselman family's early American history.

Kasselmann is a locative surname that means simply *einer aus Kassel* 'a person from the city of Kassel' in Hesse. Kassel was the site of a Roman fortification on the outer marches of the empire and takes its name from *castellum* 'little camp' then 'fortified camp' and the same word gives rise to later words like castle, château, chatelaine, and a suffix in British locations named from encampments of Roman legions, places like Chester, Doncaster, Manchester, and, home of the pungent sauce: Worcestershire.

When Casselman is a Jewish surname, it is likely to be an anglicizing of Kesselman in which the surname derives from the Hebrew male first name Yekutiel (sometimes Yekusiel), which had a pet form *Kessel* or *Kesseluh*. The Elizabethan transliteration of Yekutiel that appears in the King James version of First Chronicles is Jekuthiel, a son of the scribe Ezra. In Hebrew Yekutiel means 'fear of God.'

Casselman can also be an Englishing of the German occupational surname *Kesselmann* ultimately from German *Kessel* 'kettle, pot, boiler' and so pointing to one who made pots and pans, a boilermaker, or a coppersmith. The more common form was Kessler.

Floyd Sherman Chalmers 1898–1993

Editor of the Financial Post, *president and chairman of the board of Maclean-Hunter. Mr. Chalmers, his wife Jean, and their daughter M. Joan Chalmers have been generous patrons of many Canadian arts through the Floyd S. Chalmers Foundation, the Jean A. Chalmers Chair in Canadian Music, and other philanthropies.*

CHALMERS

Chalmers is a Scottish variant of Chambers 'son of the chamber' which was originally an occupation. The chamber was an official of a great house exactly like a chamberlain, what we might call today an estate or household manager. Middle English *chaumbre* < Old French *chambre* < Latin *camera* 'room' but originally 'room with a vaulted roof' hence 'large room, public or private' < Greek *kamara* 'anything with an arched covering' < Indo-European root **kam* 'curved, bent.' In linguistics, the symbol < means 'derived from' and the symbol > means 'is the root of, gives rise to.'

CHAREST

Un charêt.

Jean Charest 1958–
Interim leader of the Progressive Conservative Party following the federal election of 1993, the personable MP for Sherbrooke was federal Minister of the Environment (1991–1993).

Charest is a variant of Charêt, an occupational nickname for a carter, one who owned and operated *un char*, in other words a barrowman who transported goods in a handcart, a dogcart, or a tumbrel.

COCKBURN

Bruce Cockburn 1945–
The folksinger, songwriter, and political activist is the recipient of many Juno awards. His 1984 album "Stealing Fire" went platinum on the U.S. Billboard charts in 1985.

James Cockburn 1819–1883
Politician, a father of Confederation and speaker of the House of Commons (1867–1873)

Cockburn was early altered to euphemistic variants like Cobourne, and so pronounced to avoid what seventeenth-century minds thought was the vulgar meaning of 'cock.' Of course, it began innocently enough. A cock was a rooster or the male of any wild food bird. *-Burn* is often from Old English *burna* or Old Norse *brunnr* 'stream.' Thus Cockburn could mean 'a stream frequented by wild birds,' the name itself a useful hunter's mnemonic. Cock also came to mean pert lad, that is, one who strutted like a cock. It was a term of affection even as late as Charles Dickens who has Mr. Cratchit call Tiny Tim, "My little cock-sparrow." And there were Old English personal names like *Cohha and *Cocc(a) so that Cockburn may have been 'Cocca's stream.'

COHEN

Dian Cohen 1937–

The economist-commentator, journalist in print, radio, and television, has won national business-writing awards. In 1993 she was created a member of the Order of Canada. She is the author of Money *(1987).*

Leonard Cohen 1934–

Montréal poet, songwriter, novelist whose Beautiful Losers *(1966) was one of my personal literary amulets in the late sixties. Another novel was* The Favourite Game *(1963). His work includes poetry like* Let Us Compare Mythologies *(1956) and* Parasites of Heaven *(1966). Among albums of his own songs are "Songs From a Room" (1969), "Death of a Ladies Man" (1977), and "I'm Your Man" (1987).*

Matt Cohen 1942–

Kingston-born novelist who has dealt with small town Ontario life in his Salem Quartet: The Disinherited *(1974),* The Colours of War *(1977),* The Sweet Second Summer of Kitty Malone *(1979), and* Flowers of Darkness *(1981). Other works that delve into his Jewish heritage include* The Spanish Doctor *(1984) and* Nadine *(1986).*

Samuel Nathan Cohen 1923–1971

Born in Sydney, Nova Scotia, he became Canada's most influential theatre critic in the 1950s and 1960s in the pages of the Toronto Star, *as well as a popular panelist on CBC radio and television.*

Cohen, Cohn, Cahn, Kahn, Kagan, Kogan, Kaplan, Kohani, Cahana, and variants all stem from a Hebrew word for priest *kohen*. The brother of Moses, Aaron, was the first of the kohanim, priests who performed sacrifices and religious services in the simple sanctuaries during the desert wanderings and later in glory in the great Temple at Jerusalem. Post-exilic Jews passed the title of kohen down as a surname even after the specific priestly office no longer existed.

CONNORS

"Stompin' Tom" Connors 1936–
Folksy balladeer born in Saint John, N.B. whose songs include "Bud the Spud."

Connors is an Anglo-Irish version of *Ó Connor* which in Irish Gaelic means 'descendant of High Will' suggesting an ancestral nickname identifying a person of great resolution.

COPPS

Sheila Copps 1952–
Liberal politician from the Hamilton family of politicians who include her father Victor Copps, longtime mayor of Hamilton, Ontario. She has been a journalist with the Ottawa Citizen *(1974–1976) and a federal Liberal leadership candidate in 1990, and then filled various posts in Chrétien's cabinet, including Deputy Prime Minister and Minister of the Environment.*

Copps shows the common possessive *s* that makes the meaning 'descendant of Copp.' In Old English *cop, copp* meant 'top, summit, human head, hilltop, high place.' It thus can be a locative surname denoting a place the ancestor lived, or a last name based on the ancestor's nickname indicating a large head or cleverness.

COUPLAND

Douglas Coupland 1961–
Generation X novelist who popularized the phrase in his 1991 fiction Generation X, *the British Columbian has also written* Shampoo Planet *(1992),* Life After God *(1994), and* Microserfs *(1995).*

In the British county of Northumberland lies Coupland, a town founded by Vikings who seem to have bought land to settle on rather than seize it by invasion. In Old Norse or Old Scandinavian it is *kaupa-land* 'bought or purchased land.'

Mary Helen Creighton 1899–
The author is a folklorist and pioneer collector of maritime folk songs and stories in long association with the National Museum of Canada. Her books include Bluenose Ghosts *(1957),* Bluenose Magic *(1968),* A Life in Folklore *(1975), and for children* With a Heigh-Heigh-Ho *(1986).*

CREIGHTON

Creighton is a surname taken from the place an ancestor lived, here an old town in the English county of Staffordshire whose name is compounded of Old Welsh or Celtic **creig* 'cliff, big rock' whence English crag and craggy-faced and of Old English *tun* 'town, village.' Variants of the surname with the same meaning include Crichton, Crighton, and Chricton. The Scots surname Crichton stems from a place near Edinburgh where Crichton is made up of two roots that mean 'border' and 'town.'

Isapo-muxika 1830–1890
A famous Blackfoot (Siksika) chief, born a Blood but raised a Blackfoot. He co-operated with Whites when it seemed to be to the advantage of aboriginal peoples but became angry at Ottawa after the Blackfoot were settled on their Alberta reserve in 1881.

CROWFOOT

Isapo-muxika means 'Crow Indian's Big Foot' in Siksika. Interpreters shortened it to Crowfoot. His ancestral honorific name was bestowed to celebrate his bravery as a teenager in a battle.

Burton Cummings 1947–
The Winnipeg-born rock musician was vocalist for the Guess Who *(1968–1975). His hit songs include the group's only Billboard number-one "American Woman" (1970) and a solo #10 in 1977 "Stand Tall" along with "I'm Scared" and a contributing vocal on the 1985 famine aid recording "Tears Are Not Enough."*

CUMMINGS

Whether an Irish, Scottish, or English surname,

Cummings was brought to the British Isles by Norman French settlers. Various towns in France, like Comines near the French-Belgian border, may be the origin, or perhaps Bosc-Benard-Commin in the Eure where French surnames like Comin and Coumini appear in the twelfth century. Old Breton has Cunmin as a male first name in A.D. 895. All the surnames including Irish ones like Comyn, *Ó Coimín*, and *Ó Cuimín* may be diminutive forms of **cam* 'bent, crooked' either as a topographical description or a nickname based on physique.

D

DA ROZA

Gustavo Uriel Da Roza 1933–
Born at Hong Kong, of Chinese and Portuguese heritage, the influential Winnipeg architect's work includes the Winnipeg Art Gallery (1971). He also teaches at the University of Manitoba.

Da Roza is a Portuguese matronymic surname, a spelling variant of *rosa* 'rose.' The surname means literally 'from Rosa' which can be a woman's given name. Da Roza may also be a locative surname based on the place of residence of the ancestor, namely, a locality of reddish soil or rock.

DANBY

Kenneth Edison Danby 1940–
Born in Sault Ste. Marie, the popular painter of athletes and rural Ontario scenes counts among his most familiar images the masked goalie of At The Crease *(1972).*

Danby is a Yorkshire surname from one of three places in that county. In Old Norse *Danabý* means 'Danes' farm or village.' The Old Scandinavian terminal *-by* appears in dozens of British place names and thence surnames, e.g., Appleby, Derby, Kettleby, Thursby, Whitby.

DANDURAND

Ann Dandurand 1953–
She is a Québec novelist and short story writer whose works include L'assassin de l'intérieur *(1988),* Un coeur qui craque *(1990),* Petites âmes sous ultimatum *(1991), and* La salle d'attente *(1994).*

Dandurand is a contraction of the southern French

D'Andurand in which *de* is added to the surname to lend an aristocratic hue to *Andurand* which is itself an orthographical variant of *Endurant*, the present participle of the verb *endurer.* This was an ancestral nickname that meant 'patient' or 'stubborn.'

Gary Michael Dault 1939–

The Toronto writer taught the history of art at several Canadian universities and was art critic at the Toronto Star *for five years. He has written extensively on the lively arts for a number of Canadian and international art magazines and newspapers including a photography column for the* Globe and Mail *and a design column for* Canadian Art. *Among his books are* Barker Fairley Portraits *(1981),* Visions: Contemporary Art in Canada *(1983), and with Tony Urquhart* Cells of Ourselves *(1989). His* Children in Photography: 150 Years *appeared in 1990.*

    Dault is a French surname *d'Ault* 'from the town of Ault' in the Somme where *Ault* is a local variant of the Common Teutonic *alt* 'old (place).' But in the specific instance of Gary Michael Dault's name, Dault is a variant of D'Aoust from *de + aoust* 'of August' where the ancestor's nickname arises from the fact that he was a seasonal worker (of August) and in medieval France that meant he was a harvester of cereal crops who hired out in August when such crops ripened. The French surname Laoust is of similar origin.

DAULT

Florence Edenshaw Davidson 1896–?

The Haida artist and teacher of her people's culture, born at Masset on Queen Charlotte Island, worked in basket weaving, ceremonial blankets, spruce-root and cedar-bark hats.

    Her Haida names were *Jadalloz* and *g'egedngaá* 'Story Maiden.'

DAVIDSON

Robertson William Davies 1913–1995

One of Canada's greatest novelists was also a newspaperman, actor, playwright, humorous essayist, teacher and the founding master of Massey College at the

DAVIES

University of Toronto. Among his outstanding novels are the Deptford Trilogy: Fifth Business *(1970),* The Manticore *(1972), and* World of Wonders *(1975). Other works of note:* The Rebel Angels *(1981),* What's Bred in the Bone *(1985),* The Lyre of Orpheus *(1988), and* The Cunning Man *(1994).*

Davies is the most frequent patronymic from the Biblical first name, David. It means 'descendant of Davy,' Davy being the common nickname. Davies is the standard Welsh spelling of the name which is otherwise widely found in Cornwall and Devonshire.

The Hebrew name *Dovid* began as an affectionate cradle word, something like a mother cooing 'goody-woody' to a baby. From this general 'lullaby' meaning of 'darling,' David then came to mean 'friend' in general. Its Welsh popularity stems from St. David, patron saint of Wales; and two early Scottish kings bore the name. Many surnames sprang from it including Davis, Davis, Davy, Davitt, Dawes, Dawson, Dawkins, and the Scots Gaelic McTavish. McTavish is not, as the *Penguin Dictionary of Surnames* states, from 'son of Tammas,' Lowland Scots for Thomas—for the simple reason that such a derivation does not explain the mysterious disappearance of the *m*. It is rather 'son of Tavy = Davy.' But some say that in the Gaelic spelling *Mac Tamhais* the *mh* accounts for the *v* in McTavish. Then let the wee woollywallocks have their say! Scots, of course, prefer Davidson, although the Irish McDevitt or McDade are also occasionally found.

DE KERCKHOVE

High drama in a churchyard.

Derrick De Kerckhove 1944–
The writer and professor of French at the University of Toronto worked with Marshall McLuhan and is now director of the McLuhan Program in Culture and Technology at the University of Toronto; his books include The Alphabet and the Brain *(1988) and* The Skin of Culture: Investigating the New Electronic Reality *(1995).*

De Kerckhove is a Flemish surname indicating the place an ancestor lived, namely, near the *kerckhove* 'churchyard.' Compare the Dutch *kerkhof* and the German *Kirchhof* and the Scots Gaelic *kirk* 'church.'

Donald Grant Devine 1944–

A farmer who taught agricultural economics at the University of Saskatchewan and was Progressive Conservative Premier of the province from 1982, winning re-election in 1986.

Devine has two etymological strands. One Devine is Norman French (in English records from A.D. 1187) from Old French *devin* 'divine,' a nickname for an ancestor of exemplary religious character. The other is Irish Gaelic where the surname Devine is an anglicizing of *Ó Daimhín* 'descendant of Little Ox or Little Stag' or an Englishing of *Ó Duibhín* 'descendant of Blackie,' that is, 'Little Black One,' a nickname referring to complexion, hair colour, or the 'black Irish,' a term of mild opprobrium used to describe Irish people of Mediterranean appearance.

Christopher Dewdney 1951–

Poet, artist, teacher, TV commentator on TVO's Studio 2, *his works include* Fovea Centralis *(1975),* Predators of the Adoration, The Immaculate Perception *(1986), and* Concordat Provisio Ascendant *(1991).*

Sir Edgar Dewdney 1835–1916

Politician, civil engineer and surveyor-supervisor of British Columbia's Dewdney Trail constructed in the late 1860s to provide a route to the interior of British Columbia.

Dewdney is an orthographical transmutation of the Norman French name *Dieudonné* 'God-given,' itself from a Late Latin Christian first name *Deodonatus* 'given by God.'

Two semantic units in a compound name suggesting that a newborn child is a gift of God are common in the naming vocabulary of many languages. Greek, for example, has Dorothea and Theodoros where the words *theos* 'god' and *doron* 'gift' are interchanged. Slavic has *bogdan* 'God-gift' giving surnames like Bogdanovitch and feminine first names like Bogdana. Hebrew has Nathaniel 'God has given' with the verbal root *natan* 'give' and the Semitic root *el* 'god' which appears in Hebrew words like Elohim (literally a plural form

DEVINE

DEWDNEY

'gods') and in Arabic words like *al-ilah* 'the god' which is conflated to *Allah.* The Hebrew version of the root appears as the prefix in names like Elijah, Elisha, and Elisheba, the later well-known in its English form of Elizabeth.

DIEFENBAKER

John George Diefenbaker 1895–1979
The lively Progressive Conservative Saskatchewan defence lawyer became Canada's thirteenth Prime Minister (1957–1963).

Diefenbaker is a spelling variant of the German surname *Dieffenbacher* 'person from the Lower Rhine town of Dieffenbach.' The town was situated on the banks of a *dief* 'deep' *Bach* 'stream.'

DION

Céline Dion 1968–
The popular Québec singer's hits include "If You Asked Me To" and her duet with Peabo Bryson "Beauty and the Beast," as well as "Love Can Move Mountains," and "Des mots qui sonnent."

Stéphane Dion 1956–
Political science professor at the University of Montréal, appointed to Chrétien cabinet in January, 1996, as Intergovernmental Affairs Minister to deal with national unity policies.

Dion as a French surname has two sources. The ancestor may have lived in one of the half-dozen ancient French towns with names like Dion, Dions, Les Dyons, Dionne: all of them from early French *divonus* from the Celtic word for god **devos.* The Dionne quintuplets' surname has this origin too.

Dion may also be a surname based on the ancient baptismal name *Dido, Didonis* —not from the name of Aeneas' gal pal, the Queen of Carthage, but rather a Latinized form of the Germanic name *Thiodo, Diod* 'people.' The loss of the intervocalic *d* in *Didonis* to produce *Dion* indicates the word was borrowed at a very early date into French.

Thomas "Tommy" Clement Douglas 1904–1986
*One of my heroes, Mr. Douglas was a Baptist minister
who became a politician, a socialist who helped found
the CCF, precursor of the NDP, an incisive debater who
could be warm and funny, the father of Medicare and
the Canada Pension Plan, and Premier of
Saskatchewan (1944–1961). He was a plain, kind
Christian who had examined in his head and in his
heart what exactly such a label might require of a man
who found himself in the midst of the twentieth century.*

Douglas is a Scots Gaelic topographical name
made up of *dubh* 'black' and *glas* 'blue, water, stream.'
It is the name of a very old settlement in Lanarkshire.
But all over the Celtic world it was a common river
name, showing up in England as Dawlish, Dowles
Brook, Divelish; in Wales as Dulas; in Ireland and
Scotland as Douglas. Black water might mean water in
a peat bog or in a silted brook. In the late sixteenth century it was used as the Christian name of a girl or a boy.
Today it is a common first name for boys, and of course
still the proud boast of the Clan Douglas.

Garth Howard Drabinsky 1948–
*Lawyer and one of Canada's greatest showbiz impresar-
ios whose nineties company Livent Inc. has brought
large musicals to Canadians and Americans including
the highly successful revival of Kern and Hammerstein's*
Show Boat.

Drabinsky is a Polish surname from *drabina* 'ladder' + *ski,* a patronymic suffix in Polish that means 'son
of' or 'descendant of,' thus Drabinsky means 'descendant of an ancestor named Ladder,' either because he
was a renowned carpenter or because he was tall. But
this surname can also mean 'son of a rabbi' to Polish
Jews. Compare Jewish Slavic names like Rabin and
Rabinovitch. Drabinsky is an example of how Jewish
surnames could slip past anti-Semitic officials by being
disguised slightly, for there were many times in the
Jews' European history when they were forbidden to
call themselves by their true Hebrew names.

DOUGLAS

DRABINSKY

DRAINIE

John Robert Roy Drainie 1916–1966
A Vancouver-born player who taught himself to be Canada's greatest radio actor, familiar to CBC Radio listeners from 1938, until his untimely death, in roles like Jake on the CBC Radio serial of W. O. Mitchell's Jake and the Kid. *Drainie recreated Stephen Leacock reading his humorous works on stage, radio, and television. Many listeners will remember him from dozens and dozens of leading roles on Andrew Allan's* CBC Stage *series (1944–1956).*

Bronwyn Drainie 1945–
She is a journalist, broadcaster and Globe and Mail *columnist whose books include* Living the Part: John Drainie and the Dilemma of Canadian Stardom *(1988) and* My Jerusalem: Secular Adventures in the Holy City *(1994).*

Bronwyn is a Welsh given name for females that means 'white breast.' Drainie is from the Welsh word *draen* 'thorn.' An ancestor nicknamed Thorny might have dwelt near a thorn-patch or had a prickly personality.

DUCEPPE

Jean Duceppe 1923–1991
The popular Québec actor and director, best known outside of the province for his role as the long-suffering merchant in Claude Jutra's film Mon Oncle Antoine, *starred in many Québec* TV *dramas and feature films and has a theatre named in his honour at Montréal's Place Bonaventure.*

Duceppe is a French surname that means 'descendant of the jailer' where *cep, ceppe* was the wooden stake to which the iron chains that bound prisoners were attached. Its Latin root is *cippus* 'post, pillar, stake.'

DUDEK

Louis Dudek 1981—
The Montréal-born poet is a literary critic, anthologist, founding publisher of Contact Press and Delta, *a literary magazine; and longtime professor of English at McGill University, whose works include* Atlantis *(1967),* Epigrams *(1975),* Cross-Section: Poems 1940–1980, *and* The Birth of Reason *(1994).*

Dudek is Polish for 'piper' and refers specifically to one little piper, the hoopoe, a gaudily crested European bird, salmon-pink in colour, whose characteristic call has earned it the delightfully plosive zoological name of *Upupa epops*. The Polish surname may have originated as a Jewish nickname for an ancestor who was a gaudy dresser or a show-off. In Yiddish it would be *fifer* and it was not a compliment. A *fifer* might be literally 'a whistler, a piper' but it also meant 'a loudmouth, a braggart.'

The *dudek* could have been the bird on a shop sign. But Dudek also suggests a Yiddish cradle name for males *Dudel* or *Dudl* from the German and Yiddish verb *dudeln* 'to tootle, to play a pipe, to strum a stringed instrument.' The title character bears the name in Mordecai Richler's great Montréal novel *The Apprenticeship of Duddy Kravitz* (1959).

The hoopoe bird, a gaudy little piper.

Michael Dennis Duffy 1946–

Born in Charlottetown, P.E.I., Mike is an Ottawa-based television reporter on national politics for CBC TV and later CTV, once called "Marzipan Cheeks" in the pages of Maclean's *magazine by a now deeply repentant junior scribe named Bill Casselman.*

Duffy is Irish and Scots Gaelic 'black man of peace' where the Gaelic *dubh* 'black, dark' refers to hair colour or complexion of a brunette. The Erse is *Ó Dubhthaigh*.

DUFFY

Gabriel Dumont 1837–1906

The Métis leader was Riel's adjutant general during the 1885 Northwest Rebellion.

DUMONT

Mario "Super Mario" Dumont 1970–

In 1994–1996, he was the young, charismatic leader of the Québec separatist Parti Action Démocratique.

Dumont is one of the hundred most common French surnames, taken from dozens of instances as a house name in medieval France, indicating a dwelling on an elevation, literally 'of the mountain' but an apter English translation would be 'on the hill.'

E

EATON

Timothy Eaton 1834–1907
Merchant, founder of the T. Eaton Company

There are at least twenty-nine villages in England named Eaton or Eton. Bearers of this surname had ancestors who lived in one of the hamlets. Eaton has one of two sources descriptive of locality in Old English, either *ea* 'river' + *tun* 'farm, small village' or *eg* 'island' + *tun*.

EDDY

Ezra Butler Eddy 1827–1906
Manufacturer of friction-matches and other wood and paper products at Hull, Québec

Eadwig was a common Anglo-Saxon warrior name of typically Germanic compound form whose elements are *ead* 'happiness' + *wig* 'battle, war.' By the time of Middle English, Eddy had become a widespread surname.

EDENSHAW

Charlie Edenshaw 1839–1920
Born at Skidegate on Queen Charlotte Island, B.C., he was among the earliest professional Haida artisans who worked in local media like argillite and wood and in media imported by collectors like gold, silver, and ivory.

Edenshaw is a borrowed "White" name. His true Haida names were *Tahaygen* 'noise in the housepit' and *Nngkwigetklals* 'they gave ten potlatches for him.' The potlatch was an important ceremony of many Pacific Coast peoples in which gifts were exchanged, chieftains invested with power, names given, spirits propitiated, and dances performed. The word came into English from Chinook Jargon from the Nootka word *patshatl* 'a giving, a gift.' But White busybodies did not understand the complexity of the potlatch and how its sociological strands were woven tightly into band and clan life. Thus the Canadian federal government outlawed the full ceremony in its 1884 Potlatch Law. By the time the ban was repealed in 1951 during revision of the Indian Act, serious clan disruption had resulted, permanently skewing tribal identities, ranks, and statuses.

Michael Enright

Journalist and broadcaster, Michael Enright has written for the Globe and Mail, *been* Maclean's *magazine correspondent in China, director of CBC Radio news, and host of the public affairs program* As It Happens.

Enright is a back-formation from McEnright, an Irish surname which means, claims Basil Cottle in the *Penguin Dictionary of Surnames*, 'son of Unlawful or son of Attack.' Begorra! Thank goodness it isn't both, as in 'son of unlawful attack.' For that would posit a familial origin steeped in bastardy!

Sorel Etrog 1933–

The Romanian-born sculptor has lived in Toronto since 1963. Along with monumental bronze and sheet metal works, he designed the statuettes formerly handed out at the Canadian Film Awards, which were called the Etrogs.

Etrog is a Jewish surname derived from 'ethrog' which is the Hebrew name of the fruit of a Middle Eastern tree, the *hadar.* The fruit has ritual importance in *Sukkot* 'little booths,' the Jewish Feast of Tabernacles, a harvest festival. In that celebration, the etrog—sometimes translated citron, but note that it is not a lemon—makes up part of the festive *Sukkot* bouquet along with a date-palm branch, myrtle boughs, and willow branches. The surname originates as the occupation name of a fruit-seller, as a house sign name, or as a simple name of respect. For, in rabbinical symbolism, the etrog, which should be ripe and fragrant for use in *Sukkot,* may represent the pious heart, seat of emotions. The etrog symbolizes also a person of kindness, courtesy, and wisdom. As a playful *shtetl* nickname it was given to someone as short and stout as an etrog.

Joseph Fafard 1942–

F

Born at Ste-Marthe-Rocanville, Saskatchewan, this sculptor now based in Regina worked in plaster and papier-mâché portraits of people, went on to ceramic humans and animals, and in 1985 to The Pasture: *seven bronze cows at the Toronto Dominion Centre in Toronto. One of Fafard's typically impish works is* The Candidate *(1987) a sculpture of Jean Chrétien sitting on a kitchen chair in shirt sleeves.*

Fafard is a French surname based on adding a diminutive suffix *-ard* to the indigenous and onomatopoeic French root *faf* whose general sense is 'fluff, trifle, object of little value.' The root is seen in terms like *fafiot* 'small banknote,' *fafie* 'trifle' and French school slang like *faffeuerie* 'a little mistake in a lesson.' Why a forebear would be called 'a little trifle' and then choose to perpetuate the remark by selecting it as a surname is one of the many small onomastic mysteries now lost to history.

FAIRCLOUGH

Ellen Louks Fairclough 1905–
The chartered accountant and city councillor at her birthplace of Hamilton, Ontario, became Canada's first female Cabinet Minister in the 1957 Diefenbaker government, and sponsored an early bill demanding equal pay for equal work on behalf of women.

Fairclough, a common name in Lancashire, is simply fair *clough* Middle English 'dell, hollow.' A crest of a pretty ravine was the site of an ancestor's house.

FERRERAS

Sal Ferreras
A British Columbia drummer of Puerto Rican ancestry, in 1995 head of the Vancouver Folk Music festival

Ferreras 'son of the blacksmith' is a Spanish occupational surname related to Spanish words like *ferrería* 'foundry, ironworks' and *férreo* 'ferrous, made of or containing iron' and *ferrocarril* 'railway,' literally 'iron road,' all derived from Latin *ferrum* 'iron.' Compare the English noun 'farrier.' Spanish surname variants include Ferrer. Initial Roman *f* sometimes became *h* in Spanish and so another group of Spanish surnames from the same Latin root includes Herrado, Herrador; Herrero 'blacksmith,' Herreras 'son of the blacksmith' and Hierros 'son of Iron.'

Herrero or *ferrer* shoes a horse.

Donald Methuen Fleming 1905–1986
Lawyer and federal Minister of Finance from 1957 to
1962 during the government of John Diefenbaker

Sir Sandford Fleming 1827–1915
He was a civil engineer, inventor, and scientist who pro-
posed as early as 1875 the system of Standard Time
zones still in use.

Fleming is Old French *flamanc* 'person from
Flanders.' Flemish weavers migrated to various parts of
England just before and during the time that surnames
began to become well established in the thirteenth and
fourteenth centuries.

David Foley 1963–
The Canadian comedian and actor gained fame on
CBC TV as part of the comedy group The Kids in the
Hall *and later as a star of NBC TV's sitcom* Newsradio.

Foley is Folly or Folley with one *l* removed in an
attempt to disguise the underlying French origin of the
surname, namely *folie* 'madness, craziness.' The English
surname also arises from various compound English
place names whose second element is Folly. To make
one up: Smith's Folly might be a house or field name
for a property that was a financial or agricultural disaster for its original owner. Foley may also be an Irish
warrior surname from a Gaelic form like *Ó Foley*
'descendant of Plunderer.'

Megan Porter Follows 1971–
The daughter of actor Ted Follows rose to fame early in
her career starring in the CBC TV dramatized serial of
Anne of Green Gables. *The versatile actress has played*
several seasons at the Stratford Shakespearean Festival,
and starred in feature and TV films like Deep Sleep,
Terminal Station, Back to Hannibal, *and* Inherit the
Wind *(NBC TV).*

Follows is an alteration of Fallows from Old
English *falu* 'pale brown' then, by its colour, land that is
left unploughed for a season or two to increase its fertil-
ity, that is, fallow land. The naming ancestor dwelt near

'the fallows,' fallow fields. When fallow came to mean 'barren, not pregnant' and have other negative nuances, some forebears changed the spelling to Follows.

FORSEY

Eugene Alfred Forsey 1904–
Oxford-and-McGill-educated expert on the Canadian Constitution, Liberal Senator (1970–1979), witty and learned debater on Canadian public affairs

Forsey is a variant of Fursey from the Old English field name *fyrs + (ge)hæg* 'furze-fence.' The ancestor lived on or near a field enclosed by a living fence of spiny gorse bushes. Furze is a synonym for gorse. The botanical name is *Ulex europaeus* and this prickly legume still makes a deterrent hedge on the heaths of Great Britain and northern Europe.

FOWKE

Edith Margaret Fowke 1913–
Collector of Ontario folklore, folksongs, writer on Canadian folk music, teacher, longtime CBC Radio hostess whose books include Tales Told in Canada *(1986)*

Fowke is an Anglo-Norman form of the Old French *Fouques*, itself from Old German *fulco, folco* 'people.' Compare modern German *Volk* and English 'folk.'

FRASER

Blair Fraser 1909–1968
Journalist, Ottawa editor of Maclean's *(1943–1960), then for two years editor for the same magazine and finally its London correspondent with many appearances on CBC Radio and TV as political commentator.*

Graham Fraser 1946–
Blair's son is also a journalist who has been Washington bureau chief for the Globe and Mail *and is the author of* Playing for Keeps: The Canadian Election of 1988 *(1989).*

John Anderson Fraser 1944–
A music and dance critic for the Toronto Telegram and the Globe and Mail *and a foreign correspondent. Being*

China correspondent for the Globe *gave him the background for his bestselling 1980 book* The Chinese: Portrait of a People. *From 1987 to 1994 he was editor of* Saturday Night *magazine. He is now master of Massey College at the University of Toronto.*

Simon Fraser 1776–1862
Fur trader, explorer, founder of early settlements in what became British Columbia

No plausible etymology of the surname Fraser has ever been put forward, although the first of that spelling to be mentioned in Scottish records, Sir Simon Fraser (died A.D. 1306), is also named as Simond Frysel. If one wished to join the puzzled chorus, one might toss in this suggestion—although it has no textual support—of an origin in Old French *fraseur* 'one who hulls' in a kitchen, hence apprentice cook from *fraser* 'to shell beans.' Basil Cottle's nonsense about strawberries (French *fraises*) in the *Penguin Dictionary of Surnames* is the result of polyglottosis or dictionary fever, a malady that at times overcomes the best of onomasticians.

Sir Martin Frobisher 1539–1594
The explorer who discovered Frobisher's Bay was knighted not for digging up several tons of worthless ore on the shores of Warwick Sound, but for his marine gallantry against the Spanish Armada in 1588.

Frobisher from Old French *forbisseor* is a variant of furbisher and furber, a medieval occupational surname describing one who polished armour and burnished swords.

FROBISHER

Barbara Frum, née Rosberg 1937–1992
Astute interviewer on CBC Radio's As It Happens *(1971–1981) and then on CBC TV's* The Journal

FRUM

David Frum 1960–
Controversial journalist of neoconservative hue, son of Barbara and Murray Frum

Murray Frum 1931–
Dentist, real estate mogul, chairman of the Frum Development Group, vice-president of the Art Gallery of Ontario, past president of the board of directors of the Stratford Festival

Frum is a Jewish surname from the German adjective *fromm* 'pious' but standing probably for an ancestor named Avrom, short for Abraham. The *v* was pronounced *f* in some Yiddish dialects. The root was also part of pet names in Yiddish like Fruma Sarah 'pious Sarah.'

FRYE

Herman Northrop Frye 1912–1991
A professor of English at Victoria College and then chancellor of Victoria University, Dr. Frye was one of Canada's most internationally respected literary critics whose works include Fearful Symmetry *(1947),* Anatomy of Criticism *(1957), and* The Great Code *(1982).*

Frye is a common name in the southern counties of England from Old English *frig* 'free-born.'

G GABEREAU

Vicki Gabereau 1946–
Popular CBC Radio interviewer with her own network afternoon show (1988–1997)

Gabereau is a part of a French surname group with many variant spellings: Gabareau, Gabarot, Gabreau, Gaboreau, Gabbarot, Gabarret. There are two different etymological sources. The Gabereau group with a single *b* are likely to derive from the early Norman verb *gaber* 'to make fun of, to joke about' itself brought to northern France by the Vikings whose Old Norse had *gabb* 'a joke.'

With the double *b* of Gabbarot we slip south to Gascony, a former French province in the foothills of the Pyrenees, where a word in the Gascon dialect is *gabarro* 'gorse, furze' making Gabbarot a locative surname arising from the fact that an ancestor's house was in a place full of gorse, a spiny shrub which abounds on the coastal heathlands of southern France.

Is the English *gab* 'chat, idle lip-flap' also a monosyllabic borrowing from *gabb*, the Old Scandinavian word for joke? I think so. Others say gab is a back-formation from gabble or related to an Irish Gaelic word for mouth *gob* as in "Shut yer gob, yuh dirty-faced bastard!" Gab's first appearance in print meaning 'idle chat' is in eighteenth-century Scotland where one thousand years earlier Scandinavian borrowing into Scots Gaelic and Old English was extensive due to Viking invasions.

Reverend Phillip Arthur "Flying Phil" Gagliardi 1913–1995

GAGLIARDI

This colourful Kamloopsian—Yes, it's the correct designation for a resident of Kamloops, British Columbia— was Minister of Highways in Wacky Bennett's Social Credit government from 1952 to 1972. Gagliardi earned his nickname from his overuse of government airplanes—even to fly his family on vacations to Dallas. It also referred to his driving habits which caused the Minister to be ticketed frequently by police. In 1988, at the age of 75, the ordained Pentecostal minister won a mayoralty race in Kamloops.

Gagliardi is an Italian surname 'descendant of the robust one' where *gagliardo* is an Italian adjective used as a nickname. The originally northern Italian word is not from Latin, but from a Celtic root **galia* 'strength, vigour.' Compare the similar French word *gaillard.* The root named a vigorous fifteenth-century dance in triple time, the galliard (Fr. *gaillarde,* Ital. *gagliarda*).

John Kenneth Galbraith 1908–

GALBRAITH

Born at Iona Station, Ontario, the economist and writer, professor of economics at Harvard, and liberal advisor to Democratic presidents counts among his works The Affluent Society *(1958) and a childhood memoir of southern Ontario,* The Scotch *(1964).*

Galbraith is Scots Gaelic from Old Gaelic *Gall-Bhreathnach* 'stranger-Briton' where the term denoted a Welsh settler who had moved north into Scotland.

GALT

Sir Alexander Tilloch Galt 1817–1893
He was a railway mogul and developer of coal fields near Lethbridge, Alberta, Minister of Finance in the first federal cabinet (1867), and first Canadian High Commissioner to London (1880–1883).

John Galt 1779–1839
He founded the town of Guelph. Galt, Ontario, now part of the city of Cambridge, was named after this Scottish novelist and promoter of immigration to Canada.

Galt is both an English and a Scottish surname. Middle English *galte, gaute, gault* 'boar, hog' was used as a nickname, either derisive or occupational for a swineherd or operator of a piggery. The root is Old Norse *goltr* 'pig.' But some Scottish etymologists want to see it as a variant of Gall, Gaul, or Gaw, all from the Celtic word *gall* 'stranger' which was used abusively to denote lowland immigrants to more northerly parts of Scotland.

GANONG

Gilbert White Ganong 1851–1917
He founded with his brother James Harvey Ganong the well-known candy company still in New Brunswick.

William Francis Ganong 1864–1941
Son of James Ganong, professor of botany, historian, and cartographer of New Brunswick's waterways and folk ways

Ganong stems from a Latinized form of a Teutonic warrior name *Wano, Wanonis* 'one who waits' which contains the Old High German root *wân* 'a waiting' and was possibly the nickname of an army officer who deployed delaying tactics.

GARNEAU

François-Xavier Garneau 1809–1866
He was the most influential writer and historian of nineteenth-century Québec whose major work was Histoire du Canada *(1845–1852).*

Hector de Saint-Denys Garneau 1912–1943
Called by some the first modern poet of Québec, he

wrote two important works: the collected poetry,
Regards et jeux dans l'espace *(1937) and the*
posthumous Journal *(1954).*

Marc Garneau 1949–

With a doctorate in electrical engineering, he was the
first Canadian astronaut in space (1984). In May, 1996,
he took part in a U.S. space-shuttle mission and played
a key role in several Canadian experiments, including
use of the Canadarm in satellite retrieval, all part of
testing procedures involved in the eventual construction
of an international space station.

Raymond Garneau 1935–

Economist, Liberal politician, Québec Minister of
Finance (1970–1976) and elected federally (1984)

Garneau is a pet form of Garnaud from the
Teutonic male given name and officer name *Warin-wald*
'protection-ruler' suggesting one who was a captain of
the guard.

Clyde Gilmour 1912–

The popular film and music critic will in 1996 celebrate
forty years on CBC Radio's Gilmour's Albums, *the*
longest-running one-man show in CBC history.

David Gilmour 1949–

Novelist and arts critic on CBC TV's The Journal *and*
Newsworld's Gilmour on the Arts. *Back on Tuesday*
(1986) and How Boys See Girls *(1991) are deftly and*
delightfully written end-of-our-century novels of rueful
male confession about failed marriages and botched
love affairs.

Gilmour in Scots Gaelic is 'servant of Mary'
where the Gaelic word *gille* 'servant' implies religious
affection, so that the full meaning is 'devotee of the
Virgin Mary' indicating an ancestor whose favourite
saint was Mary. There is an entire class of Scots Gaelic
surnames that stem from such religious first names.
Compare:
• Gilbride   'servant of Saint Bridget'

GILMOUR

**An angel, servant of Mary, reads
the *Ave Maria*.**

- Gilchrist   'servant of Christ'
- Gilfillan   'servant of St. Fillan'
- Gilfoyle   'servant of St. Paul'
- Gillanders   'servant of St. Andrew'
- Gilmartin   'servant of St. Martin'
- Gilmichael
- Gilpatrick

The *gille* root is reduced to a lonely *l* in McLean = Mac + Gille + Ian = 'son of the servant of St. John.' Note, however, the literal serving status of the ancestor indicated in names like Gill 'servant,' Gillespie 'servant of the bishop,' and Gilroy 'servant of the red-haired one.'

GLASSCO

John Glassco 1909–1981

He was a poet, translator, and autobiographer whose works include Complete Poems of Saint-Denys-Garneau *(1975) and* Memoirs of Montparnasse *(1970). These witty musings on the state of his own being during three years he spent during the 1920s in Paris are for me the best autobiography ever written by a Canadian.* Memoirs of Montparnasse *was first published in 1970, although written in 1932. A few years after its publication, I directed a dramatized reading of Glassco's memoirs with actor Colin Fox for CBC Radio's* This Country in the Morning. *It is CBC Radio work I am proud of. If you have never ridden Glassco's surf of foaming language, I urge you to soon.*

Glassco is a respelling, Victorian or earlier, to disguise the too plain Glasgow, indicating where the ancestor lived. Glasgow is a Gaelic place name that means 'grey-green hollow,' suggestive of its original site on the River Clyde.

GOMEZ

Avelino Gomez 1928–1980

The fondly remembered Cuban-born Canadian jockey won 4,100 races in his career and earned his place in the Sports Hall of Fame.

Gomez is a typical Spanish surname with the patronymic terminal Spanish *ez* representing genitive *s* to give a meaning 'son or descendant of Gomo.' Gomo, a pet form of Gomesano, originated in the Spanish mountains of Burgos and Santander as *Gome* in the time of the Visigothic invasions of Spain. *Gome* seen in early records as *goma* stems from the Gothic word *guma* 'man,' so that Gomez means 'son of a complete or total man' with the implication of machismo. Gomez is now one of the most widely distributed Spanish surnames in the world.

Avelino is a Spanish given name from the name of an Italian Saint Andrea Avellino, himself named from Avellino, in the Italian region of Campania, which even in the days of ancient Rome was noted for the many hazelnut trees that grew there. Compare Italian *avellano* 'hazelnut tree' and the international botanical name of the hazelnut *Corylus avellana*.

Glenn Herbert Gould 1932–1982

GOULD

The most brilliant classical pianist Canada has so far produced gave up live performance in 1964 to concentrate on recordings and CBC Radio documentaries. Although his literary output was small, Gould was a genius too at wielding the English language. Read his articles and reviews.

Gould is a variant spelling of Gold found as a British surname in the west Midlands and the southwest of England generally. As an English surname derived from an ancestor's nickname, Gold is simply 'blond, yellow-haired.' The Anglo-Saxons used it as a first name for boys and girls. Gould is also used as a spelling of the Jewish surname Gold which was not always occupational for a goldsmith, but, far more often, a matronymic meant to honour a mother with the Yiddish name Golda 'yellow-haired.'

Florence Nightingale Graham 1878–1966

GRAHAM

The Canadian-born cosmetics mogul changed her name to Elizabeth Arden, selecting Elizabeth for its queenly resonance and borrowing Arden from the eponymous hero of Tennyson's 1864 narrative poem, Enoch Arden*, about unrequited love.*

Graham, a common Scottish surname, was

brought to Scotland by a Norman, William de Graham in A.D. 1127. Graham was a Norman spelling of his natal town, Grantham, a place in Lincolnshire whose name in Old English means 'village of an Anglo-Saxon named *Granta.*' This male personal name meant 'one who snarls or complains.' Old English *grantaham* can also support a meaning like 'gravel farmstead.'

GWYN

Richard John Philip Jeremy Gwyn 1934–
Political journalist, Toronto Star *national affairs columnist, frequent guest as analyst on CBC TV and TVO*

Gwyn is a Welsh surname from Old Welsh *gwyn* 'white.' Like all the given and last names in world languages that stem from a root meaning 'white,' it refers to relative fairness of hair or complexion, that is, the ancestor possessed fairer than normal hair or skin for a particular small community. Gwyn is also a Welsh male given name. The element is found in female given names like Gwendolyn. Consider too King Arthur's wife, Guinevere, with its Cornish version Jenifer. *Gwynedd* is the Welsh name for North Wales used as a female given name Gwyneth.

H

HADDAD

Claire Haddad 1924–
Toronto-based fashion designer of women's clothes, founding member of the Fashion Designers' Association of Canada, created a member of the Order of Canada (1979)

Haddad is an Arabic surname from the occupation of the ancestor. *Haddad* in Arabic means 'blacksmith, ironmonger.' The verbal root is *hadd* 'hone' so that the *haddad* is literally and originally 'one who sharpens' (knives and swords).

HAMILTON

Francis Alvin George Hamilton 1912–
Teacher, then as politician, leader of the PC in Saskatchewan from 1949, and finally by 1957 he was idea man in Diefenbaker's cabinet, serving as Minister of Northern Affairs and Natural Resources and Minister of Agriculture.

Robert Hamilton 1753–1809
Upper Canada land speculator and politician whose son George founded Hamilton, Ontario

All the surnames including the Scottish ones derive ultimately from the town of Hamilton in Leicestershire. Old English **hamel* 'cut off, maimed' + *dun* 'hill.' Compare modern English 'dune' and 'down.' It aptly describes a hill that had its top sliced off by a retreating glacier.

Stephan Handelman 1948–
Newspaper journalist, writer on international affairs, whose postings include Chief European correspondent based in London for the Toronto Star *(1981–1987)*

Handelman is a German-Yiddish surname formed to look like *Handelsmann* 'tradesman' but is actually a matronymic based on the mother's Hebrew name Hanna which among Jews living in medieval Germany could become *Hannel* or *Handel.* Biblical Hannah, mother of the prophet Samuel, is a shortened version of *Hanani* 'God has favoured me.' In its Greek form *Anna*, it gave birth to all the European and Slavic variants of Anna like Ann, Ännchen, Annette, Anja, Anya, Aña, Anita, Anushka, Nana, and Nanette.

HANDELMAN

Rick Hansen 1957–
A wheelchair athlete, Hansen raised more than $20 million for spinal cord research with his 'Man in Motion' tour (1985–1987) through more than thirty-four countries.

Hansen sports a typical Scandinavian patronymic suffix *-sen* 'son' and can be a Norwegian or Swedish surname meaning 'son of John.'

HANSEN

Michael Harcourt 1943–
Mayor of Vancouver, then NDP Premier of British Columbia whose scandal-plagued administration caused him to step down in February, 1996

Harcourt, if of Norman French origin, is a surname from the natal town of the ancestor. France has two little towns named Harcourt, in Calvados and in

HARCOURT

Eure. The *har* stems from early Germanic *hari-* 'army' and *court* 'large manor' or from Old French *hare* 'cry used to incite hunting dogs.'

There are two places in Shropshire named Harcourt, and Cottle says they mean 'falconer's cottage' and 'harper's cottage' or 'cottage where there was a salt-harp.' A salt harp was used to sift salt.

HAWTIN

Jane Hawtin
Radio and television interviewer based in Toronto, she began her own national TV phone-in program in 1995.

Hawtin is a surname based on either of two sources. The more frequent is the medieval occupation called in Old English 'hall-thane' or one who serves or works in the hall of a feudal manor. The other source is the Norman French ancestral nickname *Hautain* 'proud, haughty.'

HEALEY

Jeff Healey 1966–
Toronto-based rock guitarist, composer, singer

Healey is a variant of Irish Gaelic *Ó Healy* 'descendant of Clever' or 'descendant of 'Claimant.'' It is still among the one hundred most common names in Ireland.

HÉBERT

Anne Hébert 1916–
One of Québec's most influential novelists, also a poet and playwright, she is the author of Kamouraska *(1970), filmed by Claude Jutra, and* Les Fous de Bassan *(1982). Other recent novels include* L'Enfant chargé de songes *(1992) and* Aurélien, Clara, Mademoiselle et l'officier anglais *(1995). A collection of poetry,* Le jour n'a d'égal que la nuit, *appeared in 1993.*

Hébert is a variant of Herbert, a French surname based on an ancestor's given name, Old German *Hariberht,* made up of *harja* 'host' and *berhta* 'bright.' After the Norman Conquest it spread widely throughout Great Britain as a male given name.

HENRY

Frances Henry 1931–
An anthropologist at York University with a special

interest in Black studies, he is the author of The Caribbean Diaspora in Toronto: Learning to Live with Racism *(1995).*

Henry began as a Norman French variant of the Old Germanic warrior name *Haimirich,* a compound of *haimi* 'house' and *ric* 'ruler.' In dozens of languages it has spawned thousands of surnames, a few of which are Fitzhenry, Harriman, Harrison, Hawkins, Heinrichs, Henderson, Hendriksen, Hendry, Herriot, Parry, and Perry.

The Reverend Josiah Henson 1789–1883
An American-born slave who escaped to Canada in 1830 and founded the Black settlement at Dawn in Upper Canada. He was said to be the model for Harriet Beecher Stowe's hero in Uncle Tom's Cabin *(1852).*

Henson is an English surname, a patronymic based on the Middle English given name *Hendy* 'courteous, kind.'

Natasha Henstridge 1975–
Born in Springfield, Newfoundland, she grew up in Fort McMurray, Alberta. The beautiful young actress starred in the horror film Species *(1995).*

Henstridge is the name of a town in Somerset, in Old English *Hengest-hrycg* 'stallion-ridge' either because stallions were kept on the ridge or because it belonged to an Anglo-Saxon with the then common male given name *Hengest* 'stallion, stud-horse.'

Ben Heppner 1956–
Canadian operatic tenor currently rising to international prominence

Heppner is a German and Flemish surname that means 'person from Heppen' which is a town in Belgium, itself named after a founder with the Teutonic male given name *Heppo* related to Old High German **helfan* 'help.' Thus Heppo was a helper.

Peter Herrndorf 1940–
He is an efficient and innovative mover and shaker in

HENSON

HENSTRIDGE

HEPPNER

HERRNDORF

the administrative realms of Canadian culture. As a CBC TV executive he helped start The Journal, *sat on the board of governors of the Stratford Shakespearean Festival, was publisher of* Toronto Life *magazine, and currently heads TVO, Ontario's educational television authority.*

Herrndorf as a European village name is an example of folk etymology where the German *Herrendorf* 'village of men' stands for a much earlier *Harindorf* 'army town' or *Erindorf* 'town of a Teutonic person named *Eri* honour.'

HNATYSHYN

Raymond "Ray" John Hnatyshyn 1934–
Lawyer and Progressive Conservative politician, he has held various PC cabinet posts including Minister of Justice, and was Governor-General of Canada.

Hnatyshyn is a Ukrainian variant of *Hnatyshak* 'descendant of Hnat, Ihnat, or Ignatius,' the first name derived from one of the saints named Ignatius (see Ignatieff entry). There is also a folk etymology that the name is related to the Ukrainian verbal stem *hnatesh* 'pursue, chase.' This is spurious.

HORN

Kahn-Tineta Horn 1940–
This member of the Mohawk Wolf Clan of Caughnawaga, Québec, has been a fashion model, political activist, and civil servant, promoting the causes of aboriginal peoples outside and inside the federal Department of Indian Affairs.

Kahn-Tineta is a Mohawk name that means 'she makes the grass wave' implying she goes like the wind and is speedy. Horn is a borrowed English surname or a translation.

HOWE

Clarence Decatur Howe 1886–1960
An engineer, he built grain elevators across Canada and the world, then entered politics to become the great Liberal power-broker of the thirties and forties. As Minister of Transport for Mackenzie King in 1936 he created what became Air Canada. During World War II

*as Minister of Munitions and Supply he turned Canada
into an efficient producer of war materials, and then he
helped the economy after the war return rapidly to free
enterprise and expansion.*

Gordon Howe 1928–
*One of our finest athletes and hockey players during
thirty-two record-breaking seasons*

Joseph Howe 1804–1873
*Feisty reform journalist, politician, Premier and
Lieutenant-Governor of Nova Scotia and great defender
and proponent of his province*

Howe as a surname and place name element common all over northern England has a variety of origins. Sometimes the ancestor lived near a hill or tumulus, an ancient burial mound, and this is Old Norse *haugr* 'mound.' In other instances it is Old English *hoh* 'heel, projecting spur of a hill, steep ridge' also indicative of the location of an ancestor's dwelling. An orthographical kaleidoscope of formal variation sees Heugh, Hoe, Hoo, Hoof, Houf, Hough, How, Howe, Howes, Huff, Hughf, and even Hughff !

Mel Hurtig 1932–

HURTIG

Edmonton-based founder of Hurtig Publishers and creator of The Canadian Encyclopedia, *he is a fervent
nationalist whose passion for his country has taken
many forms including trying to start a new political
party.*

Hurtig is a German surname based on the nickname of an ancestor. The adjective *hurtig* means 'quick, speedy, agile, nimble.' However, it is likely that the founding ancestor bore the single Hebrew name of Naphtali, and that Hurtig was a translation and *kinnui* for Naphtali. Certain Biblical names like Naphtali had symbols associated with them. This symbol was called a *kinnui.* For example, in the Torah, Jacob blesses his son Naphtali and calls him "a swift-footed deer." Thus 'deer' or 'swift' becomes a *kinnui* of the male personal name, Naphtali. So it was often used to represent any

Naphtali. Thus a Naphtali among German-speaking peoples might become a Hurtig (quick) or a Hirsch (deer), as a first name to begin, as a surname later. In Biblical Hebrew, Naphtali means 'one who struggles for something.'

HUTT

William Ian deWitt Hutt 1920–
One of Canada's leading actors, associated with the Stratford Festival from its founding in leading Shakespearean roles and all of the modern canon as well, Hutt has starred on Broadway in Albee's Tiny Alice *(1964), and appeared memorably as John A. Macdonald in CBC TV's* The National Dream *(1975) and in the film of Timothy Findley's* The Wars *(1984).*

Hutt is a dialectical variant in Buckinghamshire, Lancashire, and Leicestershire of Hudd, a pet form of the male given name Hugh. Hutt may also be a severe vowel shortening in speech of one of the many Norman-French diminutives of Hugh such as Hewet, Hewit, Huitt or Huot, all meaning 'Little Hugh.'

HYLAND

Frances Hyland 1928–
One of the treasures among Canadian actors, she has played Stella in A Streetcar Named Desire, *acted with Gielgud in* The Winter's Tale, *and was invited to our Stratford Festival by Tyrone Guthrie in 1954 where her many memorable performances include an outstanding Ophelia opposite Christopher Plummer. Television, radio, and film work have kept this officer of the Order of Canada busy. In 1994 she received the Governor-General's Award for the performing arts.*

Hyland is a surname based on the ancestor's place of residence, being either High Land or, more probably, a dialectal pronunciation of Hayland, Old English *hegland* 'hay-land.'

HYSLOP

Jeff Hyslop 1951–
Singer, dancer, choreographer, theatre director, he is perhaps best known to Canadian audiences for the title role in many performances of Andrew Lloyd Webber's Phantom of the Opera. *Other roles were in such musi-*

cals as A Chorus Line, Godspell, The Fantasticks, *and* The Pirates of Penzance *(CBC TV). Younger TV viewers know him as Jeff the Mannequin on the series* Today's Special. *As director and choreographer, he's staged* Peter Pan, Irma La Douce, *and many revues.*

Hyslop is one of many variants (Haslop, Haslup, Heaslip, Heslop, Hislop) of the Old English *hæsel-hop* 'hazeltree-valley' describing one who lived in such a vale.

George Ignatieff 1913–1989
Canadian diplomat who served as Canada's United Nations ambassador and president of the Security Council in the1960s. He was chancellor of the University of Toronto (1980–1986).

Michael Ignatieff 1947–
Writer and historian, whose books include The Needs of Strangers *(1984),* The Russian Album *(1987),* Asya *(1990), and* Scar Tissue *(1993).*

Ignatieff is a Russian patronymic surname whose literal meaning is 'son of or descendant of Ignatius.' The Russian Orthodox Church approved of the first Jesuit, Saint Ignatius of Loyola (A.D. 1491–1556), founder of the Society of Jesus. Ignatia, Ignatz, and variants were given names at certain times in Russian history. But also Ignatius was a popular Latin name for saints—at least four Christian worthies were so dubbed—doubtless because of the name's meaning in street Latin: *ignatus* = *in* 'not' + *natus,* gnatus 'born.' However, the literal meaning of the elements must be added to, since the adjective did not mean 'not born' but 'low-born, of humble birth.' And so when Ignatius came to be a male given name in postclassical Latin, its humility made it an apt one for early Christians. There was also a Roman family name, a variant of Ignatius, Egnatius.

George "Punch" Imlach 1918–1987
After joining the Toronto Maple Leaf organization in

IGNATIEFF

I

IMLACH

1958 after a low-lustre career with the Québec Aces, Punch coached the Leafs when they were NHL champions in 1962, 1963, 1964, and 1967. It was said his specialty was that of a taskmaster who could squeeze hockey talent from aging players.

Imlach is a German surname indicative of where a forebear lived, namely, *im Lach* 'at or near the lake.' There is a subgroup of such phrasal surnames in German. *Imlach* is similar to *Imbach* 'near the stream,' *Imburg* 'at the fortified town,' *Imholz* 'in or near the woods,' and *Imhaus* 'in the house' with the implication that the ancestor was a live-in servant.

INNIS

Harold Adams Innis 1894–1952

At the University of Toronto he taught political economy and what today we might call communications theory, applying it in new modes in his ground-breaking books The Fur Trade in Canada *(1930),* The Cod Fisheries *(1940), and* Empire and Communications *(1950), all of which influenced Canadian scholars including Marshall McLuhan.*

Innis indicates a Scottish ancestor's residence. Scots Gaelic *Innis* 'island' is the name of a specific place in Scotland. Variants of the surname include Ennis. The Gaelic element appears widely (Innisfree, Inniskillen) in the place names of Britain and Ireland. Compare modern Irish *inis* 'island' and modern Welsh *ynys* 'island.'

Innis **means 'island.'**

J JELINEK

Maria Jelinek 1942–

The Czechoslovakia-born figure skater with her brother Otto won the world figure-skating championship in 1962, then turned professional. Another brother Henry wrote a book about this remarkable family entitled On Thin Ice *(1965). Her father owned a cork manufacturing business in Bronte, Ontario, and her brother Frank, a sports equipment plant.*

Otto Jelinek 1940–

A champion figure skater, and successful politician

elected to the House of Commons first in 1974 and again in 1979, 1980, 1984 and 1988, the Conservative MP held many federal portfolios in his long career.

Jelinek is a Czech surname meaning 'descendant of a man nicknamed *Jelen* deer,' usually because of quick-footedness. How apt a surname. It may also refer to an ancestor who was a deerhunter. The same Slavic root for deer appears in Polish *jelen* and Russian *olyen* to give surnames like Jelinski, Olyenov, Olin, Olinsky.

Claude Jutra 1930–1986
Montréal-born film director of Mon Oncle Antoine *(1971), the best Canadian feature film so far about life in a small town, and, before his untimely death, director of several superb TV features including* Dreamspeaker *(1977) and* The Wordsmith *(1979).*

Jutra is a French surname based on an ancestor's nickname. *Jut* is a popular contraction of the male given name *Just, Juste* from the very common Roman Christian name *Justus* 'just man.' Among the diminutive forms of *Jut* from which Jutra might be derived are Jutard and Juttard, both of which also produced French surnames. A much remoter possibility is a contraction of the nickname-surname *Jottereau* 'little jote' where *jote* is 'cabbage, beet, vegetable.'

JUTRA

Margot Kidder 1948–
The Yellowknife-born actress in films and TV gained fame as Lois Lane in Superman *(1978) and* Superman II *(1981). She starred in Canadian director Don Shebib's* Heartaches *(1981) and since in many made-for-TV movies and feature films.*

Kidder may be occupational from Middle English *kidde* 'bundle of twigs' hence 'wood-seller, faggot-seller.' It can also be *kidder* 'goatherd.'

KIDDER

K

Thomas Killam 1802–1868
A rich shipowner and merchant of Yarmouth, he became the first MP for Yarmouth County in 1867.

KILLAM

Construction of a giant kiln begins.

Izaak Walton Killam 1885–1955
Named after the English author of The Compleat Angler, *the Yarmouth-born financier became one of Nova Scotia's richest men, and for a time the richest man in Canada with networks of holdings in paper, publishing, utilities, and construction. His wife who survived him left multimillion-dollar bequests to many universities and hospitals (e.g., the Izaak Killam Hospital for Children in Halifax) and the estate inheritance tax of $50 million helped begin funding of the Canada Council.*

Killam stems from the ancestral residence in one of three English towns named Kilham, all from an Old English dative of location *cylnum* (at) 'the kilns.' At such large ovens and furnaces, bricks were baked, pottery was fired, grain and hops were dried, and lime was calcined.

KOFFMAN

Morris "Moe" Koffman 1928–
Master of jazz saxophone and flute in widely popular modes on many commercial recordings, Moe is also a composer of instrumental hits (his biggest: "Swinging Shepherd Blues" in 1957). His own jazz bands and combos have delighted Canadians, particularly Torontonians. His sax is one of the mellow assets of Rob McConnell's Boss Brass.

Koffman is an occupational surname, a variant of the German and Yiddish *kaufmann* 'merchant, shopkeeper.' Some of the many variants include Kauffmann, Kaufler, Koffler, Koifler, and Kuffman.

KURELEK

William (Wasyl) Kurelek 1927–1977
A visionary Roman Catholic idealist, he painted the modern Canadian prairies and our country as a paradise that had slipped from our grasp because of moral lapse. His illustrations for W. O. Mitchell's Who Has Seen the Wind *(1976, 1991) and his own children's books are masterpieces of charged folk art.*

Kurelek is a Ukrainian occupational surname possibly meaning 'descendant of the censer,' the thurifer or incense-bearer in the Russian Orthodox Church.

Compare the general Slavic and Russian root *koorel* 'smoke.'

LaMARSH

Julia "Judy" Verlyn LaMarsh 1924–1980
Lawyer, politician, broadcaster, writer, she was Liberal Member of Parliament for Niagara Falls from 1960–1968 and an important member of Lester Pearson's cabinet, helping to introduce the Canada Pension Plan and Medicare. In 1967 she headed Canada's centennial festivities, and the next year published Memoirs of a Bird in a Gilded Cage.

LaMarsh can be a locative surname from Lamarsh, a village still in Essex listed in the Domesday Book for A.D. 1086 as *Lamers*, and so from Old English *lam* 'loam' + *mersc* 'marsh.' Or, if Norman French, it's from Lamarche, the name of three localities in France which were on or near an Old High German *marca* 'frontier, border.'

LANG

k.d. (Katherine Dawn) lang 1961–
Born in Consort, Alberta, the popular singer of awesome range and beautiful voice has recorded such albums as "A Truly Western Experience" (1984), "Angel with a Lariat" (1986), "Shadowland" (1988), "Absolute Torch and Twang" (1992), and "Ingenue" (1992).

Lang is a German adjective for 'long.' It was a common medieval German nickname for tall, thin persons.

LAUMANN

Silken Laumann 1964–
The champion Canadian rower won a gold medal in single sculls at the 1987 Pan-American Games; a 1991 world championship at Vienna, a bronze medal at Barcelona in 1992, and another world cup in single sculls in Switzerland in 1991 and 1994.

Laumann is a German locative surname, a variant of Lohmann which means 'one whose house is in the woods.' It is thus semantically related to German surnames like Imlau and Imloh 'in the woods.'

A house in the woods.

LAURENCE

Margaret Laurence, née Jean Margaret Wemyss 1926–1987

She was one of Canada's most talented and compassionate novelists whose masterworks include The Stone Angel *(1964),* A Jest of God *(1966),* The Fire-Dwellers *(1969), and* The Diviners *(1974).*

Wemyss is the name of two places in Scotland, one in the former Scottish county of Fife, the other in Ayrshire. The word is Scots Gaelic for 'caves' with the addition of a supernumerary English possessive or plural marker, *s*.

Laurence and its many variants (Lawrence, Lauritz, Lavrens, St. Lawrence River, etc.) in all the languages of the West owes its ubiquity to the popularity of five saints who bore the name Laurentius 'from the town of Laurentum' named because it abounded in bay trees (Latin *laurus*). A triumphant crown of fragrant bay leaves is a laurel. A versifier crowned with such a token of honour is a poet laureate.

The most notable of the holy men who bore this name was St. Lawrence the Deacon who was martyred in Rome in A.D. 258. Among the many surnames that stem from the saint's name are De Laurentiis, Larkin, Larry, Laurenceau, Laurent, Lavrens, Lawrie, Lawson, Lorençon, Lorent, Lorenzi, and Lowrie.

LEACOCK

Stephen Leacock 1869–1944

From 1915 he was Canada's best-known writer (more than sixty books) and one of the best writers of humorous essays in the English-speaking world. He wrote Elements of Political Science *in 1906 and it became an early standard college textbook. His funny books are still funny—even when their sometimes politically incorrect biases are acknowledged—and they include* Nonsense Novels *(1911),* Sunshine Sketches of a Little Town *(1912),* Arcadian Adventures with the Idle Rich *(1914),* Winnowed Wisdom *(1926),* Short Circuits *(1928), and his posthumous and uncompleted autobiography* The Boy I Left Behind Me *(1946).*

Leacock, a variant of Laycock, is a surname based

on the location of an ancestor's home. Either of two English villages, Lacock in Wiltshire or Laycock in Yorkshire, gave rise to the surname. Both are Old English *lacuc* 'small stream' compounded of OE *lagu* 'pool, marsh, lake, creek' + *uc* a diminutive suffix. The OE root is akin to Latin *lacus* and Gaelic *loch* as in Loch Ness. The Germanic root, slightly modified, shows up in OE *leax* 'salmon' and German *Lachs* 'salmon.' The German word earlier travelled through the dialect filter of Yiddish to give *laks* 'salmon' and thence bagels and lox 'smoked salmon.'

René Lévesque 1922–1987

A compelling television commentator in the mid-fifties, he went on to help found the separatist Parti Québécois in 1968 and won power in 1976, staying as Premier of Québec until 1985.

Lévesque is a variant of *L'évêque* French 'the bishop.' This meant the ancestor worked for a bishop or in his household. Old French *évesque* stems from ecclesiastical Latin *episcopus*, a Roman transliteration of the Koine Greek *episkopos* 'over-seer' which was the term for religious superintendent or bishop among early Greek-speaking Christians. Even bishop derives from the same Greek word, after a series of alterations: Old English *bisceop* > Middle English *bischop* > modern English "bishop."

LÉVESQUE

Gordon Meredith Lightfoot 1939–

One of Canada's most successful folksingers and composers, he wrote among many others the hit songs "Early Morning Rain," "For Lovin' You," and "If You Could Read My Mind."

Lightfoot—refreshingly in English onomastic study where modern spellings disguise the meaning of so many surnames—is just what it looks like: the ancestor was agile, nimble, and quick-of-foot. Similar phrasal nicknames produced these English surnames: Lightbody, Lightburn ('nimble child' but also as a locative 'bright stream'), Lightfellow, and Lightlad.

LIGHTFOOT

LOMBARDO

Gaetano "Guy" Alberto Lombardo 1902–1977
He was born in London, Ontario. His dance band, the Royal Canadians, played "the sweetest music this side of heaven" and sold 300 million records over fifty years. Lombardo's New Year's Eve radio and television broadcasts became a North American tradition for more than 40 years.

Lombardo as a surname arises from the Italian adjective that tags an ancestor from Lombardy, a central northern region of Italy. The Lombards were a Germanic tribe living in northwest Germany by the first century A.D. They skirmished with the imperial legions of Rome from time to time, but were usually peaceful, successful farm-

A river scene in Lombardy.

ers. The Roman historian Tacitus mentions them and calls them Langobardi. The Germanic roots of their name are *lang* 'long' and *Barte* 'axe.' The Langobardi had a properly ferocious Teutonic clan name, men of the long axe.

MACDONALD

Note: The Gaelic names in Mac- and Mc- are in this listing placed first under the letter *M*.

Brian Macdonald 1928–
An inventive choreographer and director of musicals, he was a founding member of the National Ballet of Canada, worked with Hair *composer Galt McDermott on the pioneering 1957 satirical revue* My Fur Lady, *staged at McGill University and then toured across Canada. He has created dance works for ballet, directed TV, opera, and stage productions, notably a series of Gilbert and Sullivan operettas at Stratford, one of which, his* Mikado, *enjoyed a long run on Broadway.*

Flora Isabel MacDonald 1926–
*She began as PC Party Secretary, ran successfully as
MP for Kingston and the Islands and held ministerial
portfolios in the Clark and Mulroney governments.*

Sir John Alexander Macdonald 1815–1891
*Lawyer, businessman, and nation builder, he was the
first Prime Minister of Canada.*

Macdonald is Gaelic 'son of Donald' and Donald
is ultimately the Gaelic *Dhómhnuill*, a compound warrior name from Proto-Gaelic **dubno* 'world' and **valos*
'mighty.' It is among the ten most common surnames in
Scotland.

Gwendolyn MacEwen 1941–1987
*She was a versatile writer of poetry, fiction, short sto-
ries, and a wonderful travel volume* Mermaids and
Ikons: A Greek Summer *(1978). Her poetry collections
include* A Breakfast for Barbarians *(1966),* The
Shadow-Maker *(1969), and* Afterworlds *(1987).*

MacEwen is Gaelic 'son of Ewen.' Ewen is a very
early borrowing into several Gaelic languages of the
Greek saint's name Eugenios. In Gaelic it gives Ewen,
in Welsh Owen. Many minor saints bore the name; the
most famous was Saint Eugenius of Carthage (died A.D.
505). The Greek adjective *eugenios* 'well-born, noble'
also produces the given name Eugene and the sometimes abused science of eugenics.

Ashley MacIsaac 1975–
*Growing up in Inverness county on Cape Breton Island,
he was step-dancing and playing the fiddle before he
was nine. The agile Maritime folk and rock fiddler (first
CD, "Close to the Floor") combines many musical traditions in a breezy style that delights all ages and won
him, among other plaudits, 1996 Juno awards for best
new solo artist and for best roots and traditional solo
album, "Hi, How Are You Today?"*

MacIsaac is Gaelic 'Isaac's son.' The surname also
shows up with the Scots variant MacKissack, and, contracted, as the Manx surname Kissock. In Genesis, Isaac

MacEWEN

MacISAAC

is the son of the patriarch Abraham and his wife Sarah. When she hears the birth of Isaac foretold, Sarah laughs. This story is an example of Biblical folk etymology, explaining to readers and hearers of the Torah the meaning of her son's name. The Hebrew verbal root in the name is indeed *tsehook* 'laugh' but the Biblical form of the name itself, which might be transliterated *yitzchaq*, translates as 'May He (God) laugh, smile, or look with favour upon (this child).'

MacLEAN OR McLEAN

John Angus MacLean 1914–
For twenty-eight years, MP for Queens County, he won victory in 1979 and was Premier of Prince Edward Island until 1981.

John Bayne Maclean 1862–1950
The magazine publisher created Maclean's *and* Maclean-Hunter.

John Duncan MacLean 1873–1948
The politician was Premier of British Columbia in 1927–1928.

James Stanley McLean 1876–1954
He created Canada Packers Ltd. in 1927 and ran it until 1954.

Robert "Bob" McLean 1933–
Windsor-born Canadian talk show host and broadcaster with a long and varied career in Canadian radio and television and, briefly, in the United States where he replaced Tom Snyder at Philadelphia's KWY TV. Bob hosted radio talk shows at CKBB in Barrie, CKO in Vancouver and Toronto, and CKXM in Edmonton. He was host of The Bob McLean Show *and* McLean at Large *on CBC TV, riding the network noon hour for eight years. He then hosted* McLean & Company *at CKCO-TV in Kitchener, Ontario for many years. His wife Willa has produced his shows for the last twelve years. Bob and Willa McLean have been good friends to Canadian books and their authors, having interviewed*

every ink-stained wretch who ever stumbled into a TV *studio clutching his or her latest volume, and that includes your humble deponent.*

MacLean as a Gaelic surname combines Mac + Gille + Ian to mean 'son of the servant of John.' All that remains of the *gille* root is the el. The most famous gillie in history was probably a personal servant of Queen Victoria who, after the death of Prince Albert, accompanied the grieving queen on so many occasions that scandal-mongering whisperers suggested the old Queen might indeed be amused and perhaps aroused by the presence of the handsome, burly Scot. But let us abandon that coarse rumour, leaving it to echo down the imposing corridors of Windsor and Balmoral. Gillie could also mean 'devotee,' one devoted to a saint. So it is probable that the originating MacLean ancestor was the son of an early Christian who held pious regard for St. John the Baptist. Ian or Eoin or Iain are Gaelic variants for John.

Rita MacNeil 1944–

The popular singer from Big Pond, Nova Scotia (pop. 175) in 1995–1996 hosted Rita & Friends, *her own musical variety show on CBC TV. She has received the Order of Canada and many Juno and Canadian Country Music awards.*

Bill McNeil 1924–

Cape Breton Island's gift to CBC Radio, Bill was a Glace Bay miner when he finally won an audition as announcer at CBI in 1950. His long and generally happy career included years of hosting Assignment *and the Ontario regional program* Fresh Air *until the early nineties.*

MacNeil is Scots Gaelic 'son of Neal.' But Neal as a given name for more than one thousand years has had a whirligig circumnavigation of northwestern Europe that might have made Erik the Red himself too pooped to pillage. It began as Old Irish *Níall*, an affectionate diminutive of *niadh* 'champion.' The early Viking raiders of Ireland carried the name to Iceland where it

MacNEIL OR McNEIL

shows up in *Njálssaga*, the title of the best Icelandic family saga, called also *The Saga of Burnt Njál*, probably compiled late in the thirteenth century. The invading Norsemen introduced the given name into Norman French as Nel or Nele where it produces later French and Flemish surnames like Neelen, Neilz, Nel, Nélat, Nelet, Nelis, Nelles, Nellon, Nesle, Nieloux, Niles, and Nille. These names **are not** all pet forms of Cornelius, as Marie-Thérèse Morlet states in her usually brilliant *Dictionnaire étymologique des noms de famille* (1991). Even the Italian surname Nelli comes from this root. But that is not the terminus of Neil's travels, not by a long oar. Among Latin-writing Norman scribes who re-introduced Neil to the British Isles, the name, when recorded in official documents, was turned into Latin *Nigellus*, because their folk etymology thought of it incorrectly as a diminutive of the Latin adjective *niger* 'black.' That spelling produced the given name Nigel. English surnames from the root include Neal, Nelles, Nelson, Nielson. In the Scandinavian languages one sees forms like Nielsen, Nielsholm, and Nilquist. The modern Irish version is still Niall.

McCLUNG

Nellie Letitia McClung, née Mooney 1873–1951

The Canadian pioneer for women's economic rights wrote sixteen books including an early Canadian bestseller Sowing Seeds in Danny *(1908). She raised five children, campaigned as a suffragist across Canada, was a Liberal MLA for Edmonton from 1921 to 1926, sat on the first CBC board of governors, and was a delegate to the League of Nations in 1938.*

McClung is Gaelic *mac* 'son of' + *long* 'ship, boat' where Ship was the nickname of a fisherman or sailor.

Son of the fisherman

Herbert Marshall McLuhan 1911–1980

One of the pertest minds to ever saunter into the groves of Canadian academe, McLuhan taught us that the form in which information is delivered deeply affects our perception and interpretation of it. The medium, McLuhan argued, rather determines than transmits meanings (messages). The popular slogan "the medium is the message" marks an extension of this basic principle. His seminal, still vibrant books are: The Mechanical Bride *(1951),* The Gutenberg Galaxy *(1962),* Understanding Media *(1964),* The Medium Is the Message *(1967), and* From Cliché to Archetype *(1970).*

McLuhan is an alternate Anglo-Irish spelling of MacLoon. Early members of the family didn't like the loony look of it. McLuhan is a Galloway name of Irish origin, in Erse *Mac Giolla Éoin* 'son of the servant of (St.) John' and thus a variant of MacLean.

McLUHAN

Antonine Maillet 1929–

Born in Buctouche, New Brunswick, the foremost Acadian playwright and novelist counts among her masterworks La Sagouine *(1971),* Pélagie-la-Charrette *(1979),* Le Huitième Jour *(1986), and* Évangéline Deusse, *her new play that debuted in 1996, reuniting a Maillet script and the great Québec actress Viola Léger who first created Maillet's famous Acadian washerwoman,* La Sagouine.

Maillet is a pet diminutive form of Maille, a French surname that arose either as a nickname "Chain mail" or an as occupational descriptive for one who made chain mail, that is, an armourer. A medieval tax was collected on armour made of these linked metal rings and the French surname Maillard names such a tax collector.

MAILLET

Knights in chain-mail joust.

MIRVISH

Edwin "Honest Ed" Mirvish 1914–
Toronto department store entrepreneur and theatre owner-producer of the Royal Alexandra and The Princess of Wales theatres in Toronto, and the Old Vic in London, England.

Mirvish is a variant of the Yiddish Mervitz or Mervis from a place name, *Mierzwica*, which occurs with spelling variations dozens of times throughout Russia and Lithuania. If the settlement was Slavic, the components of the place name are lexical items like Russian *mir* 'hamlet, small community in pre-revolutionary Russia' + descriptives like *vika* 'vetch, tares' to give 'little place where vetch grows.' Vetch was then a common fodder crop used to feed domestic animals. If the place was founded and named by Jewish settlers, one may look for *shtetl* names transformed by Slavic spelling conventions. Then the initial component may be the founder's name Meir (variants: Meyer, Mayer, Meier) from Hebrew *me-ir* 'one who shines.'

MUNRO

Alice Munro 1931–
She is the best writer Canada has ever produced. Certainly Munro writes short stories in English as well as any living author. Her collections, often themed, include Dance of the Happy Shades *(1968),* Lives of Girls and Women *(1971),* Something I've Been Meaning To Tell You *(1974),* Who Do You Think You Are? *(1978),* The Moons of Jupiter *(1982),* The Progress of Love *(1986),* Friend of My Youth *(1990), and* Open Secrets *(1994).*

Munro is one rare example where linguistically accurate family history has preserved the precise meaning of a complex surname. Munro details the founding ancestor's place of residence. The Munroes came from Ireland from the foot of the river Roe in County Londonderry. Irish Gaelic is *Bun-Rothach* 'man from the foot of the Roe.' In Scots Gaelic, in the Scottish county of Ross, the family name was altered to *Munrotha* due to known linguistic transformations that need not concern us here.

Anne Murray 1945–
The popular singer from Springhill, Nova Scotia, had hits with "Snowbird," "Danny's Song," "You Needed Me," and many others.

    Murray is a variant of Moray, a province of Scotland. Aptly enough, Gaelic Moray means 'seaside settlement.'

James A. Naismith 1861–1939
The doctor and physical education director who invented basketball in 1891 was born at Almonte, Ontario.

    Naismith is an Anglo-Saxon occupational agent noun, *knif-smið* 'cutler, one who makes knives.' Note the possibly unfamiliar Old English letter ð called eth which in earlier Anglo-Saxon manuscripts represented the sound of *th* in modern English words like whether. With the advent of printing, ð was replaced by *th*, which was how Roman copyists chose to transliterate the Greek letter theta.

Nanook (Nanuq)
Nanook was an Inuit hunter of the Canadian arctic who "starred" in American explorer Robert Flaherty's silent film Nanook of the North *(1920). It is often called the first documentary film. But scenes were rehearsed over and over again, and Flaherty did retake after retake. Thus artifice and flim-flam shroud even the earliest examples of this so-called truthful mode of cinema and now television. Truth is always compromised by editing, camera angles, artificial lighting, and the other falsifying paraphernalia of image recording. Flaherty's years in our arctic were financed by Revillon Frères, a French fur company. Nanook came to a bad end in his dealings with southern Whites. Meanwhile, Flaherty, ever the itinerant con man, sailed off to the south seas to film more tropical truths.*

    Nanuq (a better transliteration than nanook) means 'polar bear' in Inuktitut.

NASH

Cyril Knowlton Nash 1927–
The writer and broadcasting administrator is best known as a CBC TV journalist and newsreader. One of his many books is The Microphone Wars *(1994) about protracted management follies at the Canadian Broadcasting Corporation.*

Nash is from an ancestor's homestead or a place name which in Middle English was the phrase *atten asch* 'at the ash tree' where the initial *n* was actually the old dative case ending of *at* which became attached to *asch* so that newcomers to such a community thought it was called Nash and perhaps never knew that the place was founded amid a stand of ash trees. There are half a dozen British hamlets called Nash.

NUNZIATA

John Nunziata 1955–
He was elected to the House of Commons for York South–Weston in 1984, 1988, and 1993 where he has proven himself among other roles an excellent opposition critic. In April of 1996 he was expelled from the Liberal caucus for voting in the House of Commons against the government's budget proposal.

Nunziata is an Italian surname based on a familiar Italian epithet of the Blessed Virgin Mary, *L'Annunziata* 'Our Lady of the Annunciation.' The angel Gabriel who made known to Mary news of the Incarnation is also known as *l'angelo annunziatore*. These terms and the office of papal *nunzio* and the English words announce, announcer, and announcement all derive from Latin *nuntiare* 'to report, to bring a message.' The earlier noun *nuntius* 'messenger' is possibly a contraction of **nouentius* from two roots **nou* 'new' and *uentum* 'having come' so that a nuntius was someone who came with new things (like news?).

The angel Gabriel foretells to Mary the birth of Jesus.

Michael Grattan O'Leary 1889–1976

Political reporter, then Progressive Conservative editor of the Ottawa Journal. *Prime Minister Diefenbaker tossed in the reward of a senate seat in 1962.*

O'Leary is an occupational surname from the Irish *Ó Lao-ghaire* 'descendant of calf-keeper.'

Sir William Osler 1849–1919

One of the greatest clinicians Canada has produced, Osler helped establish current postgraduate training methods for physicians, published widely, and was the author of a standard textbook The Principles and Practice of Medicine *(1892, many revisions). A Victorian of daunting energy, he also knew the value of humour in education and in patient care: "The chief thing that separates human beings from animals is the desire to take pills."*

Osler is a medieval occupation name from Old French *oiseleur* 'fowler, bird-catcher' or Old French *oiselier* 'poulterer, seller of game birds.'

Manly hunters in a noble sport shoot dangerous pheasants.

Richard Ouzounian 1950–

"Ouz" is a witty writer of revue songs, director, producer, and general gadfly of the Canadian theatre scene, who has run Theatre Manitoba, theatre companies in Vancouver and Toronto, and also been a drama critic for CBC Radio and a television administrator in charge of the arts at TVO (1995–1996).

Ouzounian is an Armenian surname with the standard Armenian patronymic suffix *-ian* 'descendant of, son of' borrowed from the Hellenistic Greek surname suffix *ianos*, itself from a common Latin adjectival suffix *-ianus*. In Armenian *ouzon* means 'tall' and Ouzounian 'descendant of the tall man' refers to a specific heroic ancestor who defeated a Turkish foe in times past.

PALLISER

John Palliser 1817–1887

He explored western Canada from Lake Superior to the Okanagan Valley as leader of the Palliser Expedition (1857–1860) whose reports and maps were invaluable to planners of the Canadian Pacific Railway and others opening our west. Palliser's Triangle of semi-arid prairie and Palliser's Pass are named after him.

Palliser is a medieval occupational surname widespread in northeast England's County Durham. A palliser was one who made fences or palings. Compare the word *palisade*.

PALMER

Daniel David Palmer 1845–1913

The popularizer of chiropractic manipulation of the joints, especially of the spine, was born in Port Perry, Ontario. In 1898 he opened the Palmer School of Chiropractic in Davenport, Iowa, to teach his techniques. An early patient of Palmer, a Reverend Weed, coined the word chiropractic which has the general sense from its Greek roots of 'doing things with the hands.'

Palmer is an early medieval honorific that harks back to the times of the crusades when a pilgrim returning from the Holy Land always brought back a palm-branch because of its association with the story of Jesus. In Old French a *palmer* was also one who set out on one of the crusades.

PARIZEAU

Jacques Parizeau 1930–

He joined the Parti Québécois in 1969 and worked his way to Party President by 1988. The reward? Premier of Québec from 1994 to 1996.

Parizeau is a pet form of Patrice, and so it's similar to Patty or Paddy. The name was popularized by *saint Patrice*, Saint Patrick.

Gérard Pelletier 1919–
A lifelong enemy of Québec Premier Duplessis, he gained attention reporting on the 1949 Asbestos Strike for Montréal's Le Devoir. *As a labour activist he helped Pierre Elliott Trudeau and Jean Marchard found* Cité Libre *magazine and then entered Liberal politics to hold cabinet portfolios under Trudeau and later ambassadorial posts.*

    Un pelletier was a medieval French occupation, the name of one who made and sold prepared animal skins and furs, from the Late Latin *pelletarius*. Compare the English word *pelt*.

John Whitney "Jack" Pickersgill 1905–
A very influential policy wonk—as we might say today. He was right-hand man to two Canadian prime ministers, Mackenzie King and St. Laurent, and his written history of that era is still of value.

    A Yorkshire surname, Pickersgill means almost literally 'den of thieves.' Pickersgill Lane is a place in Killinghall in the west riding of Yorkshire. Gill is from Old Norse *gil* 'ravine' and a picker in Middle English was a petty thief who stole things easily picked up. This ravine of the cutpurses must have been a dangerous dell indeed. Perhaps the founding ancestor lived up on the ridge of the ravine whence he could observe the robbers below at their nefarious deeds.

Edwin John Pratt 1882–1964
A boy of the Newfoundland outports, he became through twelve volumes of verse one of Canada's most anthologized poets and a professor of English at Victoria College (1920–1953). His best narrative poetry is steeped in Newfoundland and Canadian history.

John Christopher Pratt 1935–
Critic Joan Murray calls this austere stylist "one of the great classicists of contemporary Canadian painting."

PELLETIER

PICKERSGILL

PRATT

Mary Pratt, née West 1935–
A painter of what one critic called "domestic photo-realism tempered by lush delight in surfaces," she was married to artist Christopher Pratt.

Pratt is an ancestor's nickname from an unattested Old English adjective **prætt* 'cunning, tricky, astute.' However the noun *prætt* 'guile, a trick' is in print from A.D. 1000. It is highly unlikely that the surname derives from the British slang term *pratt* 'buttocks' since this does not appear in print until 1567, and Pratt as a surname shows up in a document dated 1179. Still, this does not prevent British residents with the name from having to abide a certain amount of schoolyard joshing.

R

RAE

Robert "Bob" Keith Rae 1948–
The leader of the Ontario NDP from 1982 (MPP, York South) when he resigned his federal seat. He was Leader of the Opposition in the Ontario legislature (1987–1990) and then NDP Premier of Ontario (1990–1995).

Rae is a Scots variant of Roe from Old English *ra* 'deer, roe.' The ancestor might have received the nickname because of his hunting ability, his swiftness-of-foot, or even for certain bashful, retiring ways.

RANKIN

*A popular family of five singers (**Cookie, Heather, Jimmy, John, and Raylene**) from Mabou on Cape Breton Island with a background in the Celtic music of our Maritimes, they have recorded CDs that include "The Rankin Family" (1989), "Fare Thee Well Love" (1990), and "North Country" (1993).*

Rankin was a popular first name for men in medieval England. *Ran-kin* is a pet or diminutive form of the compound Old English first name Randolph, from *Rand-wulf* 'shield-wolf.' The first and last name Randal is from the same source.

RASKY

Harry Rasky 1928–
Co-founder of the news-documentary department at CBC TV (1952–1955), he is the maker of award-

winning television documentaries and biographies, shown on CBC TV and internationally, whose subjects include Marc Chagall, Robertson Davies, Northrop Frye, Yousuf Karsh, Raymond Massey, Arthur Miller, George Bernard Shaw, Teresa Stratas, and Tennessee Williams. He has published books based on his TV documentaries and been honoured with many awards.

Rasky appears Slavic but is a Jewish matronymic surname honouring a mother named Rachel. A common nickname for Rachel in Russian Yiddish is *Raske* (in German Yiddish it's *Reichel*). *Rachel* 'ewe' is a very ancient Hebrew given name for women.

Keanu Reeves 1964–

The actor has become a superstar of Hollywood films. He is Canadian though born in Beirut to an Hawaiian father and an English mother. His feature films include River's Edge *(1987)*, Point Break *(1991)*, Much Ado About Nothing *(1994)*, Johnny Mnemonic *(1995), and* Speed *(1995). In a rare theatrical outing Reeves played Hamlet in 1994 at the Manitoba Theatre Centre.*

Keanu is Hawaiian and means 'cool breeze.' *Ke-ahe-anu* is literally 'the breeze cool.'

Reeves is a possessive surname from the medieval occupation of reeve, who at various times and places could have been a bailiff, an overseer, or a magistrate. Reeves 'of the reeve' could also denote one who worked in the house of a reeve, or who was the son of a reeve.

Roy John Romanov 1939–

A successful NDP politician in Saskatchewan, he has been Premier of the province since 1987.

Romanov is a Slavic patronymic surname meaning 'descendant of an ancestor named Roman.' For more than eight hundred years Roman has been a popular male given name in many Slavic languages, including Ukrainian, Polish, and Russian.

Patricia Rozema 1958–

Canadian director, writer, and producer whose feature films include I've Heard the Mermaids Singing *(1987),*

White Room *(1990), and* When Light is Falling *(1995).*

Rozema is a Dutch surname, a matronymic 'descendant of Roza.' A much more remote possibility is a pet form of *rozemarijn* 'rosemary.'

RUBES

Jan Rubes 1920–

The Czech-born operatic bass has contributed hugely to the development of opera in Canada, chiefly through his work with the Canadian Opera Company. He has directed theatre and opera, and as an actor he has been memorable playing an Amish farmer in the Hollywood thriller Witness *(1985) directed by Peter Weir. He has acted in many Canadian television features including* Charlie Grant's War *(1984).*

Rubes is a locative Slavic surname based on an ancestor's house being located on a boundary or border. Compare Russian *rooBESHCH* 'border' and Ukrainian *ruBEEZH.*

S SCHREYER

Edward Richard Schreyer 1935–

Born at Beauséjour, he entered the Manitoba legislature at age twenty-two, becoming by 1969 NDP provincial Premier. In 1979 Trudeau made him Governor-General of Canada, a post he held until 1984, when he became Canada's High Commissioner to Australia for four years, before returning to private life.

Schreyer is a German name denoting the important medieval occupation of *Schreier* 'town crier,' one who walked through the central streets of a town declaiming the latest news and government bulletins. There are also German records indicating the noun was sometimes the humorous nickname of an ancestor who was a loudmouth, a real windbag.

SHAMAS

Sandra Shamas

Born in Sudbury, the brilliantly funny stand-up comedienne based in Toronto is of Lebanese extraction. One of her early gigs was as puppeteer for the CBC/Jim Henson television series Fraggle Rock *(1984–1986). After comic monologues at Toronto venues like the Back*

*Room at the Rivoli, Ms. Shamas has had national and
international success with one-woman shows like "My
Boyfriend's Back & There's gonna be Laundry" and
"Wedding Bell Hell."*

Shamas is an occupational, religious surname
from Arabic *shammas*. The shammas can be a layperson
who performs duties similar to a sexton, or, in Middle
Eastern Christian rites, the shammas may be an acolyte
or liturgical cantor.

Tatanga Mani 1871–1967

*The Stoney Indian leader, statesman, and philosopher,
born in the Bow River Valley of Alberta, had the English
name of George McLean. His thoughts on world peace
are worth fresh consideration.*

Tatanga Mani in the Stoney language is literally
'buffalo walking.' Canadian aboriginal actor Graham
Greene has a memorable scene in the film *Dances With
Wolves* trying to guess the charade as the Kevin Costner
character imitates a buffalo–badly–but Greene's character does understand and says, "*Tatonka!*" which is the
similar word for 'buffalo' in the language of the Lakota
Sioux .

Veronica Tennant 1947–

*Her great technique and intensity made the ballerina
one of the greatest stars of the National Ballet of
Canada.*

The popularity of Veronica as a female given name
is due to Saint Veronica, a woman of Jerusalem whom
pious legend states stood along the *via dolorosa* and
took pity on Jesus and his suffering as he was led to his
crucifixion. Veronica stooped down and wiped Christ's
sweating brow with her veil. Later she noticed that the
cloth now bore a true image of the face of Christ. At St.
Peter's in Rome such a cloth, claimed to be the original
veil of St. Veronica, may be seen among the holy relics
in the Vatican collection. July 12 is St. Veronica's feast
day, and girls born on this date are sometimes baptized
with the name in the Russian Orthodox, Greek

TATANGA **T**

TENNANT

Orthodox, or Roman Catholic churches.

One standard but dubious etymology of Veronica arises from this story, and is the origin found in many, poorly researched "names-for-your-baby" books. Monkish folk etymology posits that the name is a contraction of the Latin phrase *vera iconica* meaning 'true image,' from the same Greek root that gives us the word for a religious painting, icon. Such a derivation is linguistically unlikely.

Much more probable is the derivation of Veronica from a medieval Latin adjective *veronicus* that meant 'a person from the Italian city of Verona.' Veronica would mean a woman of Verona, a suitable name for a girl because the women of that city were considered to be among the most beautiful in all of medieval Italy. Shakespeare places Romeo and Juliet "in fair Verona where we lay our scene." But Verona also claimed to possess the veil of St. Veronica at one point during the Renaissance! Sixteenth-century Italian referred to this as *la veletta veronica* 'the Veronese veil.' This, I believe, is the origin of the feminine first name. Véronique is the French spelling. In some Slavic tongues, it is Veronika or Beronika. The fact that one of the Catholic Stations of the Cross commemorates St. Veronica's kindness to the suffering Jesus insures the name's continued popularity in all languages of the western world.

Another doubtful source of the given name Veronica is the female first name Berenice (often shortened to Bernice), originally a Macedonian form of the Greek *Pherenike* 'bringer of victory.' The vowel shiftings and interlingual gradations necessary to support this bizarre transformation may happen on Mars, but have not so far occurred on earth, except in the frantic noggins of certain desperate etymologists.

Tennant as an English surname originates as tenant. A putative ancestor might have been called John the tenant, a man who held land in one of various forms of feudal tenure. In form, it's *tenant*, a Norman-French participial form from *tenir* 'to hold.' By the end of the period of Middle English, about A.D. 1500, when some British surnames had assumed their final form, tenancy came to refer to renting a piece of land for a specified time by lease. The spelling *Tennant* is not, of course, an attempt to disguise the fact that the founding ancestor did not own any land outright. It merely reflects how variable English spelling was, before the rise of dictionaries and widespread literacy combined to regularize orthography. The surname appears as Tennant, Tennent, Tennents. Tennant is common in Yorkshire and southern Scotland.

TILLEY

Alexander Tilley 1938–
Inventive Canadian designer of outdoor and travel clothing and originator of the Tilley hat.

Leonard Percy de Wolfe Tilley 1870–1947
The New Brunswick lawyer and politician was premier of the province from 1933 to 1935. He was the son of the father of Confederation listed next.

Sir Samuel Leonard Tilley 1818–1896
Born at Gagetown, New Brunswick, he began in the drugstore business and rose to political fame as a staunch advocate of New Brunswick's inclusion in Confederation. He was Macdonald's politically astute point man in the province and held many cabinet portfolios in both Macdonald governments.

The origins of Tilley as an ancient British surname are complex. The earliest form of the name appears as Ralph de Tilio in the Domesday Book of the English county of Derbyshire in A.D. 1086. This man was of Norman-French extraction, and a recent arrival from France—remember the Norman Conquest of 1066 a few years before. The founding ancestor of this family took his name from the place he lived in France. There are five little towns in northern France that may be the locality of origin: Tilly-sur-Seulles in Calvados, Tilly in Eure, Tilly in Seine-et-Oise, one in Meuse, and one in the Pas-de-Calais. Only a rigorous genealogical search might determine the precise locative origin of the family.

This Norman Tilley has many spelling forms both

in England and in France, among which are: Tillie, Tilly, Tiley, Tily, Tylee, Tyley, Tilhet, Thillet, and Thiellet! Why is this particular name and its variants so widespread over northern France? Because it belonged to a Teutonic tribe who controlled much of the area, long before the Romans conquered northern Gaul. The area was known to Gallo-Romans as *Tilliacum* and that term was based on the tribe's name in Old Germanic *Tielo*, short for *Theod-ilo*, and that word contains a Germanic rootword *theod* that means 'the people.' So Tilley harks all the way back to a word at least two thousand years old and means 'the people.'

Is that it then, for Tilley? Unfortunately no. Several hundred years later in England, Tilley was coined as a new matronymic surname based on the nickname of an ancestral mother. Till and Tilly were pet forms of Matilda. Some English Tilleys also stem from Middle English *tilie* 'one who tills the fields,' a forebear who was a husbandman.

TOBIN

Brian Tobin 1954–
The feisty Newfoundland Liberal made a big splash as Chrétien's Minister of Fisheries, then in 1996 he quit federal politics to return to his native Newfoundland where he won a huge majority to become Premier of the province in February of 1996.

Tobin can be a Norman-French surname or an Irish one. If Norman French, it stems from *Tob-in* 'little Tobias' or 'Toby.' Tobias is the Koine Greek form of the Hebrew male name Tobiah 'Yahweh (God) is good.' As a Christian first name it is the source of surnames like Tobey, Tobin, and Tobyn. If Tobin is of Irish provenance, it may derive from *Ó Tobán* 'descendant of Washtub' where *tobán*, the Gaelic word for tub, is the nickname of an ancestor who took in washing or who was squat as a tub. More austere etymologists suggest Irish *Tobin* stems from a Norman surname St. Aubyn or St. Aubin, originating in Brittany.

TREMBLAY

Michel Tremblay 1942–
He is the leading French-Canadian playwright of the

second half of the twentieth century whose vivid, joual-
flecked dialogue sparkles in such plays as Les Belles-
Soeurs *(1968),* A toi, pour toujours, ta Marie-Lou
(1971), Hosanna *(1973),* Albertine en cinq temps
(1984), and Le gars de Québec *(1985). In the mid-
seventies Tremblay turned increasingly to fiction in a
series of continuing novels under the series title* Plateau
Mont-Royal *which nevertheless move through the same
world as his plays, the working-class neighbourhoods of
Montréal. He did not abandon theatre however, as
shown by his most recent play* Messe solennelle pour
une pleine lune d'été *'High Mass for a Full Summer
Moon' which debuted early in 1996 at Montréal's
Théâtre Jean Duceppe.*

Tremblay beats out Smith as the most common
surname in Canada. In 1995, there were 180,000
Canadians with the last name Tremblay. One out of
every 50 Québécois is named Tremblay. Many families
with the surname settled early in *la Nouvelle France*. At
least six towns in France are called Tremblay or
Tremblais. The place name stems from the Gallo-
Roman adjective *tremuletum* 'place abounding in trem-
bling aspen trees' from the earlier Latin adjective *tremu-
lus* 'shivering, quaking.'

Joseph Philippe Pierre Yves Elliott Trudeau 1919–
*The constitutional lawyer and Liberal writer became
the fifteenth Prime Minister of Canada and the first
born in the twentieth century. Holding the Prime
Minister's office in 1968–1979 and again in 1980–1984,
Trudeau became one of the most influential figures in
modern Canadian history.*

During his years of political power, a hoary folk
etymology, very common and very wrong, made the
rounds about Trudeau. You could ask anyone on the
street in Québec and be told that Trudeau was, *bien
entendu*, from *trou d'eau*, a supposed old term for
water-hole. And of course there were vulgar jokes told
that depended on this spurious etymology. Trudeau as a
surname goes back to an ancestor who bore the
Teutonic warrior name *Trudo*. The root is Old High

TRUDEAU

German *drud* which meant 'strong, hardened, tough, mighty.' So frequent a first name was it in very early French that we even find it in ancient church records with a full Latin declension: *Trudo, Trudonis*, etc. Quite the opposite with our little water-hole *trou d'eau* which is **never** found in print. *Trou* was simply not used like this in early French. *Trou* indicated always an absence, a hole that was empty. Even in the most recent French coinages using the word, this holds true. For example, the English astronomical term "black hole" is translated in current French by *trou noir*.

TWAIN

Eileen "Shania" Twain 1965–
The million-CD-selling country-and-western singer-composer grew up in Timmins, Ontario, as Eileen Twain and got her start singing at Ontario's Deerhurst Inn. She has won many awards for her work, e.g., 1996 Junos, Country Music Awards, and Grammies.

Her adoptive father, Jerry Twain, is full-blooded Ojibway. Shania was the name of a girl she worked with at the Deerhurst Inn, and, when it came time to confect a show-biz name, she changed it to Shania (pronounced sha-NYE-a) which is Ojibwa for 'on my way.'

There seems to be no mention of Twain as a surname in print until the American satirist Samuel Langhorne Clemens (1835–1910) used it as his pseudonym and called himself Mark Twain based on the shout of a Mississippi riverboat deckhand who called out water depth from a sounding line sunk in the turbid waters of the river. When the line showed a depth of two fathoms, the mate shouted out to the pilot of the boat, "Mark twain!," that is, the mark is twain, i.e., 'two.'

U URQUHART

Anthony "Tony" Morse Urquhart 1934–
No artist's work can be summed up in a phrase, but this southern Ontario painter, sculptor, and draughtsman had a well-titled retrospective that toured Canada in 1988–1989. It was called Worlds Apart: The Symbolic Landscapes of Tony Urquhart.

Jane Urquhart, née Carter 1949–

Born in Geraldton, Ontario, this novelist of warm, poetic insight counts among her works The Whirlpool *(1986),* Changing Heaven *(1990), and her greatest storytelling to date* Away *(1993).*

Urquhart is the name of half a dozen places in Scotland. The linguistic origin of the name is not clear. It may be Old Celtic, a pre-Roman language of the British Isles, and it may mean 'on the wood-side' denoting the habitation of an ancestor who dwelt on the forested slope of a hill. Onomastician Basil Cottle says the places in Fifeshire named Urquhart have a Scots Gaelic root that means 'cast' or 'shot' and that refers to some lost incident in history that was memorable enough to name the place in which it happened. Professor Reaney's contention that all the Urquhart surnames go back to the barony of Urquhart in Inverness is, simply, unsupported by any historical proof. Here's one name whose origin appears forever lost.

Guy Vanderhaeghe 1951–

VANDERHAEGE

Born in Esterhazy, Saskatchewan, the novelist and short-story writer has published such works as Man Descending *(1982), which won the Governor-General's Award for Fiction,* My Present Age *(1984),* Homesick *(1989), and* Things As They Are? *(1992).*

Vanderhaeghe is a Dutch surname of a familiar topographical type in the Netherlands. *Van der haeghe* means 'of the hay(field)' in Dutch. Such a locative tag named the position of an ancestor's house within a small community. The locative tag began to be written down in registers of marriage, birth, and death, and soon became an inherited surname.

Georges-Philéas Vanier 1888–1967

VANIER

A lawyer, soldier, diplomat, and a great Canadian citizen, he served as founding officer of the Royal 22e Regiment, the famous Vingt-Deux's, *and as Canada's ambassador to France during the Second World War. From 1959 to his death in 1967 his moral dignity and compassion made him one of the best Governors-General Canada has ever had.*

Jean Vanier 1928–

The son of Georges Vanier founded L'Arche *(the ark), a series of homes for handicapped men that now stretches over Canada, France, India, Africa, and the United States. He is also the author of several books of spiritual guidance including* Community and Growth *(1979).*

Vanier is an occupational French surname. A *vanier* or *vanneur* made *vans*. In medieval French a *van* was a sort of flat basket in which grain was sold.

Norman girl with flounder in a *van* 'basket.'

Mary Walsh 1952–

Satirist and comedienne on Maritime stages and on CBC TV's This Hour Has 22 Minutes.

Walsh begins as a word expressing Anglo-Saxon xenophobia. In Old English it was *wælisc* 'foreigner, stranger.' The invading Anglo-Saxons called any Celtic peoples they found in Britain by this adjective, in particular the Welsh who dwelt in Wales, Old English *Wealas* 'land of the foreigners.' The Welsh call themselves *Cymry* and their land *Cymru*. This insulting adjective gave rise to a number of common surnames. But the adjective became obsolete in late Middle English, and so the surnames survived without any obvious semantic opprobrium attached to them. These surnames include Wallace, Walles, Wallice, Walch, Walsh, and Welsh. Wallace is the Scottish form, while Walsh is Irish and is still one of the fifteen most common names in Ireland.

WALSH W

Larry Zolf 1934–

Larry Zolf is the major gift of Winnipeg's North End to Canadian journalism. A longtime CBC host and producer of public affairs television programs, Larry is also the author of a wonderfully satiric look at Canadian journalism, a 1989 novel entitled Scorpions for Sale. *Zolf is a laugher. Zolf is smart and funny. So seldom does this trio of felicities occur together that many of his friends have long since declared him a Living National Treasure.*

Zolf is most likely a Yiddish variant of the Polish *zólw* 'turtle.' In strict Polish orthography the *z* is surmounted by a dot, indicating a sound for this dotted *z* much like the *si* in vision. And note that Polish *w* is pronounced like English *v*, except at the end of a word where it is almost as hard as English *f*. An ancestor might adopt a surname like Turtle because it was an identifying sign on his house or his shop. Does that mean he sold turtles? No, it probably indicates he was a jeweller, who would have used tortoise-shell inlays in making personal adornments and ornamental boxes. For

ZOLF Z

this use, compare the German and Yiddish surname *Schildkraut* or *Shyldkrot* which meant 'turtle' and 'tortoise-shell.'

Three other remoter possibilities exist as origins for the surname Zolf. *Zol* was a variant for Saul among Polish and Russian Jews. Zolf could be a later contraction of a surname that began as Zolov 'descendant of Saul.'

In the Volkovysk district of Grodno, near Bialystok, in what became known as the Pale of Settlement, was a little *shtetl* called Zel'va. This gives Jewish surnames of place like Zelvensky, Zelvin, Zelfin, Zelver, and Zilvin. Note the gradations of the first vowel in these names. A form like Zolfin with a short *o* could arise from such gradation.

The final possible derivation of Zolf is from Zelfman, a person who made soap, from a Yiddish word *zeyf* 'soap.' This root produced Jewish occupational surnames like Zelfman, Zelfin, and Zeyfman. Zolf could be a shortened variant of one of these names.

That is my admittedly selective romp through some Canadian surnames whose origins provoked my interest. Any conclusions to be drawn? Yes. Our tolerance of racial difference should increase. Look at all the fiercely French surnames that turn out to be Germanic warrior names. Look at the given and last names of anti-Semites—none of whom except Hitler are knowingly mentioned in this book—anti-Semites whose very names spring from Biblical Hebrew! The contemplation of this wonderful, tangled root mass of human names behooves all of us to smile more often upon our neighbours and to dismiss ignorant extremists who blat of racial and linguistic purity. In the naming habits of the chief languages of the Western world there is no such purity. All languages blossom from much hybridized seed. So have we.

CHAPTER SEVEN

CHIMO! & OTHER GREETINGS

Klahowyah, *old chum.*

ecognition of the arrival and departure of another person takes many verbal forms, and salutations spring from surprising sources. Hello, as we'll discover, began with a human imitating the howl of a hunting dog. In this chapter we look at expressions of greeting and farewell in English, in some foreign languages, but chiefly at greetings in Canuck parlance. On the TV series and in the movie versions of *Star Trek*, the Vulcan Spock says, "Live long and prosper." Ancient Romans had the somewhat abrupt *ave atque vale* 'hello and goodbye,' which always reminds me of the ditty that comedian Groucho Marx used to sing, "Hello, I must be going." The Latin is literally 'hail and be well' and might be the source of Spock's bye-bye. Bye-bye is a contracted and then duplicated form of goodbye, itself a centuries-in-the-making compression of 'God be with you.'

AVE ATQUE VALE

The Romans used *ave* and *avete* by themselves for saying hello or goodbye. Later *ave* was a morning greeting, and *vale* was used when leaving someone in the evening. In classical Latin *ave atque vale* came to be a

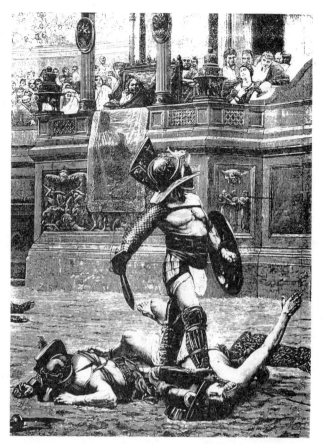

Ancient Rome had few Retired Gladiator Homes.

formulaic farewell to the dead, as in the touching obituary poem that the lyric poet Catullus addressed to his departed brother: *Atque in perpetuum, frater, ave atque vale* 'now for all eternity, my brother, farewell.' When the slaves and criminals who made up the ranks of Roman gladiators were about to enter the arena to almost certain eventual death—ancient Rome had few Retired Gladiator Clubs—they marched past the V.I.P. box and saluted the emperor with this formula: *Ave, Imperator, morituri te salutant* 'Hail, Emperor, those who are about to die, wish you health.' Darn nice of them too—when one considers they were being sacrificed only to ensure the emperor's popularity as a provider of spectacle for the Roman mob, or, in the famous phrase of the satiric poet Juvenal, as a provider of *panem et circenses* 'bread and chariot races.'

Like *ave* were the classical Greek *chaire* and *chairete* which were used both on meeting and on leaving a person. Their root meaning was 'rejoice! be happy!'

HELLO

Before we examine distinctly Canadian greetings, let's look briefly at two others—hello and *ciao*. Hello appears to have arisen in its first instance as an imitation by hunters of a hunting dog's yowl. It is marked "echoic" in many dictionaries, which then add its early forms like halloo from medieval French *halloer* 'to pursue game with shouts and cries.' Compare, too, the Old High German verb *halôn* 'to hail a ferryman by shouting halloo across the water.' Halloo, hullo, hello are a few of many variants which include the reduplicated hullabaloo.

CIAO

The very informal and familiar Italian *ciao* can be used as a greeting or a farewell. *Ciao* sounds approximately like our food word chow. *Ciao* came into standard Italian from a Venetian dialect where *ciao* is a condensed variant of *schiavo* 'slave' in the longer formal greeting *schiavo suo* 'your slave,' itself a reduction of *sono il suo schiavo, signore* 'I am your servant, sir.' How very close to the Victorian English greeting, "Your servant, Mr. Scrooge." You can still hear such a greeting in Latin in the common Austrian greeting *Servus!* with stress on the last syllable. *Servus* harks back to the days of ancient Rome when slavery was in force, and slave servants had to greet their masters with the lick-spittle sibilance of *servus sum* 'I am your slave.'

SLAVE

The word slave and its Italian form *schiavo* merit two paragraphs. They are both from a medieval Latin word *Sclavus* and its slightly later form *Slavus*, both of which referred first to any person who belonged to the large group of peoples of central and eastern Europe who spoke Slavonic languages. Medieval Latin borrowed the word from the Slavs' own name for themselves. In Old Slavonic *Slovëne* was the word for a Slavic person. It means literally 'speaker' from Old Slavonic *slovo* 'word.' They were the people of the word, i.e., they spoke a Slavonic language. The rest of the world spoke gibberish. Almost every linguistic group on earth has words insulting those who do not speak their tongue. The word for baby talk, nonsense, and goo-goo in very ancient Greek was *bar-bar.* The Greeks thought if you were not speaking Greek, you were just uttering gibberish words like *bar-bar.* Such non-Greek speakers were the original *barbaroi* 'barbarians.' Even the philosopher Plato divided mankind into Greeks and Barbarians.

When did Slav come to mean slave? In the tenth century, during the eastward expansion of the Franks under Otto I (A.D. 913–973) many speakers of Old Slavonic were in fact conquered and enslaved. The change in meaning from Slav to slave occurred a little later in Italy, after the raids made by Venetians upon

Slavonia during the time of the Crusades. By the time *schiavo* was reduced to *ciao*, it meant simply 'servant.'

CANADIAN GREETINGS AKSUNAI

Aksunai or *auksuai* is the traditional phrase of greeting and of farewell among the Inuit of the eastern arctic. In their particular dialect, one of the nine of the Inuktitut language, its literal meaning is 'be well, be strong, won't you?'

BITAEMO

Pronounced *vee-tie-amo*, it's Ukrainian for 'welcome' and the motto of Canada's National Ukrainian Fesitval held every year early in August at Dauphin, Manitoba, a pleasant and prosperous town about 310 kilometres northwest of Winnipeg and just north of Riding Mountain National Park. The verb of greeting in Ukrainian is *veetati* with its related noun *veetanya.* By the way, don't let residents of this active tourist centre on the Vermilion River hear you trying to say the name of their town as if it is the French historical title for the eldest son of the King of France. It is true that explorer Pierre Gaultier de Varennes et de La Vérendrye and some of his four sons canoed by in 1730, may have stopped to build a small fort or post, and named the place to honour their king's offspring. Dauphin's pro-nunciation had a French cast to it then,
but later immigrants from Ontario and the Ukraine pro-duced a new Manitoban sound to the name. This is Dauphin pronounced doffin. Since the early 1960s, Ukrainians, who first settled the area in 1896–1898, have celebrated their folk customs and delicious foods each summer in Dauphin at the National Ukrainian Festival.

BO JO, BO JO

In 1836, Anna Brownell Jameson, née Murphy, a Dublin-born writer, early feminist, and later a popular art historian, came out to Toronto for eight months to be with her husband who was a judge in Upper Canada. She kept a diary of her sojourn in our wilds, and published it once back in England. *Winter Studies and Summer Rambles in Canada* (1838) contains a scathing portrait of early Toronto, but an enthusiastic account of a trip through Ontario up to Sault Ste. Marie and back. She paid some attention to pioneer greetings: "The form of salutation in common use between the Indians and the whites is the bo-jo borrowed from early French settlers." It was also spelled Bo Jou, making plain the origin in French *bonjour* 'good day.' This traditional greeting was almost always said twice when aboriginal peoples, trappers, traders, and voyageurs met. As late as 1941 it was noted in *Beaver*, the Hudson Bay Company magazine, as "Bo Jo, Bo Jo. An Indian greeting."

CHIMO

A widespread and ancient Inuit greeting, *chimo!* may be accompanied by a gesture of salutation as well, namely moving the left hand in a circle on the area of the chest over the heart. Variants as heard by white explorers include *teyma*, *tima*, and *timah*. Some early explorers were told that *chimo* came from an Inuktitut root that meant 'trade, barter' and that the only greeting implied in the word when spoken to white southerners was 'let's trade.' Even if that is true, today *chimo* is exclusively a warm greeting and is used in our North as a toast before drinking.

The number of discrete sounds utterable by the human vocal apparatus is finite. Consonant and vowel repertoires vary from language to language, but it only takes learning three or four new languages, before the student begins to hear words that sound the same in two languages but have quite different meanings. I heard about such a mix-up concerning chimo from my friend, broadcaster Vicki Gabereau. Vicki had an acquaintance who liked the cheerful sound of Chimo (chee-mo) and so this female friend named her dog Chimo. The dog was obedient and learned to respond to his name when called by his owner. When the lady got a job in Japan that was to last several years, she did not want to be parted from her dear Chimo, and so decided to take her pet with her to Japan, which she did. Things worked out well as Chimo had the run of a little fenced yard beside the lady's residence in quite a posh suburb near Tokyo. Now Chimo was good-natured but frisky, and occasionally jumped the fence. But the lady had only to call him by name, and eventually he would come trotting home and jump back inside the little yard. The lady did notice that when she called him loudly, any Japanese neighbours who might be in hearing distance would turn away and avoid her. This happened every time she shouted, "Chimo! Chimo!" Then people of the neighbourhood began crossing to the other side of the street or roadway whenever she came along. It was months until a Japanese friend explained that the way she pronounced chimo made it sound exactly like a Japanese word for 'pubic hair.' She had been running up and down the street for months shouting "Pubic hair! Pubic hair!" Her Japanese neighbours had been too polite to inquire if she was merely crazy or was experiencing a late but joyful puberty.

I promise that is the only shaggy dog story in this book.

Chimo had long tenure as a Canadian place name too. An Innu community on the Koksoak River just south of Ungava Bay was called Fort Chimo from 1831 until 1981 when the name was changed to the traditional one, Kuujjuaq. *Koksoak* means 'big river' in western Inuktitut. Would anyone go skinny-dipping in the Koksoak?

KLAHOWYAH

Klahowyah! is hello in Chinook Jargon. Chinook Jargon was a trading language, a lingua franca based on the speech of the Chinook Indians, with words from French, English, Salish, Nootka, and other local tongues. Springing up to help speed transactions in the fur trade, Chinook Jargon was used from the 1830s until the turn of the century by first nations and white traders on the Pacific coast. Like all pidgins, it had simplified grammar and a tiny vocabulary of about seven hundred words. Some of its words entered British Columbian slang and place names. A high muckamuck is a bigshot. Skookum is 'big, mighty.' Fifty years ago, a Vancouver radio newscaster began his nightly broadcast with the Chinook Jargon greeting, "*Klahowyah, tillicums!*" 'Hello, friends.' Some say *klahowyah* actually condenses the English greeting "How are you?"

NITCHIE

Nitchie, with many variants like *neche, nee-chee, neejee,* and *nidge*, is a general term in many Algonkian languages for 'friend, person, native.' It was used among Algonkian-speaking aboriginal peoples to greet one another. The root appears in the Ojibwa word *Anishnawbe* that is used by Ojibway people to name themselves. It means 'first (original) people.' A collective form in general Algonkian is *Anishnabeg*. But as early as the 1840s fur traders and other Whites had turned the cheerful *nitchie!* into yet another derogatory synonym for 'Indian,' thus permanently reducing its use among Whites who did not want to offend first peoples.

An interesting new Canadian word, which is a blend of English and Ojibwa, was pointed out by Toronto-based writer and dramatist Drew Hayden Taylor in his occasional column in the *Toronto Star*. This pun on *Anishnawbe* is used by certain native people to describe the growing aboriginal middle-class in major Canadian cities. If they seem too white to other native people, they are termed 'Anish-snobs.'

TAKE OFF!

Forty years ago one could knock on the screen door of a farm house in Ontario or the Prairies, have the door opened by a smiling resident, and be told: "Don't stand there. Take off." A city slicker might think he was being told to go away. Many a time an urban visitor started down the porch steps in a huff, only to be summoned back with an explanation. "Take off" meant 'take off your coat or heavy outerwear, come on in, sit down, and be welcome.' They had confused the urban American dismissal "take off" with a standard rural Canadian welcome. The meaning of the expression was influenced also by "sit down and take a load off."

WACHEE!

Cree speakers often hailed Whites with '*wacheya!*' British and Scottish trappers and fur traders falsely believed that *wacheya* and *wachee* were borrowed directly from the eighteenth- and early nineteenth-century British salutation "What cheer!" implying 'what cheer to meet you.' But it's a Cree greeting that only happens to resemble an English phrase. *Wachee* is in print as early as 1872 in Robert Ballantyne's *The Pioneers—A Tale of the Western Wilderness*, and as late as this example from 1964 in Canadian writer Jock Carroll's *The Shy Photographer*: 'Watchee!' cried Shorty to Mad Pierre, using the Swampy Cree greeting."

CHAPTER EIGHT

PROVINCIAL & TERRITORIAL WORDS

When Brian Tobin was elected Premier of Newfoundland early in 1996, he promised to seek a constitutional amendment to change the official name of his province to Newfoundland and Labrador. Most Canadians thought that was already the case, that Labrador was legally and undisputedly and forever a part of Newfoundland. Maybe not? Behind the seemingly innocent expansion of the provincial name is a centuries-old territorial squabble. In his speech from the throne on March 20, 1996, marking the opening of the first session of the Newfoundland legislature with Tobin as Premier, the Lieutenant-Governor Frederick Russell said, "It is time to change the name of our province to reflect the reality that it is made up of two equally important parts, Newfoundland and Labrador." And Labrador is more vital a part than ever before. With the decline of the fish stocks off our east coast, the massive find of mineral deposits at Voisey's Bay in Labrador has become a pivot on which the economy of Newfoundland may turn around. Scheduled to start in 1998, the mining operation will tap one of world's largest caches of nickel, copper, and cobalt. The multi-billion-dollar bonanza has

A NEW NAME FOR NEWFOUNDLAND?

the added benefit of being a lode that will be relatively easy to mine. The smelter for Voisey's Bay ore will be in Newfoundland. So will trans-shipment depots for off-shore oil finds, like the Hibernia project in Bull Arm where already five thousand jobs have been created, and the Terra Nova oil field off Newfoundland's west coast. These megaprojects will bring new jobs and growth to a province in need of such a boost.

But a long-standing Labrador boundary dispute between Newfoundland and Québec has sizzled on the skillet of history for more than two hundred years. The boundary in contention does happen to be our longest interprovincial border: 3,500 kilometres long—a territorial limit that has never been surveyed or marked *on the ground*. A time-line of the dispute makes clear its persistent appearance in Québec-Newfoundland relations.

- 1763 Britain acquired Labrador by the Treaty of Paris, and all other French territories in North America except the two little islands of St. Pierre and Miquelon. The vaguely defined area of Labrador was included within Newfoundland chiefly to cut off Québec from east coast access and fur trade of eastern origin. Acadia being annexed to Nova Scotia served to isolate Québec too. Also in 1763, Thomas Graves, the governor of the British colony of Newfoundland, was given by royal commission jurisdiction over the coasts of Labrador. Constitutional experts claim that Newfoundland's ownership of Labrador can be traced back to this year. However, a further royal proclamation later in the same year placed Labrador under Governor Graves' "care and inspection" for fishing purposes only.

- 1774 Labrador became part of Québec (Lower Canada) by statute.

- 1783 The Peace of Paris divided up British territories in North America after Britain lost the

American War of Independence. While Cape Breton, the Gulf of St. Lawrence, the Labrador coast, and Newfoundland stayed British, Great Britain ceded to the Americans vast fishery rights, not only to the Grand Banks, but also to fishing inside the then three-mile limit of British territorial waters, and to going ashore anywhere on British territory, including Labrador, to dry their catch.

- 1809 Labrador is returned to Newfoundland by statute.

- 1825 Part of Labrador is returned to Québec (Lower Canada).

- 1902 Newfoundland issued a licence to a private company to cut timber near Labrador's Churchill River. Québec protested ownership.

- 1904 Québec succeeded in getting the federal government to submit the question of ownership of Labrador to the Judicial Committee of the Privy Council in London, England.

- 1927 After twenty-three years of wrangling, the Privy Council set the present boundary between Labrador and Québec, and decided in Newfoundland's favour, that is, that Newfoundland could claim Labrador as its own territory "inland to the watershed line."

- 1949 Newfoundland joined Confederation as Canada's tenth province. The territory of Labrador was defined in the Terms of Union, now called the Newfoundland Act. And this was re-enshrined in the Constitution Act of 1982.

- 1971 Québec set up a royal commission to study complaints since 1949 that Labrador's boundary was not settled. Its own commission ruled against such Québec claims.

- 1990 The dispute is still a good way for a federal back-bencher to get some press, and so in October of 1990, a Montréal MP introduced a constitutional proposal that would have divided Canada into five regions, one of them to bear the quaint title *Québec and Labrador*. Some honourable members objected, among them a Newfoundland MP, Brian Tobin, who rose in the house to denounce any such rejigging of Canada's boundaries.

In one of his literate columns on Canadian affairs, which grace the pages of the *Toronto Star* and other newspapers, that wily sage of New Brunswick, Dalton Camp, once wrote: "The awesome perils of reorganizing societies by redrawing maps have been proclaimed through history. It was a mistake, perhaps, to have so much of Labrador made up of what might have been Quebec." Indeed. But striving to unaccomplish any fait accompli is a popular millennial hobby. Therefore it seems unlikely, as we squirm here in the foreshadow of future separation referenda, that Canadians have heard the last of this litigious bickering over Labrador. What's in the new name of Newfoundland and Labrador? Well, mineral wealth and hydro-electric power, for starters.

NEW BRUNSWICK FROLIC

Pioneer neighbours rallied around to help put up a barn, make quilts, dry apples. What might be a quilting bee in Upper Canada was a quilting frolic in New Brunswick's early days. A stick-to-your-ribs meal, dancing, and several cups of good cheer might follow all the communal hard work. British immigrants brought the term to New Brunswick. Frolic came into English from Dutch *vroolijk* 'happy, joyous.' Compare its cognate synonym in German *fröhlich*, as in the German for Merry Christmas, *Fröhliche Weihnachten!* The Indo-European root **fro* means 'hop.' It has descendants like German

Freude 'joy' and even English *frog* whose root meaning is 'the hopper.' Classical Sanskrit, ancient tongue of India and sacred language of Hinduism, has the related *pravate* 'it hops.' So a frolic is semantically close to a high-school hop of the 1950s.

HERRING-CHOKER

This old slang term for any Maritimer was applied usually to New Brunswickers, probably because the Bay of Fundy has a run of spring herrings (alewives, a good bait fish) that come in to spawn in April and May. In the fall, a herring run of a different species more highly prized for eating arrives, as A. Murray Kinloch points out in "The English Language in New Brunswick 1784-1984," his lively tour of the topic that appears in *A Literary and Linguistic History of New Brunswick* (1985).

INTERVALE

This word, also seen as "interval," brought up to our Maritimes by immigrants from the New England states, is a synonym for bottomland, the rich alluvial soil in the flood plain of a watercourse. New Brunswick's many rivers rejoiced in deep intervales, sometimes called riverbottoms. Here's a pioneer quotation from around 1780: "The interval lands on the St. John are wonderful, not a stone, and black mold six feet deep."

JILL-POKE

In the jargon of New Brunswick lumbering this noun named a major nuisance for log drivers: a timber pole that had one end stuck in the mud of a riverbank and the other projecting dangerously out into the current. Jill-poke was also heard in early Maritime lumber camps as a label for anyone in camp who was a 'pain-in-the-ass.' "Get that drunken jill-poke's face out of the molasses!" It's a nifty, jabby chop and should be resuscitated for use in political invective. Why, two or three of our glorious, jill-pokey leaders come to mind almost immediately.

LUCIVEE

It was the Canada lynx or its pelt. This is a New Brunswick variant of the French and Acadian *loup-cervier*, a direct borrowing from medieval Latin *lupus cervarius* 'the wolf who attacks deer.' The European *loup-cervier* is not the same species as our lynx. But English did a multiple mangling of the word. It appears as *lucerver, lucervi, lucifee,* and the magnificent *lucififer,* a local name on the upper St. John River at the turn of the century.

PEAVEY

This is a lumbering tool invented in the New Brunswick woods where the first important commercial logging in North America took place. A peavey is a long pole (up to 7 feet) with an iron point and a hinged hook. Lumbermen used it to guide logs on a drive. Certain Maine etymologists claim that a J. B. Peavey of that state invented the instrument. The only slight fly in the American ointment is the total lack of any printed record that any person of that name ever existed. I don't want to be peevish, but—tough hook, guys.

RAMPIKE

A British dialect word of unknown origin gave us this sturdy noun that names a dead but standing tree burnt in a forest fire. Joshua Fraser, a nineteenth-century Scottish immigrant, in his 1883 *Shanty, Forest, and River Life in the Backwoods of Canada,* gives this description: "In backwoods parlance these are called 'rampikes' and make you think of the crowbars which the Titans may have used to pry up the rocks, with which they tried to pelt Jupiter out of Heaven."

RAPPÉ PIE

A hearty Acadian dish, literally 'grated pie' from Acadian French *tarte râpée* or *pain râpé,* this *tarte à la râpure* was the traditional meal served after a pioneer quilting frolic in New Brunswick. Among the ingredients inside the pastry were potatoes, onions, chicken or black duck or rabbit, lard, salt, and pepper.

RIPS

Where New Brunswick rivers ran fast and shallow, white waters were 'rips.' Rips called for deft canoeing, log-booming, and bateau-ing. The more usual English word was "riffle," and perhaps rip is a shortening of riffle. The Rips is a local tag for white-water rapids at several places in New Brunswick.

SAW-WHET OWL

This little owl of eastern North America, *Aegolius acadicus*, was named by New Brunswickers who thought its characteristic cry reminiscent of the sound made when filing or whetting a saw. Also known as the Acadian owl, it was dubbed "the sawyer" in pioneer Ontario. A citation from Upper Canada in 1822 states that it was sometimes called the "whetsaw."

SCRIPTURE CORD

Many early New Brunswick farmers took to the woods in winter to work in lumber camps or as independent lumberjacks. When in the spring the trimmed wood was sold, Scripture cord was cut timber that measured more than the invoice indicated. It was a lumbering equivalent of a baker's dozen, in which the good Christian selling the wood, mindful of scriptural injunctions about generosity, gave the buyer a little extra *bois* for good measure, perhaps with the practical benefit that the buyer would return for more small bargains.

SHEDIACS

Oysters from Shediac, New Brunswick, suffered a few sea changes when subjected to the metamorphosis of pioneer spelling. Here's how the succulent molluscs saw print in 1835 in the pages of *The Novascotian*, a weekly published in Halifax : "Where have you been all your days, that you never heard of Shittyack Oysters—I thought everybody had heard of them." Shediac was named by the Mi-'Kmaq people from Micmac *esedeiik* 'running far back,' referring to the bay's indentation from Northumberland Strait.

SLOVEN

New Brunswick carters invented the sloven, a cart with a crank axle and a very low floor that facilitated loading and unloading. Its practicality saw use spread to all of the Maritime provinces. In his 1941 novel *Barometer Rising*, whose climax is the 1917 Halifax explosion, Hugh MacLennan writes: "Grinding on the cobblestones behind a pair of plunging Clydesdales came one of Halifax's most typical vehicles, a low-slung dray with a high driver's box, known as a sloven."

TOGUE

The popular name of a tasty lake trout of our Atlantic provinces, also seen as "tog," well illustrates one of the trade-offs people make in using common names—since togue can refer both to a freshwater fish (also called grey lake trout, mackinaw trout, mountain trout, and salmon trout) and also to a saltwater fish, an Atlantic wrasse, the tautog (*Tautoga onitis*). Tog and togue all stem from an eastern Algonkian plural *tautauog* 'black fishes' which gives an American common name for the saltwater species 'blackfish.'

TREE NAIL

Eighteenth-century homesteaders did not have a ready supply of iron nails unless a blacksmith had set up a forge nearby. So, early New Brunswick building timbers were fastened together with wooden pegs dubbed in pioneer lingo "tree nails."

WANGAN & WANIGAN

New Brunswick lumbermen used this raft or scow to transport to a new site personnel and camp supplies. The cook shack could be on the boat too with a floating mess hall, until facilities on shore were set up. Whites borrowed the term from local Algonkian-speaking peoples. In Ojibwa *wa'nikka'n* was a storage pit containing a cache of odds and ends that might be useful for trade. Montagnais has *atawangan* 'trade storage' related to *atawan* 'to trade,' the same Algonkian root that named the Ottawa people, the trading band that gave its name to our capital city. In the Abnaki language *waniigan* is a 'pit trap' or 'a container for sundries.'

"Running the wangan" was taking a loaded boat downriver. In *Seven Rivers of Canada*, Hugh MacLennan writes of lumbering on New Brunswick's St. John River: "Within three weeks the Wangan boat men clear the river of stray logs all the way from Beechwood to Maugerville."

A wangan box was a large chest in which New Brunswick lumberjacks kept clothing, pipes, tobacco, and other camp necessities. Out west, logging company stores were called wanigans where the logger could buy bush clothes and supplies. During the gold rushes wanigan was used to name a one-room shed on skids

that was used as instant accommodation in boom towns.
Up north, huts mounted on sleds with runners and tow-
able by Bombardiers were called wanigans. And the latest use of this all-purpose term can be found in a 1966
western edition of *Eaton's Fall & Winter Catalogue*:
"Natural sheepskin wannigans for wear under over-
boots." This wannigan is a short-laced,
leather-soled boot. Adaptable wear. Adaptable word.

"When the state has withered away" Karl Marx prophe-
sied, there would come into being a workers' paradise.
It hasn't happened yet, *mein Kärlchen*, although neo-
conservatives all over the world bray for the decline of
the nation state (big governments getting smaller and
governing less) to make the world a CEOs' paradise.
Some of us who have observed the current behaviour of
multinational conglomerates and of the glut of mam-
mons who control them think turning the planet over to
such greedsters is a very bad idea. William Butler Yeats
in his poem *The Second Coming* wrote: "And what
rough beast, its hour come round at last, slouches
towards Bethlehem to be born?" Well, I can just begin
to make him out, W.B. He's white, has a copy of the
Globe and Mail's "Report on Business" under one arm,
and is wearing a $3,000, dark-blue Armani suit. And
we're not. So we ought to worry. Everywhere in the
West is a yearning to downsize, a scurry to amalgamate,
an urge to merge provinces and territories, an obscene
frenzy to reduce the unit price of each human being.

Such low motives give rise from time to time
among the councils of Canuck Great Ones to calls for a
union of our Atlantic provinces. When this happens,
proponents go to the dusty word cupboard of Canadian
Confederation, open its rickety doors, and withdraw for
one more wheezing go-round that tired old term,
Atlantica. In 1995 and 1996 Atlantica squawked into
view once more, flapping its preposterous wings like
some gangly pterodactyl. Strident cries to blend Nova
Scotia, New Brunswick, Prince Edward Island, and perhaps Newfoundland too, come almost exclusively from
outside the Maritime provinces—from Ottawa, Toronto,

NOVA SCOTIA + NEW BRUNSWICK + PRINCE EDWARD ISLAND = ATLANTICA

Calgary, and Vancouver, where deficit-obsessed neo-conservatives foresee vast savings of subsidy money in such a union. A weakened Canada can't afford all these separate provinces is one of the siren-songs on the amalgamators' hit parade. No real proof of fiscal benefit is offered, and the banner with a strange device (Atlantica) is hoisted over the coastal ramparts so Bay Street may drool at the prospect.

On Monday, January 1, 1995 the *Globe and Mail* began that new year with a long editorial entitled "Welcome to Atlantica, Canada's ocean province." It was a blurb of prose soaked in Globespeak, a mishmash of school-marmish exposition and neocon flapdoodle quite common in its editorials. I considered putting comments on that editorial into another chapter of this book, "The Canadian Museum of Bafflegab and Gobbledygook," but decided it belonged here among provincial words and territorial phrases. I have no plan to dignify the Globe's cheerleading for the dissolution of four provinces by picking through each sentence. First, I don't have the heavy rubber gloves required to keep my hands clean. Second, only a few of the more distended Globules in the editorial need to be aspirated. The editorial is a summary of the supposed economic boons of union. But, sprinkled throughout—like fly shit in stale pepper, hence difficult to discern—are several bits of word trickery and logical sham worth attention.

The editorial trots out "a survey" saying Maritimers approve of union. That can be safely poll-axed and sent to the hell reserved for statisticians—I envisage an endless array of Cray computers, all on the fritz, with data being fed into them by bleary programmers who have to jolt one another with electric cattle prods as they nod off at their keyboards. The editorial continues: "That putative province—we'll call it Atlantica—would have a population of. . ." Clever, how the writer implies that he and/or the *Globe and Mail* invented the term Atlantica. The word is 131 years old, at least, appearing in pre-Confederation word lists for suggested new names for parts of what would become Canada. Atlantica appears sprinkled throughout

Hansard for the last 100 years. The *Globe and Mail* did not invent the term. How much of the rest of this editorial's "statistics" can we believe?

A few sentences later, biting its lip with a grimace of stern maturity, the editorial opines, "Of course, there are always historical and romantic reasons for remaining a province." Note the neocon delight in meanness. Sure, people want their place of birth to endure—for picayune, bourgeois notions like home, family, land, blood. "Atlantic union. . . a tough sell on emotional grounds" continues the snotty blather a few paragraphs later.

Among the reasons for jackhammering the foundation of our country, the *Globe and Mail* has the effrontery to list this one: "In some cases, companies have decided against locating in the Maritimes because they were put off by hostile relations between suitors [provinces competing for a new plant]." Imagine giant corporations being "put off." Awwww. Now there's a darn good reason to dissolve a province.

The *Globe and Mail* continues its cheesy sell-job by offering the European Union as an example of the advantages that would heap up after Maritime union. Have Globers checked any Reuters wires from that continent lately?

To sum up: the editorial writer takes a long walk on a short pier of fact. I suggest the scribbler of this hymn to disintegration continue to the end of the pier and go jump in his Atlantica.

PRINCE EDWARD ISLAND
FLYING AXEHANDLES

No one seems to know the origin of "the flying axehandles" as a vivid rural synonym for diarrhea. Field research has been understandably limited. However, exaggeration is part of folk metaphor, and the handle of a short axe is probably here being compared to a piece of feces. Compare "log-jam" as a comic synonym for constipation—but perhaps you would rather not.

In any case, the flying axehandles is an evocative phrase to put beside other Canadian and North American pioneer expressions like "the green-apple two-step, the blueberry runs, the skithers, the back door trots." Variants include "slippy axehandles, wild axehandles, throwing axehandles."

SCUT

The *Oxford English Dictionary* suggests this opprobrious epithet for dismissing a contemptible person—"You dirty scut! You mean old scut!"—is a dialect variant of "scout," itself in use as a term of contempt from 1380 to 1869. In Anglo-Irish a scut was a rabbit's tail or a nasty person. In his *Dictionary of Prince Edward Island English*, T. K. Pratt found it in limited use on the Island among older rural residents. But scut is a fine, spittable, corrosive monosyllable that should be revived and spread about to bolster the tired stock of insult words in Canadian English. "Scut work" for any low, disagreeable task is widespread across Canada.

SONSY

One of Lucy Maud Montgomery's cherished Islandisms describes a full-figured, healthy woman, a lady of proportion, the Edwardian ideal of womanhood, big and buxom. In *Anne of the Island* (1915) Montgomery writes of "Mrs. Lynde...sonsy, kindly, matronly, as of yore." Sonsy came over as a Scots Gaelic adjective and may be related to Erse *sonas* 'luck' so that the sense extension is 'lucky, thriving, healthy, robust.' Sonsy is a fine figure of a word.

A sonsy bride.

STOG YOUR FACE

It's a slangy way to say "go eat" on the Island. The British dialect verb *stog* meant 'to stuff.' It was brought to Newfoundland and Prince Edward Island by immigrants and used in the original sense there, as shown by a definition in Devine's *Folk Lore of Newfoundland*: "Stog—to chinse moss between the logs of a log house to keep out draughts." But *stog* developed extended meanings in our Maritimes, e.g.,"to stog (stuff) the Christmas turkey" and "to stog your gob (to stuff one's mouth full of food)." On P.E.I. one can also hear, "Stog the cattle with grain."

A TEDDY OF SHINE

In the dry times of Prohibition on the Island, bootleggers used long-necked green beer bottle empties to hold homebrew illegally sold to the public. A teddy of (moon)shine might cost a dollar in those days. T. K. Pratt says some of his linguistic informants claimed a teddy of shine was the bribe used in certain election shenanigans which from time to time besmirched the honesty and fair name of Island politics.

This noun names a product used in the P.E.I. potato business. A vent-view is a potato bag with plastic mesh covering a hole so that customers can see and palpate through the mesh the potatoes inside the bag.

VENT-VIEW

Something no lobster fisherman or any commercial fisherman wants to see in his nets, a whore's egg is a type of sea urchin, a sea-thistle, a spiny shellfish also called Aristotle's lantern. T. K. Pratt ingeniously suggests a derivation from French *oursin* 'sea urchin' combined with English sea egg. *Oursin* stems from Latin *ursinus* 'bear-like' possibly from the bristly nature of a sea urchin's spines which resembled stiff, matted hair in the fur of a bear cub (?).

WHORE'S EGG

Canadian history's most adaptable patriot is Bloc Québécois leader and Premier of Québec Lucien Bouchard. The glum monopode stumps through our nightly news and our nightly nightmares. No matter how one views Bouchard's plans for national fission, one notes with awe the man's dexterity as a political quick-change artist. He's trickier than a chameleon on a tartan. So those of us who do fret about the integrity of Canada observe any discomfiture of Bouchard with some equanimity. It was good to see him blustering and coughing when, just before the 1995 neverendum, the word "Nunavik" stuck in his throat.

Nunavik, a useful place name, gained country-wide prominence as the correct term for one-quarter of Québec, the northern Ungava peninsula and an area south of Ungava Bay, where 7,000 Inuit live, and where their ancestors lived and hunted long before whitemen came. In Inuktitut, Nunavik means 'our place,' and the

QUÉBEC & NUNAVIK

locative suffix -*vik* appears in other northern place names like the town of Inuvik 'place where Inuit live' and Aklavik 'grizzly-bear place.'

That area of northern Québec was part of the Northwest Territories at the time of Confederation, and did not fall under a provincial jurisdiction until the Boundary Extension Act was passed by Parliament in 1912. If the Inuit of Nunavik vote to stay in Canada after Québec decides to deconfederate, it will reduce by one-quarter the realm under the sway of Bouchard.

Nunavik should not be confused with its neighbour Nunavut that lies across Hudson Bay to the west. Nunavut was created by act of Parliament in 1993 as a new Canadian territory, slated to be fully operational by April, 1999, and made up of land in the mid-arctic that used to be part of the Northwest Territories. Nunavut will hold one-fifth of Canada's land. The word is Inuktitut for 'our land.'

ONTARIO

CARIBBEAN ENGLISH

MAS

Mas bands draw a million people to Toronto every summer during the Caribana festival, boosting the economy by hundreds of millions of dollars, and boosting summer spirits in the city with their inventive, polychromatic floats and lively dancing. Mas is a Caribbean short form of masquerade. In its widest sense, mas can refer to the carnival or festival itself, then to the procession or parade, and finally, in its most focused meaning, to one of the bands themselves. Toronto's Caribana is almost thirty years old and is solely responsible for introducing non-Caribbean Canadians to the joys of mas. A mas band is a group of people who work together to create intricate costumes, floats, and road dances. Some years at Caribana more than thirty-five separate mas groups take part in the parade.

Masquerade is a word borrowed into standard English from early French, which in turn picked it up from Italian *mascherata*, itself from an Italian word *maschera* which is the source of "mask" and "masque." *Mascherata* came into the early Sicilian dialect of Italian when Sicily was ruled by the Moors who spoke

Arabic. One Arabic word for buffoon is *máskharat*. Its Arabic verbal root is *maskara* 'to ridicule, mock' with interesting related words like the Arabic noun *mask* 'transformation, metamorphosis' and the Arabic adjective *mask* 'transformed into an animal.' The last adjective is also used as a noun in Arabic to mean 'freak, monster.' These meanings are all part of the origin of ancient traditional clowning.

Yes, professional buffoons in every culture dress up, imitate totemic animals, cavort, mock those in power, and often wear heavy comic makeup. When the Arabic word *máskharat* travelled farther north in Italy, it made a stop in Tuscany where it was used to name a colour "Tuscan red" which became a favourite hue for darkening the eyelashes. That resulted in our current word for eyelash cosmetic, mascara—not so far away from the antic spirit of Caribbean mas bands brightening a summer day in Toronto.

ONTARIO'S REAL McCOY

The real McCoy is the genuine article, and there are three origins that all contributed to the spread of the catchphrase. Closest to home and perhaps the earliest to be attested is Canadian and American railroaders' jargon where the real McCoy was the nickname for a railway car coupling invented by an African Canadian named Elijah McCoy who was born in Colchester South, Ontario.

But the phrase was alive in Scotland too, as "the real Mackay," a superior Scotch whisky made by the Mackay company. The phrase appears in print in Scotland by the 1870s and also in a slight variant as "the real McKie." Even in America, Mackay's whisky had brand clout, and was advertised widely as "the clear Mackay" which by prohibition times was whispered in American speakeasies as "the real Mackay"—an amber distillate far superior to the illegal, watery rotgut being peddled in most honky-tonk dives of the era.

Both those usages predate the origin that gave wide currency to the expression in the United States. A boxer named Norman Selby (1873–1940) took the ring name of Kid McCoy in 1891. He won the world welterweight championship in 1897 and two years later in a spectacular boxing match that went twenty rounds McCoy knocked out heavyweight Joe Choynski. A headline the next morning in the *San Francisco Examiner* written by their sportswriter William Naughton blared: "NOW YOU'VE SEEN THE REAL McCOY!" The catchphrase raced across American newspapers and stuck in public speech as a synonym for 'the goods, the authentic thing.'

McCoy himself did not last long on the canvas. In 1900 he saw stars the hard way when he was k.o.'d by Gentleman Jim Corbett. In *The Real McCoy*, a racy biography of the boxer, Robert Cantwell traced the man's sad decline. He tried running a saloon in New York City. It failed. He tried showbiz, appearing as a boxer in an early and classic silent film, *Broken Blossoms*, directed in 1919 by D. W. Griffith. He tried marriage—ten times. In 1924 he tried nine years in San Quentin for manslaughter. The judge disagreed, but most people attached to the case figured McCoy murdered his mistress. It seems ten wives did not completely occupy his free time. He committed suicide in 1940 and left a note which he ended with this signature: "Norman Selby." At the end, even the real McCoy was sick of his own moniker.

HAW EATERS OF MANITOULIN

Haw eaters are Canadians born and raised on Manitoulin Island. Their local word for themselves comes in three forms: run together as haweater, with a hyphen as haw-eater, and primly discrete as haw eater. They like hawberries, the dark-red fruit of a species of hawthorn common in northern Ontario. Haws can be lovingly ovened in pies, tarts, and strudels. Visitors to Manitoulin buy tasty haw jams too.

The word was brought to Canada by early immigrants from England and Scotland. One of the oldest berry names in English, haw pops up plump and ruddy in a glossary dated around A.D. 1000. Hawberry and hawthorn share an initial element which is cognate with Old High German *hag* 'enclosure.' The first meaning of haw in English was fence. Hawthorn bushes were early used to fence yards, hence hawthorn is fence-thorn. Our later word "hedge" is related to haw, and still hemming and hawing in some rural English dialects is church-hawe for churchyard.

By the fourteenth century, 'enclosed yard' and 'pen for domestic animals' were common meanings for the word. Geoffrey Chaucer (A.D. 1340–1400), the first great poet in English, used it that way, in "The Pardoner's Tale" from his *Canterbury Tales* written in Middle English: "Ther was a polcat in his hawe, That... hise capons hadde yslawe." There was a polecat in his yard that his castrated roosters had slain [by pecking it to death]. A polecat is a smelly European weasel. Charming vignette. Chaucer used the word in its fruity sense in *The Former Age*: "They eten mast hawes and swyche pownage." They ate acorns and chestnuts (mast), hawthorn berries, and such pannage (pig food).

A Dutch cousin of haw, Middle Dutch *hage* 'ground enclosed by a fence, park' gives both of the two names of the capital city of the Netherlands: *'s Gravenhage* 'The Count's Haw, or Park.' Modern English "The Hague" stems directly from the other name of the city in Dutch *Den Haag* 'the hedge.' Both names refer to woods that were a royal hunting grounds surrounding a medieval palace. Such pleasant ripples in the pond of words waft us back to Lake Huron and the largest freshwater island in the world.

DEBAJEHMUJIG, TELLER OF TALES

Manitoulin Island is home to two of the most imaginative storytellers in Canada, De-ba-jeh-mu-jig and Terry Griggs. Is narrative magic aloft in island air, spun of mystic wisps only haw eaters may gather? Seems so. The Ojibwa word *debajehmujig* 'storyteller' is used to name an inventive Ojibwe theatre group based in "Wiky." Some of the actors and craftspeople belong to the local Obidgewong band. Wiky is Manitoulin's affectionate short form for the Wikwemikong Unceded Reserve at the eastern end of the island. *Wikwemikong* means 'bay of the beaver.' Note the adjective "unceded" in the reserve's name. Thereby hangs a tale. In 1836 the stoutly named Sir Francis Bond Head, Lieutenant-

Governor of Upper Canada, put his signature to a treaty that ceded Manitoulin Island to the Ojibwe and Odawa peoples for their sole occupancy. But—surprise! surprise!—in 1862 the white government cancelled the treaty and allowed white settlers to homestead almost anywhere on the island. The aboriginal leaders of the Wikwemikong peninsula said no, and Wiky remained unceded.

In August of 1994 the De-ba-jeh-mu-jig Theatre Group staged a performance piece called *The Manitoulin Incident*, written by Alanis King-Odjig, local playwright and artistic director of the company. Acted smack-dab in the ruins of a Jesuit mission at Wiky where some of the white duplicity had actually taken place, the play was a night of marvels: giant thunderbirds on stilts, a woman impishly playing Sir Francis Bond Head, three languages—Ojibwa, English, French—ricocheting off the Jesuitical bricks, puppets, drums athrob in the dusk, masked dancers. See this astounding company if you can. They usually perform in conjunction with the Wikwemikong pow wow held on the first weekend in August and each production runs for a few weeks on Manitoulin before a fall and winter tour. Their hits have included a 1990 piece, *Toronto at Dreamer's Rock*, and one that wowed me, King-Odjig's 1993 *If Jesus Met Nanabush*. Nanabush is a shape-shifting half-mortal and trickster god of the Ojibwe. He smiles on this company, and so will you.

TERRY GRIGGS

If you are the kind of reader who memorized "Fern Hill" by the poet Dylan Thomas just for pleasure in his consonant thwack and vowel ease and ooze, if you return to the Circe or Nighttown episode in *Ulysses* to lap up James Joyce's gaudy vaudeville of word music, if you are bored to virtual autism by the bland cast of current English prose, if the soup-label monosyllables of journalese pop the top of your ennuiometer, then delight awaits in the work of Canada's most remarkable new writer. Her name is Terry Griggs. *Quickening* is the title of her first short story collection, published in 1990 by The Porcupine's Quill. *The Lusty Man* from the same publisher in 1995 is Grigg's first novel. Terry is a haw eater, born at Little Current on Manitoulin Island, and raised there until the age of sixteen at a tourist camp owned by her parents. Listen to her write of a rural gossip: "News came to him steadily like a wind trained to heel." Here a girl peruses an old roof: "I let my eyes take a spider-walk down cracks and minute paths getting lost for awhile in smaller erosions and the cunning creeping politics of rooftop weeds." In "Suddenly," one of the short stories from *Quickening*, Terry Griggs catapults me back to my Dunnville High, as she writes in the voice of a Manitoulin high-school girl hydroplaning down the slicked road of life:

> Even the long death of high school has its moments, and here was one: Biology, we're doing cows, if you can believe it. Some farm kid's brought one into class divvied up in about four or five green garbage bags. I think I'm going to be sick. I've got the lyrics of "Johnny Angel" running nonstop through my head like a purring engine to keep me from keeling over. Buck is sitting behind Trudy, as per usual, fanaticizing (you got it) about her swivelly hips, her ample tail piece smothering the lab stool that with luck could be his face, I know he's thinking. His hand darts out and sinks into pink angora. He hooks a finger around her bra at the back and pulls it out like a sling shot. Lets it go and snap! Funny? Everybody turns to smirk at Trudy and even Mr. Dandy, who floats at the front of the room like he's pickled in formaldehyde, seems to wake up.

The girl's hormonal gusto, the exuberance of the telling, the preservative image of the biology teacher— they're all pure Griggs, who, as her other stories prove, is a writer eager to detect magic in Manitoulin's peoples and woods and words. She pleasures the reader with words. She strokes dolphin-smooth nouns, pricks with spiky adjectives, revs up the body heat of verbs to make them hum. Want to go awording with her on the island? Read her books.

It means 'spirit island,' isle of God, Gitchi Manitou, the Great Spirit in the Sky. Ojibwe legend recounts the

MANITOULIN

creation of Manitoulin. The Great Spirit first dreamed the cosmos, made the elements, then the stars and the earth, and finally the friends, the children of earth, the Anishnabeg 'friends made of the void.' Now while the Great Spirit was forming earth, he kept aside certain choice morsels of his creation: the most shining water, the fields and woods most abounding in game and food, the most sun-dappled shores, the freshest breezes. He piled these up beside him to delight himself as he completed the rest of the earth. Then he fashioned a great island from his mound of treasured keepsakes and floated it upon Lake Huron where breezes blew it to snuggle against the north shore, the green island set off by the stark, rocky coast. With a thunderbolt and a lightning flash, he fixed the island in the lake forever, and called it Manitouminiss 'island of the Spirit.'

MANITOWANING

The best guide book to the island, *Exploring Manitoulin* by Shelley J. Pearen, is published in paperback by the University of Toronto Press. In it, Pearen gives this origin: "The Wikwemikong Peninsula is separated from the rest of the island by two bays, South Bay and Manitowaning Bay...Manitowaning received the Ojibwe name for 'den of the Great Spirit.' The bays are separated by a three-kilometre neck of land containing, according to native legend, a secret underwater passage which the Great Spirit uses to travel between the bays."

MUSKOKA'S GORBIES

A localism in the central Ontario tourist area of Muskoka is "gorby" used by some inhabitants of the area, mostly younger people, to describe loud tourists of the yahoo persuasion. "Oh-oh. Another busload of gorbies!" This does not imply that visitors, upon whom much of the Muskoka economy depends, are treated badly by locals. Muskokans are polite to a fault, in the view of this visitor. But it is pleasant to know they have a little phrase to dismiss the vulgar litterbugs and motorboating cretins who happen through the district now and then. The origin of gorby is, I believe, in the 1950s camping slang term G.O.R.P., an acronym that stood for Good Old Raisins and Peanuts, a trail mix suitable for canoe nibbling, easily packed, and not subject to immediate spoilage. However, when people who were practically born paddling a canoe across a small lake to a store see a tourist and canoeing neophyte set off on the same trip with thousands of dollars worth of yuppie camping equipment and three pounds of G.O.R.P.—to sustain them in their fifteen-minute canoe trip across the lake—then it seems natural that gorpy, later gorby, might arise as a mild put-down.

ONTARIO HYDRO

The Hydro-Electric Power Commission of Ontario began small in 1910 and grew to a once-efficient monopoly under the bullying promotion of power mogul Sir Adam Beck. His dream of getting cheap electric power from Niagara Falls also influenced Ontarian and then Canadian English. Although the adjective hydro-electric had been coined in Britain by 1832, Beck gave it wide currency in Canada at the turn of the twentieth century. As the giant utility grew, and delivered on its promise of safe, inexpensive electricity, Ontario customers shortened the name to "hydro" (in Canadian print by 1916) and introduced many combinations like hydro bill, hydro power, hydro man, hydro service, and hydro wires. If you ask an Englishman or an American, "Has your hydro ever been turned off ?" they may look puzzled. It's a completely Canadian usage which has spread as a name for other utility services to other provinces.

TORONTO STREET SLANG

Two scraps of street lingo heard in Toronto in the 1990s are new to me. One was a synonym for petty theft: "the five-finger discount" and the other was similar to "take shank's mare," the very old English phrase to describe walking somewhere as opposed to another means of transportation. "Goin' by subway?" asked one student. "No," came the reply, "I'll take the shoelace express."

MANITOBA
BUNGEE

Like Chinook Jargon on our Pacific coast, Bungee was a trading language or lingua franca used in the Red River area before Manitoba became a province of

Canada in 1870. Bungee was made up of words from English, Cree, and from the local Ojibwa dialect of the Saulteaux people, with words from Orkney Gaelic, Scottish English, and French tossed in as needed. The word "Bungee" comes from the Ojibwa *penki* 'small, little' and there are several explanations. One claims it arose simply because Bungay, Bungee, Bungie, and Bungy were slang terms for the Saulteaux who did use the lingo in dealings with local Whites. Another reason might be that it was *penki* 'small' talk because the grammar was simplified and the vocabulary was minimal. Like all trading languages and pidgins in the world, the number of words was "small."

Bungee arose in Métis families where the mother was often Cree or Saulteaux and the father was Scottish or English. In "The Red River Dialect" from *The Beaver*, the magazine of the Hudson Bay Company, S. O. Scott and D. A. Mulligan give examples of Bungee:
• By me I kaykatch killed two ducks with one sot ('shot'). Cree *kaikach* 'nearly.'
• He fell off the rock chimmuck in lake. Cree *chimmuk* 'head over heels.'
• keeyam = never mind, don't bother. (Cree)
• neechimos = sweetheart, honey. (Ojibwa *neeshee* 'friend')
• slock the candle = snuff out the candle. (Slock is a Scottish dialect verb.)

Bungee has vanished from our Prairie soundscape, but trace phrases and stray words are heard now and then.

COTEAU

This continental French noun meaning 'small hill, slope of a low hill' came early to Québec, and is still there in place names like Coteau-du-Lac and Coteau-Landing. Voyageurs and trappers spread it across our west where coteau is still used today in Canadian English and Canadian French to describe high prairie. A coteau is a plateau or a series of low ridges. In 1843 in his *Narrative of the Discoveries of the North Coast of America*, Thomas Simpson described a "route...through a more open country, consisting of rising grounds, or 'côteaus,' [sic; there is no circumflex on the *o* of coteau] with bare ridges, and sides clothed with dwarf poplar and brushwood." The word came into medieval French from Late Latin *costellum* 'little side, hillock, slope of a hill,' itself a diminutive of the Latin word *costa* 'rib, side, sea-coast.'

This term for dried buffalo dung used as a fuel began as a loan translation from the Canadian French of early voyageurs and fur trappers where it appeared—at first humorously—as *bois de vache* 'cow wood' and also in the slightly more refined phrase *bois des prairies* 'prairie wood.' Buffalo chips were called bodewash too, which is a direct Englishing of *bois de vache* that shows up in the Manitoba folk saying "squished flatter 'n a bodewash chip." Anyone who could find the chips of buffalo dung strewn about the prairie used them since there was little wood available. The dried dung of cattle burns with a very heavy odour. Buffalo chips are relatively odourless and in plentiful supply, a fuel just lying there in the early "buffalo days" of prairie settlement before the vast herds were slaughtered.

COW CHIPS

Two thousand years ago Greek map makers thought of drawing imaginary lines on the earth to help locate places for travellers and sailors. This grid of lines is now made up of meridians of longitude and parallels of latitude. A meridian of longitude is half of an imaginary circle around the earth drawn from north to south, passing through both poles. On our Prairies, early surveyors who were laying out townships and parcels of land for settlement selected a meridian line a few miles west of Winnipeg from which to begin and called it the First Meridian. Townships in Manitoba were numbered to a second initial meridian east just east of Lake of the Woods, and to a second initial meridian west just west of the Saskatchewan-Manitoba border. The term, highly suitable for our Prairie surveys, is a little confusing since geographers also call a line of longitude that passes through Greenwich, England, the prime (or zero)

FIRST MERIDIAN

meridian. This was selected in 1884 as the meridian from which to start measuring how far east or west a location was.

HERE'S A HO!

When all glasses are charged with bubbly or suds, this drinking toast can still be offered in Winnipeg and other places in Manitoba, and some among those tippling will remember the origin. "Ho!" was the word used to begin the attack in great community buffalo hunts of yore. In those early days (pre-yore or post-yore), a buffalo's horn was commonly used for certain ceremonial toasts and that may have influenced the choice of "Ho!" Sodbusters and stubble-jumpers would toast that way to make sure no one mistook them for a bunch of high-falutin' *cigarette dudes* (old Prairie slang for a 'city slicker').

NUISANCE GROUNDS

From the Alberta-British Columbia boundary right across the Prairies to northern Ontario one can still hear this euphemism for garbage dump. In print since 1889, it popped up in the *Edmonton Journal* in 1958: "In Banff, the best place to see bears is the 'nuisance grounds'—the preferred title [for the] garbage dump." In the short story "Where the Wind Began" from her collection *Heart of a Stranger* (1976), Margaret Laurence wrote: "The town dump was known as 'the nuisance grounds,' a phrase fraught with weird connotations, as though the effluvia of our lives was beneath contempt but at the same time was subtly threatening to the determined and sometimes hysterical propriety of our ways." Margaret Laurence here pinpoints one of the chief sources of euphemism in her insightful phrase "hysterical propriety."

SASKATCHEWAN BUTTE

Frenchman Butte, Butte St. Pierre, Belbutte, and Central Butte are all in Saskatchewan. But this word for a hill with a flat top is in general use in all three of our Prairie provinces. Although the geological formations are particularly common in southern Alberta at places like Picture Butte, buttes abound elsewhere, for example, on the outskirts of Paradise Hill in northern Saskatchewan near the Alberta border, one of which is Frenchman Butte. In the Nahani country of northern British Columbia and the Northwest Territories, a butte is a low, rounded mountain. Pronounced to rhyme with cute, butte often is the northern equivalent of the Spanish-American topographical noun *mesa* 'tableland of a flat-topped hill or mountain.' Butte came into Canadian English from early trappers' French.

GRID ROADS

You know you're in Saskatchewan when you hear this term describing the best system of municipal roads in Canada. Incidentally, Saskatchewan has the longest road system in Canada: more than 200,000 kilometres! The grid roads were laid out 1 mile apart east to west and 2 miles apart north to south, with a *correction line*, a little hop every 24 miles in the north to south line to compensate for the difference between the line as surveyed and the true meridian of longitude.

MEDICARE

Saskatchewan officials coined the now endangered word "Medicare" and introduced the world's first universal prepaid medical care in 1962, but only after a bitter strike by Saskatchewan doctors. Medicare is one Saskatchewan word that has been borrowed into American usage. In the United States, medicare usually refers to government-sponsored health care for elderly citizens. Saskatchewan's CCF government under Tommy Douglas had introduced free hospital care in 1947. Douglas was Premier of the province longer than any other politician (1944–1961), and the nastiness surrounding the introduction of Medicare was one of the factors that cost him the 1961 election.

MINA: CREE FOR 'BERRY'

Here's a Cree root that appears in three well-known Prairie place names, two in Saskatchewan. Saskatoon was named by early settlers because the original site had many saskatoon berry trees. The Cree word for these tasty purple berries is *mi-sakwato-min* 'tree-of-many-branches berries.' The name of the town of Moosomin in southeastern Saskatchewan is from the

Cree term *mongsoa minan* 'mooseberries' or 'high bush cranberries' which abounded in the area. In our western provinces, mooseberry can also be applied to low bush cranberries. Another Cree phrase for high bush cranberries *nipi-minan*—literally 'summer berries'—was heard by early French explorers as *pembina* and was much used as a place, river, and commercial name. The Pembina River is still an important waterway in southern Manitoba near the Pembina Mountains, and Pembina was one of the settlements founded by Lord Selkirk that did not endure. Alberta has a long and important Pembina River as well. Still heard in the west is pembina berries for high bush cranberries.

PRAIRIE

To a visiting botanist, prairie is a vastness of grasses, and of xerophytes, plants adapted to intermittent drought. To a homesteading newcomer in 1876, prairie might have meant "the first land anyone in my family ever owned." Later such a drylander might decide to sow a domesticated grass called wheat. To a writer like W. O. Mitchell, born at Weyburn, Saskatchewan, prairie might resound in his heart like the great chord of words that opens his novel *Who Has Seen the Wind*: "Here was the least common denominator of nature, the skeleton requirements simply, of land and sky— Saskatchewan prairie. It lay wide around the town, stretching tan to the far line of the sky, clumped with low buck brush and wild rose bushes, shimmering under the late June sun and waiting for the unfailing visitation of wind, gentle at first, barely stroking the long grasses and giving them life..."

Who first applied the word "prairie" to the rolling grasslands in the middle of North America? Canoe-stiff French adventurers dubbed it, early in the eighteenth century. Rough explorers they were, China-hungry, gold-thirsty, fur-crazy, paddling the continental interior by unknown lakes and rivers. They had no exact French word to label the grassy plains whose immensity and reach had startled their sense of geographic proportion, based as it was on the populated density of their native Europe. But there was a French word for grazing land, sometimes used to describe dry scrub in the south of France. *Prairie* 'grassland' had entered Old French by A.D. 1180. Its first meaning in French was 'pasturage,' any field with plants that were suitable fodder for domestic animals.

La prairie may have arrived directly from a Late Latin phrase like *terra prataria* 'meadow-land.' Compare such borrowing in other Romance languages where Italian has *prateria* and Spanish *pradera.* The classical Latin root was *pratum* 'meadow.' But *pratum* had come into French earlier as *pré* 'meadow' and so French prairie may simply be an extension of *pré* formed by adding to it *-erie* to produce *préerie* which is actually one of the early spelling variants. *-Erie* was a noun suffix, giving *préerie* the sense of 'a considerable area of meadow-like land suitable for pasturing cattle and sheep.'

A few hundred years later, when French surnames began reaching some of their final forms, a person whose house was beside a *pré* might have become known as Jacques Dupré, giving one of the commoner modern French surnames with continental French regional variations like Duprey, Duprat (note retention of the original Latin *t*), and Dupraz. Once the name reached the New World, we see American variants like the original Louisiana spellings Dupree and Dupry. Famous bearers of the name include French organist and composer Marcel Dupré and the American cellist Jacqueline Dupré. These surnames are semantic equivalents of English ones like Meadow and Meadows.

Canadian French produced a diminutive of prairie, *prairillon* 'a small tract of grassland,' which enjoyed a brief vogue in Canadian English, sometimes spelled prairion.

In France, Bastille-stormers took up *prairie* too. French Revolutionists wanted everything ancient and stinking of noblesse to be dumped, including the old calendar. They made up a clumsy new one that lasted a short time. The ninth month of the Revolutionary calendar, which fell between May 20 and June 18, was called *Prairial* 'meadow-month.' In the third year of the

Republic June 8, 1795 appeared as 20 *prairial, an III*. Oh, it was a really *new* month name—if you consider one thousand years old to be new. *Prairial* in fact was a Republican scholar's sneaky translation of one of the earliest month names in proto-Germanic languages. Even among the Anglo-Saxons one name for what became the month of July was *meadmonath* 'meadow-month,' the time when northern meadows throve. How very revolutionary.

Back home, where the buffalo roamed, later Canuck sodbusters were coining a variety of phrases:

- Bald-headed prairie   rolling plains with no trees
- Prairie itch   a dermatitis produced by contact with nasty micro-organisms called fresh-water polyps of the genus *Hydra* found in prairie potholes, ponds, and ditches.
- Prairie oyster   best cure in the West for a hangover: open a fresh egg, sprinkle with pepper, drop it into a double shot of rye, drink at once while invoking any hovering deity. Bacchus may deign to quell the throb.

• Prairie wool   wild fodder for sheep
                                 consisting of graminaceous
                                 goodies like spear-grass,
                                 bunch-grass, and buffalo-grass

Prairie popped up in England in the local slang of late Victorian and Edwardian London in the phrase "a bit of prairie: which, until 1914, was in common use to describe a bare stretch of roadway during any short lull in carriage and automotive traffic in the Strand. J. Redding Ware in his 1919 *Passing English* quotes a London cabby saying, "Bit o' prairie—go!"

This little gopher-scurry over our Prairies concludes with a question. If you dwell in the south of Alberta, Saskatchewan, or Manitoba, do you ever tire, when asked where you're from, of answering "I live on the Prairies"? Just for fun sometime, raise a listener's eyebrow by responding, "I am pratincolous." Your listener will probably snort and say, "Seen a doctor about that yet?" But stick to pratincolous, with stress on the second syllable and a hard *c*. It's such a delightfully obscure word. Pratincole was coined by an ornithologist in 1773 and is still the correct name of an Old World swallow-like bird of the plover family, with related species also found in Australia. But it was made up of Latin *pratum* 'meadow, prairie' + *incola* 'inhabitant.' So it can perfectly well be transferred to humans who live on a prairie. With a wee bit of jiggery-pokery a verb is possible too. Yes, my forefathers came to Canada and pratincolated near Saskatoon. On second thought, maybe not.

Athabasca was originally applied to the large, reed-ringed lake that straddles the northern Alberta-Saskatchewan border. 'Reed beds' in Cree are *athapaskaw.* The Athabasca boat, in print by 1824, was a speedy canoe useful to early fur traders in the area. There was also a clumsy wooden barge in use on the river of that name called an Athabaska scow. Once its cargo was unloaded, the crude planks making up the scow were dismantled and put to shore use. The Cree

ALBERTA
ATHABASKA

word also appears in the zoological name of Canada's largest land animal, the wood bison of Wood Buffalo National Park in northern Alberta and the N.W.T. Big male wood buffaloes can weigh 900 kilograms. The park is Canada's biggest, more than 44,000 square kilometres, and contains the largest herd of bison in the world. The scientific moniker of the nobel beast is *Bison bison athabascae*, which is no sillier a name than Henry Wadsworth Longfellow.

BLUFF

Bluff came to North America as a nautical adjective that meant 'broad-faced.' British navigators first applied the descriptive in such phrases as "bluff-headed ship, bluff cliffs, a bluff headland" and then in North America bluff was used as a noun to mean the cliff or headland itself. Nautical metaphors were in common use among early explorers of our plains. Consider a frequent synonym for prairie 'the sea of grass' and 'prairie schooner' for a pioneer wagon used by homesteaders.

Entirely Canadian in origin is the Albertan and Prairie use of bluff to designate a stand of trees, a little grove of trees alone on the generally treeless prairie. In our West, a bluff can be the high, wooded bank of a river, giving place names like Oak Bluff in Manitoba and Poplar Bluff in Saskatchewan. Canuck too is the infrequent adjectival form found in phrases like 'rolling, bluffy prairie.' This Canadian sense of bluff has been heard in some northern American states like North Dakota, Montana, and Wisconsin. And *le bluff* has entered the Canadian French spoken in some of our Prairie provinces.

COULEE

French *coulée* gave us a word for the deep, dry bed of a stream or river, the bed having sloping sides unlike a canyon's steeper, perpendicular sides. Coulee has a southwestern American synonym in gulch or dry gulch. British trappers called them dry sloughs, but the French-Canadian voyageurs' term stuck. *Coulée* 'the running, flowing of a liquid' entered continental French from Latin *colare* 'to run liquid through a strainer.' Alberta has a community called East Coulee, and an interesting doublet occurs in southern Alberta's Etzikom Coulee, where *etzikom* is the Siksika (Blackfoot) word for coulee.

Tar sands is an Alberta coinage known by every Canadian. The vast Athabasca tar sands appear in print by 1897 as "tar sand-beds." The tar sands lie under more than 31,000 square kilometres of the north and contain a cache of recoverable synthetic crude oil estimated at more than four billion cubic metres. A Canadian chemist named Karl Clark pioneered the hot-water process for recovering oil from tar sands that was used successfully in 1967 at Fort McMurray by Suncor Ltd. and later by Syncrude.

These extensive deposits of oil sand containing bitumen are quite close to the surface around Fort McMurray and the extraction plants there on the banks of Alberta's Athabasca River helped turn the little village that began as a post of the North West Company (a syndicate of fur trading firms absorbed into the Hudson's Bay Company in 1821) into an important economic centre. By the late 1960s, Fort McMurray had become "a company town" which is a phrase totally Canadian in origin, describing a settlement built and controlled by a business to house its employees. It is likely that company town originated as a description of the outlying buildings around early Hudson's Bay Company posts. But the word has not always been music to the ears of Canadian workers' unions. Some company towns live in infamy, like Murdochville in Québec. Even certain residents of Fort McMurray were not entirely enamoured with life under company rule. During the slump in world oil prices in 1987, bitter strikes and lockouts produced unrest there. But as the only game in town, the oil industry managed, even in a year beset with labour strife, to increase levels of production. Some in Fort McMurray claim there can be too heavy and too wide a hand laid upon the lives of employees when one or two corporations have the final say about almost everything that happens in one locality. But Fort McMurray is now a thriving city of more

FORT McMURRAY & TAR SANDS

than 35,000 inhabitants, and the diversity of aims its citizens have brought to this northern Alberta outpost, have made company town less applicable a label.

HOODOO

Hoodoos

Who grew that hoodoo that you knew came from voodoo? Every kid who ever traipsed the badlands of Alberta near Drumheller and saw hoodoos has played comic variations on silly hoodoo sentences. Hoodoos are oddly shaped pedestals of earth or pillars of rock that develop through erosion by wind and water, especially in areas where the sedimentary layers alternate between soft and hard material, for example in horizontal strata of shale and sandstone. You can see them in Alberta's Dinosaur Provincial Park, down in the border country near Alberta's Milk River, on the banks of the Columbia River north of Cranbrook and in the Okanagan Valley in British Columbia. I saw small hoodoos on a raft trip I once took down the Kootenay River. And there are plenty in Hoodoo Valley near Leanchoil on the edge of Yoho National Park in B.C. French-Canadian voyageurs called them *demoiselles* 'young ladies.'

Hoodoo is general across the west of North America, and is not of Canadian origin. *The Dictionary of Canadianisms* (1967) states that hoodoo is "of African origin, related to voodoo." No, it is not related as a word to voodoo. In the eighteenth and nineteenth centuries, black slaves of Hausa origin brought with them to their enslavement in the American south a distinct magic practice called "hoodoo." The word comes directly from the Hausa language where the verb *hu'du'ba* means 'to arouse resentment, produce retribution.' Note that the word *voodoo* comes from another African language called Ewe where *vodu* refers directly to a specific demon or tutelary deity. Voodoo passed into American English by way of Louisiana Creole *voudou.* Very early in America, hoodoo came to mean 'jinx' or 'cast a spell on' as a noun and a verb: "Something hoodooed me out in the swamp last night. I think it was my ex-husband."

American aboriginal peoples of the northwest

picked up the word from English-speaking fur trappers and, like them, used hoodoo to refer to any malignant creature or evil supernatural force. That's how it came to be applied to the curious columns of earth or rock. For they were thought to be evil in the mythologies of many first peoples. For example, in Siksika (Blackfoot) mythology, the strange shapes were giants whom the Great Spirit had turned to stone because of their evil deeds. Deep in the night, the petrified giants could awaken and throw boulders down upon any humans passing nearby.

Alberta had several local words for money, now chiefly historical. The visitor can still hear "shinnias," derived from the Cree *shoneya* 'money' and also hear *meakskim* from the Siksika (Blackfoot) language. Other Albertan terms for cash are "the velvet" and "otter-skins."

SLANG FOR MONEY

From the "sawdust nobility" of lumber barons to the humble "whistlepunk" who relayed signals from workers with axes, to those running donkey engines used to pull cut timber, B.C. loggers' lingo has a long provincial history, a stock of jargon that has words now obsolete, together with words fresh as the aroma of a Sitka spruce bough. The west coast forest industry depends on Canada's tallest and broadest conifers, the chief commercial trees being Douglas fir, western cedar, balsam fir, hemlock, and Sitka spruce, whose coastal stands thrive in the mild, wet climate and make up 40 percent of Canada's commercial lumber potential. Charles B. Crate, one of the editors of the *Dictionary of Canadianisms* (1967), has done much pioneering study of British Columbian localisms, including those from logging.

BRITISH COLUMBIA
LOGGING JARGON

Scotsmen brought the verb "birl" to Canadian lumbering. In Scots dialect, to birl is to spin something, like a coin on a table, so that it makes a noise. Birl, especially with a thick burr of the *r*, originates as an imitation of

BIRLING

the whirring sound made by a spinning object. It was a natural verb to apply in Canadian logging to the practice of spinning a floating log while remaining balanced atop the log. Logs are spun to propel them out of shallow water, off snags and sandbars where they have become stuck, and to make it easier to change their direction. Birlers were competitive. Competition at a local camp soon led to district log-rolling contests where the deftest act of birling could win big bucks.

CRUMMY

Crummy meaning 'lousy, of poor quality' derives from an extension in mid-nineteenth-century American English of *crumb* 'body louse.' In B.C. logging areas, from the late 1930s, a crummy was an old box car or caboose in which loggers were transported from towns to the current cutting site at the logging camp. A bit later, beat-up buses and trucks that hauled forest labourers were crummies. Now in British Columbia crummy can mean a school bus, or any vehicle that carries workers to and from distant work sites. This usage has spread down into the state of Washington too.

DAVIS RAFT

The Davis raft met special conditions of west coast logging. Sometimes booms had to be towed by tugboat to saw-mills across rough ocean. Even if the tow was short, rafts sturdier than those used in eastern lumbering were needed, and one was invented in 1913 by a Mr. Davis of Port Renfrew, B.C. The Davis raft consisted of layers of logs "choked" into bundles by withes and chains. In Old English a withe was a tie made of several slender willow shoots twisted together. The Davis raft was almost 500 feet long, 30 feet deep, 16 feet above sea level, and held an astounding 3,600,000 board feet of timber.

HIGH-LINE LOGGING

The size and height of B.C. trees like the Douglas fir made necessary new logging techniques. Skyline or high-lead logging involves the use of a spar tree. A standing tree is topped and trimmed and given extra support from guy cables anchored to the ground. It is then rigged with a series of high cable-lines and pulley-blocks by which the logs cut afterward are hauled from the cutting area to the yard. In very large operations there are now mobile spar trees that are gigantic Diesel-engined cranes that do all the complicated skylining. The lively world of B.C. logging terminology can be further examined in some of the specialized journal articles and books devoted to this corner of verbal Canadiana.

JAW BONE

Unemployed loggers sometimes had to "live on the jaw" or "call my jaw." Jaw was short for jawbone, a word widespread in the Canadian west, a synonym for credit obtained at a store. Its first appearance in print is 1865 in the pages of the *Cariboo Sentinel*, the feisty newspaper of Barkerville, near the Willow River east of Quesnel, B.C. Barkerville was the terminus of the Cariboo Gold Trail which began in 1862 with William Barker's rich strike. The slang term arose because one had to use his jawbone in trying to talk a line of credit out of a merchant. Matthew Macfie visited the interior from England during the Fraser River Gold Rush and wrote this in *Vancouver Island and British Columbia* published in 1865: "Credit is 'jaw-bone'; and in one store on the road to Cariboo, the full-sized jaw-bone of a horse is polished and suspended on the wall, with the words written under: 'None of this allowed here.' "

THE NORTH
BOIL-UP

A boil-up is a stop on the trail to brew some tea and take a brief rest. It's used as a verb too: "We'll boil up at the next ridge." Boiling places and boil-up places that are used frequently are sometimes marked as such on company or individual maps. Similar terms in the Canadian north are mug-up and smoke-up. Drink-up is saved for the return to town. Another early (1806) term for a rest-break was a 'pipe.' In the days of the fur trade and later, from voyageurs' French *une pipe*, English picked up 'pipe' as a measure of distance. A pipe to explorers like Simon Fraser was the distance rowed or traversed between rest breaks. During such breaks but not en route, men would smoke a pipeful of tobacco.

BRUCK

This word is a blend of bus and truck to name a northern bus with passenger seats in the front and an expanded baggage and freight area in the rear. Its first appearance in print was in 1961 in the *Edmonton Journal*, but was it a nonce coinage, or is bruck still heard in the north?

CATSKINNER

Drivers of giant caterpillar tractors used in northern construction projects particularly for clearing trail invented this Canadian term in the early 1930s. It was formed by analogy from mule-skinner, a phrase of brutal origin that meant in its first instance a mule-driver who used the whip so frequently that it might flay the poor beast of burden. Catskinner is also used in abbreviated form in the north, as 'skinner.'

CHEECHAKO

Prospectors heading north to the Klondike gold rush of 1898 brought this Pacific coast word for 'greenhorn' or 'newcomer' with them. Cheechako is Chinook Jargon, *chee* 'new' + *chako* 'come.' Another definition of a cheechako was a prospector who had never seen the ice go out in the spring. Such tenderfoots were different than old gold-rush hands who called themselves sourdoughs, even if they had only been in the Yukon gold fields for a few months, even if they had not yet staked one claim. Sour dough was dough fermented with yeast; a portion of this leavened dough was saved to start the next batch of bread. Both terms were widely introduced into Canadian and American English by the popularity of Robert W. Service's books of frontier poetry, especially *Songs of a Sourdough* (1907) and *Ballads of a Cheechako* (1909).

LA FOULE

The French word for 'crowd' was used by French-Canadian trappers to refer to the great autumn migration of caribou from the Arctic Ocean south for food and shelter in the pinelands. And *la foule* is used in northern Canadian English to describe this massing of caribou.

A white-out is an arctic meteorological condition during which diffused light from a cloudy sky is equal to that being reflected at the same time off ground snow. The resulting whiteness dazzles the eye and obscures landscape features, even the horizon. White-out also refers generally to the height of a blizzard in which thick snow cuts visibility severely.

WHITE-OUT

This humorous bit of slang for the derrière of a cooked bird, usually a chicken or turkey, has variants like the parson's nose and the pope's nose. None of these comic metaphors is Canadian in origin, but all are used here. Sometimes such terms are offensive. I would like to offer a Canadian compromise, a term that lessens any possible offence and yet maintains a little humour. Just use the technical word in ornithology for the fleshy protuberance on a bird's butt that supports the tail feathers. The parson's nose is the uropygium, from Greek *ouropygion* literally 'tail-rump-let, little tail-rump.' A uropygial gland opens dorsally at the base of the tail feathers on the uropygium and secretes an oil used by the bird in preening its feathers. The bird transfers oil from this gland to its bill and then coats and waterproofs each feather as needed. "A slice of white meat, dear? A drumstick? How about the uropygium?" The pope's nose has a *locus classicus* in modern literature, and mentioning it will raise the tone of any discussion about the phrase. Use of the expression begins a family agrument in the first scene of James Joyce's seminal novel *Portrait of the Artist as a Young Man*.

CANADA-WIDE PHRASES
DEACON'S NOSE

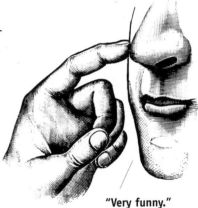

"Very funny."

This pure Canadianism began in political backrooms where one party agreed not to run a candidate in a certain riding, if the second and opposing party agreed not to run their candidate in a riding where the first party was certain of victory. Saw-off now has broadened its scope to mean any mutual concession or trade-off. In *Our Own Voice: Canadian English and How It Is Studied*, R. E. McConnell shows how it can even refer to a draw in a hockey game, by quoting a *Vancouver Sun* headline: "Canucks Manage Saw-off."

SAW-OFF

SHIT-DISTURBER

Should we be proud that Canada has contributed to English a common synonym for trouble-maker, "shit-disturber"? Eric Partridge in his 1961 *Dictionary of Slang and Unconventional English* marks the phrase "Canadian" and says it's a variation of the earlier British "shit-stirrer."

SHITE-POKE

Also Canuck is "shite-poke" as a Canadian term since roughly 1880 for that reclusive bird of reeds and bull-rush beds, the bittern. In southern Ontario I've heard a heron referred to as a shite-poke, and in certain rural communities it is a synonym for shit-disturber, often one of the political persuasion. Eric Partridge explains why certain birds of the heron family are called shite-pokes by quoting an ornithologist who says they were so named because they habitually defecate when taking flight after being frightened.

CHAPTER NINE

TRADEMARK CANADIAN WORDS! EARN BIG BUCKS!

Don't shrug. Just tug. Introducing the Jack Pine Posture-Maker!

Stoopers, don't be stupid. **Slouchers, shoulder-shruggers**, get pert military bearing!. Enjoy anatomical perfection! Attain the posture-perfect stance of steroid-drenched Hollywood behemoths! Just tug gently on our safety-tested series of pulleys and winches. Invented in Canada by Honest Sid Procrustides at the back of a used car lot in east Toronto.

CAUTION: Use only as directed by our small print. May break your neck or crack your spine.

Should we Canucks get all moist in the armpits about the continuing sellout of our Canadian heritage, even some of our words, to foreign moguls? After all, the word "Canada" is safe, eh? Think so? Did you know that at EXPO 86 in Vancouver, British Columbia, during the preparation of our national pavilion on Canadian soil the federal government of Canada was not allowed to use the maple leaf logo and the name Canada until it had humbly applied for permission from the Ace Novelty Company of Seattle, Washington? The good folks at Ace Novelty had been granted exclusive use of the name Canada and the maple leaf logo at the exposition. Now there's word-watching with a vengeance. Interesting, how in specific venues a country might not own the rights to its own name! O Canada, indeed.

The following section is NOT a home guide to registering a trademark. The relevant law is complex (I present here only a summary) and registration should be handled by a lawyer who knows trademark law or by one of many registered trademark agents who must train and

HOW TO TRADEMARK

pass an exam and who are listed in the federal Trade Mark Rules. But let's say that you or your lawyer or one of the professional name-search businesses like Idealogic Searchhouse or ABC Namebank International, both of Toronto, have invented a name and already run your putative trademark through NUANS, a computer database of trademarks, business, and corporate names. NUANS is an acronym for New Updated Automatic Name Search. A name-search company may charge you from $1,500 to $20,000 or more to invent a new brand-name or trademark.

A common legal principle operates when registering a trademark. It might be called discovery by elimination. The law states which kinds of trademarks cannot be registered. If your trademark escapes these restrictions, it is registrable. In general, you can register a trademark (for a fee) if you have used it in Canada, or intend to use it in Canada within six months of your application, and if you have made it known in Canada.

To register that trademark, one applies to the Canadian Intellectual Property Office at Place du Portage in Hull, Québec, where some 450 federal

The trademark for this nineteenth-century patent medicine has lapsed.

bureaucrats do the paper waltz and the microchip two-step each working day. If the name isn't taken, isn't obscene, doesn't sound similar to existing trademarks or in any way infringe upon them, and the initial examination of the application is okayed during discovery by elimination, which *may* take years, then the name to be trademarked must be published in the *Canadian Trademarks Journal* (CTJ) put out by the Canadian Intellectual Property office. Here myriad, beady eagle-eyes will peruse it, seeking reasons to oppose your application—although the registrar has performed his official discovery by elimination. They have two months after the date of publication to draft an objection. The fee to file such an objection with the registrar of trademarks will set you back about $250.

But the fees are a pittance if you feel a new trademark infringes on one you have registered. In 1988 Sunlife Fresh Juice Ltd. was ordered by the Supreme Court of Ontario to change its name when the Sun Life Assurance Co. of Canada assured the court that apple juice would be confused with insurance policies by Ontarians (we're not that bright, apparently). Anyhow, the Supreme Court agreed with the insurance company's objection and—abracadabra—the juice company found a new name.

ORIGIN OF BRAND NAME

Brand-new is old. The compound adjective appeared in print more than four hundred years ago. At first, brand-new described newly struck swords hot from the armourer's forge. Shakespeare had used "fire-new." Old English *brand* 'act of burning something' is cognate with German *Brand* and Dutch *brand*. The same root, modified, appears in "burn." Like most words that endure over many centuries in a language, brand added new meanings. It came to mean 'a burning log or stick,' the "flaming brands" of old adventure stories. From brand-new, it acquired the meaning 'sword.' Thus Tennyson wrote "the brand, Excalibur" when he named King Arthur's magic sword. By A.D. 1400 the verb "brand" meant to burn with a hot iron for identification.

The first things branded in English were human beings. Convicted criminals, even harmless wanderers, had their flesh seared with the branding iron. In the Tudor period of English history, vagabonds had the letter *V* burnt into the skin of their chests. "Fray-makers in church" received an *F*, the hard way. A British law in the reign of King William III ordered thieves to be branded on the left cheek. In *Uncle Tom's Cabin*, Harriet Beecher Stowe reminded Americans of how they treated African slaves when one black character had "been branded in his right hand with the letter H." Branding of criminals was not abolished in England until 1829. In the British army, as late as 1879, cads and bounders who had the bad form to desert were branded with a big *D* just under the left nipple. The army's "bad characters," in a further show of Victorian solicitude, had the initials *BC* burnt into their bodies. Branding horses is at least as old as the Dorian invasions of ancient Greece, and probably much older, perhaps reaching back to humans' first herding of wild horses. Branding domestic animals began with agriculture. Sheep were early branded with hot pitch. The first use of brand in print is 1827 as "brand mark" to mean trademark, when such proofs of ownership were burnt into wooden casks of wine and liquor, then into timber, metal, and finally printed on paper products and labels.

Pioneer hero with flaming brand descends rapids in a burning canoe to rescue onlookers who, however, seem a tad non-chalant.

ALBERTA UNBOUND

In 1994, booze maker Alberta Distillers Ltd., owned by Jim Beam Distillers in the United States, applied to restrict use of the word "Alberta" to its products which included the popular brand, Alberta Vodka. A Calgary trademark agent objected. In a public letter, Victor Arcuri of Arvic Search Services Inc. stated: "Alberta Distillers claims that the word Alberta has become so well known in relation to their alcoholic beverages that the average Canadian consumer has come to think of the word Alberta in association with their...beverages rather than in association with any other product or service." The Canadian Intellectual Property Office usually rejects a trademark that includes a geographic location unless long and distinctive association with a particular product is proven. I wasn't aware that Jim Beam owned or had any right whatsoever to the name of a province of Canada. I personally never think of Jim Beam when daydreaming of Alberta and, say, the surge of spring fever that an invigorating chinook can summon. Much kickier, by the way, than a slug of vodka.

MINDING THE "NET"

In 1992, Bell Canada through its subsidiary Worldlinx Telecommunications Inc. made application to trademark the words "The Net," a common synonym for the Internet. In August of 1995, their application was published in the *Canadian Trademarks Journal* seeking exclusive Canadian rights to use the words "The Net." Hell hath no fury like Internet cyberspace threatened with commercialization. Some of the tens of millions of international computer users who employ the short form every day, told Bell in strident terms to ring off. The Net is a package of software and services Bell Canada wanted to flog. But the company checked with its lawyers and decided that "the net" had become a generic nickname for the Internet. Because this commonplace term was already in wide general usage, trademarking it might induce undue contention. So Bell said officially, "In deference to this usage, the application to trademark The Net will be withdrawn." Bell will continue to call its package The Net but will not prevent others from using the term. I guess not. In 1995, sixty-eight Canadian companies made applications to use a trademark containing the word "Internet." A couple of arrogant hopefuls tried to copyright "Internet" alone.

YOUR CALLING CARD? NO.

In a name spat with Unitel in 1994–95, Bell Canada lost a few other cherished brand names when the Federal Court of Canada expunged some Bell trademarks because they were not distinctive enough to warrant proprietary rights. Opened to public domain when Bell lost their exclusive use were the following terms: "Calling Card, *Carte D'Appel*, WATS, 800-Plus, Inwats, Outwats, and *Le Service 900*."

ICING THE BUCK

Labatt Breweries of Canada lost a trademark infringement case early in 1995 when a jury of the U.S. District Court of St. Louis, Missouri, ruled against Labatt's claim that the terms "ice beer, ice brewing, and ice brewed" were trademarks. The jury's decision was in favour of Anheuser-Busch, a licensing partner of Labatt. Labatt makes the brand Budweiser™ in Canada. Anheuser-Busch had introduced its own brand of ice beer, "Ice Draft." Labatt sought damages of $61 million. Anheuser-Busch had brought a lawsuit earlier against Labatt, charging false advertising and publishing an "injurious falsehood" (publication of a false statement causing financial loss). Anheuser-Busch objected to suggestions in certain Labatt advertisements that any other "ice" beer was a fraudulent copy of Labatt's brand. The American jury agreed with the American company in their February, 1995, verdict and awarded the American beer giant $5 million in punitive damages.

The jury agreed with Anheuser-Busch lawyers that "ice" beer was a generic word for a category of beer. Labatt still plans to licence other brewers in the world market to use the ice beer process. During the U.S. trial, Labatt lawyers said that Labatt invented ice beer and the brewing procedures to make it. It is manufactured at temperatures lower than normal and this causes ice crystals to form resulting in flavour and drinkability improvements. But appeals are possible and this complex matter is ongoing.

ICE SCREAM

One verbal result of that case was a rush to the Canadian trademark registry of brand-names using "ice." Leafing through the *Canadian Trademarks Journal* issues dated from June 1995 to January 1966, one finds these trademarks applied for in Canada but not necessarily yet granted:

• "DRY ICE"   for men's and women's footwear

• "EXTREME ICE"   a Hong Kong company wants this for an alcoholic beverage. Could "ice" become also an adjective meaning 'desirable, good, trendy'?

• "ICE MODEL TALENT MANAGEMENT"   casting, modelling, and talent service. But would an ad agency wish to employ an "Ice Model"? Aren't most models cold and stiff enough to be begin with?

• "ICE SMOOTHNESS"   for alcoholic beverages, wearing apparel for men and women—sunglasses, lighters, umbrellas, T-shirts

• "ICE SPICE"   for men's toiletries

SUDS & DUDS

Brand-names for new beers listed in the same issues of the *Canadian Trademarks Journal* prove that some popular motifs in current beer marketing are totemic animals and demonic symbols to suggest machismo and a subliminal, devil-may-care attitude which may accrue to any who quaff a tankard of a particular foaming brew. This trendlet may have been started by Red Dog beer.

• "BREWTUS"   a pun on Brutus with its hint of 'brutal.' Pretty scary, eh?

• "DIABLO"   for alcoholic beverages and wearing apparel (the T-shirts, etc.)

• "HORNED TOAD"   yes, some aspirant brewer of beer thinks I'll swagger up to the rail and call out, "Barkeep, a pint of your finest Horned Toad, and I'll punch out any dude who snickers."

• "POWDER HEAD"   a beer, suggesting it's a real blast like powder keg?

• "WILDCAT DRY"   for a beer and its attendant T-shirts, tractor caps, posters, key chains. This one will certainly need a growling cat logo, because the words by themselves summon images of desiccated pumas and bleached carcasses of dead mountain lions—or have I missed the snarly gnarly of it all?

But the applied-for beer and ale name that I like best is "Truly Naked" (*CTJ*, Dec. 20, 1995). Will this be a "clear" beer? Or has the "clear, back-to-nature" mythos, now so pervasive in mineral waters and soft drinks, reached nigh unto breweries yet? Just how Edenic and pristine does one want a guzzle of swill to be? Beer names fizzle when subjected to such hyper-yuppification.

EEK! ECO-NAMES

Consumers want to assuage their guilty, polluting consciences these days by "buying green." Eager-to-please entrepreneurs have stepped forth to assist them with a tidal deluge of ecological brand-names like these from the *CTJ*:

• "CLUB ECO" for the operation of a retail store selling clothing, etc., with this brand-name
• "ECO-BASICS" children and infant wear
• "ECOLEC" electric panel and convection heaters, previous U.K. registration
• "ECOLINE" biodegradeable fishing line? Excellent.
• "ECOLUX" interior lights and fixtures
• "ECOSAVE" a magnetic water-conditioning plastic ball used in washing machines, dishwashers, and to fit over a tap
• "ECOSKI" international sporting gear and wear, already registered in Italy
• "ECO-STIK" pens, pencils, various writing instruments
• "ENVIRO BLEND" bird feed and animal fodder
• "ENVIROFRIEND" cut timber, "lumber including but not limited to western red cedar, green hemlock fir and green douglas fir." Yeah, and I bet when you thump one of their logs, they are really "Clayoquot" sound.
• "ENVIROMAX" residential furnaces, air conditioners, and heat pumps
• "ENVIRO-MIX" bituminous coatings
• "GENVIRONETICS" featuring the Trauma hook, being a picture or piece of jewellery in the shape of a fish hook to be used during psychotherapy and person-

al development workshop/seminars; also includes heal-ing dolls used as tools for well-being. I like the Trauma hook, but only if I can sing "Flycasting my blues away" as I sink it into the instructor's wagging finger.
• "NATURAL SELECTION"   Scott Paper Ltd. wants this as a brand-name for certain paper towels, facial tis-sues, and hand-care towelettes. Would Charles Darwin frown on this binge of eco-fetishism?
• "THE NATURAL SOLUTION"   pharmaceutical cleansing liquid for contact lenses. Note the pun on solution: both the solution (answer) and the solution (liquid cleanser) are natural.
• "SEACOLOGY"   hair care, soap, and aromatherapy products so evocatively named that dialogue from a play I will never write comes to mind:

> *Bruce, the skin-careologist*: "Mmmm. Smell that essence of kelp, Mrs. Wells. Isn't it just too, too divoon? Your gaping nose pores are closing down nicely, dear."
> *Mrs. Wells:* "They're okay, Bruce. But first, get this Trauma hook out of my mouth. Now."

THE NAME GAME

I must share a few final gleanings from the *Canadian Trademarks Journal*. In the June 14, 1995, issue some-one seeks to trademark a Canadian board game named "Referendum." Tired of the real thing, Canucks? Try the game! It is a game, isn't it?

"ANTI-FLIRT" UNDERWEAR

In the same edition is a coin-operated amusement game machine called "Great Greed." Later issues offer "Spit A Pit" catering and take-out food services. I am not making this up. "Wet Yourself" is applied for as a brand-name for non-alcoholic carbonated and non-carbonated beverages, and related wearing apparel, namely the T-shirt. "Bahama Mama" is a brand of processed meats, perhaps an allusion to the Boney M song. A clothing and underwear maker desires to put the brand "Anti-Flirt" on his wares. What would "Anti-Flirt" underwear be? A bulge-suppressing elastic codpiece? A chastity belt with a dead bolt—but done in pleasing, shell-pink leatherette?

THE FIZZ BIZ

Oxfam Québec, a nonprofit charity, sells as a fund-raiser the Canadian product with my favourite punning brand-name. Their bottled water is called "*Eau Secours*" which suggests *eau* 'water' and the French phrase *au secours!* 'help!'

Of course, some inappropriate drink names do appear. Manufactured in British Columbia, and perhaps elsewhere in Canada now, and quite legally for sale is "Original New York Seltzer." It is not seltzer. It did not originate in New York City, but in California. It is no more "original" than any other soda pop. Authentic New York seltzer has no sugar and no salt, just plenty of artificial carbonation for a light, healthy fizziness. So how do the makers of "Original New York Seltzer" get away with such a claim. Well, it is not the brand-name of the product! "Original New York Seltzer" is the name of the company. Classy, eh?

NEW TREND: CACONYM

One late-nineties trend in brand-names is so strange that I am compelled to make up a generic term for such trademarks: caconym. A caconym (Greek 'bad name') is a nasty, blunt brand-name whose unpleasantness is thought humorous or appealing to a certain market segment. One is a Canadian trademark application for a commercial wine called "Rotting Grape" (*CTJ*, Aug. 9, 1995). And there is "Freaks" footwear including kiddies' boots and shoes, already registered in the Netherlands. Another is the "Dead Cow" brand of leather mitts and gloves (*CTJ*, August 30, 1995). I close this chapter with a brand-name (*CTJ*, Dec. 20, 1995) for a line of women's clothing and fashion accessories called "Lifestyle Has No Limits." Now there's a terrifying concept.

CHAPTER TEN

HAY IS FOR HORSES, BUT EH? IS FOR CANADIANS

Eh?

I magine this statement by a gentleman
of the Canadian persuasion fresh from a
psychiatrist's office: "So I go to this
shrink, eh, and he goes like I don't have
no confidence, eh? I go, 'No way, man.'
He goes I should take assertiveness training. Weird, eh?
Like I'm always supposed to be seeking approval, eh,
from, you know, other people? I felt like he could kiss
my Royal Canadian, eh? But, sayin' it woulda been too
pushy. Dyuh think?"

Eh comes in two basic flavours, two broad categories of usage: final interrogative eh? with a rising
intonation, and narrative eh with a sustained or flat intonation and found in the midst of spoken Canadian
English sentences. Pop culture icons like Bob and Doug
Mackenzie, those two hosers on SCTV played in the
1970s to the 1980s by Rick Moranis and Dave Thomas,
popularized and used eh? repeatedly as a marker of
Canadian speech. The two actors were simply reproduc-
ing what they heard in everyday Canadian life. But the
popularity of SCTV in the United States also helped
some Americans and more Canadians become aware
that eh was a characteristic of Canuck talk. Long before
the hosers, of course, academics were writing their

eh-says too. Professor Harold B. Allen in "Canadian-American Speech Differences Along the Middle Border" (*Journal of the Canadian Linguistic Association*, 5 [1959]:20) wrote "Eh?...is so exclusively a Canadian feature that immigration officials use it as an identifying clue."

It is natural that we Canadians share a proprietary need to claim certain speech habits as our own. Differentiating ourselves from Americans is important to our notoriously fragile sense of self. But we cannot go too far and claim eh is exclusively Canadian. Chaucer used it, eh? That's Geoffrey Chaucer, English poet, author of *The Canterbury Tales*, written between A.D. 1387 and 1400. Chaucer used Middle English ey? and variants in some of the same ways Canadians still do. The interjection is well over six hundred years old. I know it hurts but, no, three rink rats did not meet in a secret cellar under a hockey arena in Sudbury one night back in the forties after a game and too many brews to coin the evocative particle. Yeah, but only Canadians use it. Oh, right! Check out these famous Canadian usages:

Charles Dickens, eh?

"And who is to look after the horses, eh?"
(Emily Brontë, *Wuthering Heights*, 1847)

"So you think he might be hard on me, eh?"
(Charles Dickens, *Bleak House*, 1852)

"I suppose you're a smart fellow, eh?"
(Henry James, *The American*, 1867)

"Breakfast out here, eh?"
(George Bernard Shaw, *Arms and the Man*, 1894)

"Breathe—fresh air. Good, eh?"
(Joseph Conrad, *Typhoon*, 1903)

"Didn't come, eh?"—"No."
(Ernest Hemingway, *The Sun Also Rises*, 1926)

"So this is Brooklyn, eh?"
(Arthur Miller, *Death of a Salesman*, 1949)

"Oh, she's coming, eh, Ma?"
(Paddy Chayefsky, *Marty*, 1954)

"Not like some people we know, eh?"
(J. D. Salinger, *Zooey*, 1957)

"Let this cup pass from you, eh?"—"Right."
(Harper Lee, *To Kill a Mockingbird*, 1960)

"Eh, Nat, ain't that so?"
(John Fowler, *The French Lieutenant's Woman*, 1969)

O RARA AVIS!

Of course Morley Callaghan, Robertson Davies, Margaret Laurence, Stephen Leacock, W. O. Mitchell, Farley Mowat, Mordecai Richler, and dozens of other Canadian writers use eh as well. Its usage is widespread. Australian and South African novels contain the interjection. The examples from British and American authors quoted above, which demonstrate many of eh's categories of usage, were collected by a great Canadian lexicographer, the late Walter S. Avis; and they appear in his definitive article "So eh? is Canadian, eh?" (*Canadian Journal of Linguistics*, 17, no.2 [1972]: 89–104). It is well worth perusal. Professor Avis's view is the scholarly and the commonsensical one and I quote it: "Eh?...did not originate in Canada and is not peculiar to the English spoken in Canada....On the other hand, there can be no doubt that eh? has a remarkably high incidence in the conversation of many Canadians these days...in Canada eh? has been pressed into service in contexts where it would be unfamiliar elsewhere. Finally, it would appear that eh? has gained such recognition among Canadians that it is used consciously and frequently by newspapermen and others in informal articles and reports." Earlier in the same study, Avis writes "eh? is a feature Canadians share with Britishers but one which some Americans consider unusual."

Americans say huh? more often than eh?

So what is eh? In the always magisterial (and often correct) words of the *Oxford English Dictionary*, eh is "an exclamation of instinctive origin...an interjectional interrogative particle often inviting assent to the sentiment expressed." Wordy, eh? An interjection is a marginal lexical item like oops, ouch, wow, tut-tut, tsk-tsk, ugh, and yuck. It is a part of speech thrown into a sentence for emotive effect. Compare its Latin origin in *interiectio* 'something thrown in between.'

FUNCTIONS

Eh has many functions in Canadian speech. By itself it often asks the listener to repeat something not heard: "Eh? Yes, my hearing aid works. Isn't it wonderful about those Dead Sea squirrels? They found more of them. People were putting them in desserts. What did you say?" Canadians use it very frequently as a spoken question mark, inviting the agreement of the person they are speaking to. "Mike Harris, the Mother Teresa of Queen's Park, eh?" It is a question tag much like the French terminal *n'est-ce pas?* or the German *nicht wahr?* Of course, eh? along with *eh bien* and *hein?* has been an interrogative tag in Parisian and Québécois French for many centuries.

In English, subtle shades of expressive connotation occur in the manifold uses of eh. Avis distinguishes eight main categories of usage. Here are three examples chosen by Professor Avis from the short stories in Margaret Laurence's *A Bird in the House* (1970):

1. There is the eh? that seeks agreement after an elliptical statement of something observed by the speaker. "Taking life easy, eh?"

2. There is the eh? that reinforces an exclamation. "Gee—what a night, eh?" "What an admission, eh?"

3. There is the eh? that reinforces an imperative. "Yeh, I know," Aunt Edna sounded annoyed. "But let me say it, eh?"

All those uses caught by Margaret Laurence's ear for Canadian speech also display a quality in the way Canadians overuse eh that Professor Avis neglected to mention. The many ways we toss eh into sentences show us constantly attempting to involve the persons being spoken to, to draw a response from them, to seek their agreement. It is a residual, uniquely Canadian, pioneer bashfulness, a polite hesitational spacer in daily discourse. What do you think, eh? Sure, I can keep right on spieling like a snake-oil barker selling Kickapoo Joy Juice, eh, but I'm also very concerned that you are listening, that you are not offended, and that you are in general agreement with the drift of my conversation. It's a way of being nice, eh?

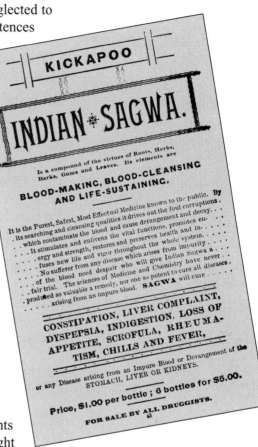

One must not fail to include the ehs repeated *ad nauseam* in the slovenly speech of the unlettered oaf and the shambling halfwit. That use is not nice. Professor Avis put it well and more temperately: "Its frequency of occurrence is high generally— among some individuals so high as to pose a threat to communication."

Moreover, some of the British immigrants who first brought eh to Canada had been taught over 'ome that using eh was rude—and, sir, a damned impertinence! We know this from several, centuries-old expressions of reproach that became common in Britain. In fact, in print as early as Jonathan Swift's *A complete Collection of polite and ingenious Conversation* (1740) is a catch-phrase said by their superiors to vulgar persons who used eh or hay. Upon having her ears affronted with such a low interjection, the pearl-encrusted dowager would shake her wattles, look with scorn through her tortoise-shell lorgnette at the varlet who had dared to utter the particle, and dismiss him with: "Hay is for horses." If the particle spoken was eh, a variant Cockney response was: " 'Ay is for 'orses." All forms of eh and hay continued to be branded vulgar well into the 1930s in England. Thus, as Eric Partridge reports in his *Dictionary of Slang and Unconventional English* (1984), we have a British RAF retort: "Eh? to me! Why, you'll be saying 'arseholes' to the C.O. next!" Later British army slang had "Eh? to me, you offensive little twit; next you'll be saying 'balls' to the Queen. GET OVER HERE!"

So, say eh for aye, if you like. Just don't flog it.

CYBER EH?

For a short time, cybernauts could have checked out a delightful, giggle-filled page on the World Wide Web called "The Canadianizer," the brainchild of Rob Stanley and Andrew Chak who created the web page for a contest they won that was sponsored by The Mix, a Toronto radio station and InContext, the Toronto software company that came up with Spider, a program that helps automate making your own web page. "The Canadianizer" used to call up any web page you requested and, before displaying it, insert into its text playful Canadianisms. The best example was the Canadianizer's own introduction: "G'day eh? And welcome to The Great Web Canadianizer eh? I got sick and tired of those American hosers messin' around with our Canadian identity and stuff eh? So I got me this computer machine and made myself this web hURLer that'll add some back bacon to the net! Beauty eh? Take a looksie at the control bar below eh? In the 'Go to:' window you can enter any http URL and it will Canadianize that web page."

A URL is a Uniform Resource Locator that uniquely identifies each file on the web by specifying its name, what server it's stored on, and where it is in the server's directory structure.

Wordy, eh?

Unfortunately, the Canadianizer web page has been discontinued. Ominous?

IS YOU IS OR IS YOU AIN'T USIN' ENGLISH?

WHY I AM NOT A WORD COP

I'm a word-nut, not a word cop. Nothing spoken or written in English is alien to my linguistic interest, except the fine print on packages of hemorrhoid medication and the writings of David Frum. Frum, like suppositories, wants everything Canadian to shrink. Word-nuts want to describe, not prescribe, how humans use language. Some readers of my first book urged me to include in this second volume long lists of bad grammar and words misused by Canadians. But quarrelsome language pedants have their ordained venue. Their fretful quibbles appear in letters-to-the-editor in many of our newspapers. You know their peevish tone: "Proper English is in decline. I have been much troubled of late about the wanton use of the semicolon in the novels of Jane Urquhart. If only everyone would write and speak precisely as I do, the virginal purity of our noble tongue would be preserved in its ancient and pristine form." Well, first, virginity is something most healthy human beings don't want to preserve forever. Second, there never was, nor is there now, a pure English. Our language began as a West Germanic dialect transported to England around A.D. 450. Over the next fifteen hundred years this dialect grew into a

"I have been much troubled of late about the wanton use of the semicolon in the novels of Jane Urquhart."

271

language as it borrowed and was influenced by Old Scandinavian loanwords, Norman-French vocabulary, and scholarly Latin and Greek. English was—may it always be!—the great thief of tongues. It grabbed new words and concepts whenever they appeared useful.

Word cops pine for an English mummified in amber, like some Jurassic mosquito. They pine for a golden age of unchanging literacy where perfumed verbal dandies exchanged exquisite ripostes in Shakespearean blank verse, while outside their mullioned windows the *profundum vulgum* trudged to its loathsome chore of growing the dandies' food, serving it to them, and cleaning up after the dandies consumed it. Word cops would like to stop language from changing. In a world where social change is fast and frightening, so they seem to say, we'll carp and cavil and try to prevent English, at least as we learned it, from any alteration. But words don't work that way. If the spirit of a living language could give tongue to its quintessence, it would shout: "Alive from lips to lips of humankind I go awinging!" In that translabial exchange, living language "morphs" and "polymorphs," in a rich sea-change caused by usage through time by smaller and larger groups of speakers, often separated by geographical, political, and social distance. That change produces dialects and varieties, hybrid speech and writing whose diversity is its glory, whose Protean habit makes it a joy to study.

Language change is not shoddy slippage. Change is programmed into the complex systems that comprise a language. It is inevitable, natural, linguistically healthy. The languages we can study through their history begin with small vocabularies and complex syntax and grammar, and then evolve toward larger vocabularies and simpler syntax and grammar. English has been so evolving for a thousand years. As I showed in chapter five in the entry on the gobbledygook word "nordicity," the only languages that do not change are dead languages. Word cops want English to be dead. For when a language is all rouged and lip-sewn and pickled in formaldehyde like some glum stiff in a funeral parlour, why, then it will never alter and present new words and grammatical ploys to the horrified eyes and ears of the word cops. These fussy pontificators would enjoy life much more if they would embark on a study of some dead tongue, not Latin and Classical Greek which can be studied to see how "dead" languages can be "alive" in modern vocabularies, no, but, say, ancient Egyptian. Learn hieroglyphics instead, you defenders of English against change, and then curl up for a comfy evening with *The Book of the Dead*.

Here is a letter bitching about someone who has had the effrontery to use a new verb. The miscreant had written: "We'll brainpick in the morning session, and present formal reports in the afternoon." "Brainpick" is a fresh, terse verb formed, like many in the history of our language, by compressing a longer verbal phrase 'to pick one's brain' into tighter form. Delightful! But not to the letterwriter who "could find it in no dictionary." Awww. Maybe, if it gains wider usage, the dictionary will have to include the vivid *brainpick* in a futute edition? Might that be the chief function of a dictionary? To describe how we currently use our language? A dictionary is not some immutable linguistic pattern-book against which all speech and writing must be measured. Unfortunately, that is how word cops use dictionaries, as a Procrustean bed. In Greek mythology Procrustes was a sadistic bandit who kidnapped travellers and made them fit into his special bed. If they were too tall, he cut off their feet. If they were too short, he stretched them on the rack that was his bed. Word cops like to do this to other people's varying use of English.

But the word cops are wrong. English glories in variety. To paraphrase the Bible, in the house of language there are many Englishes. Only the impaired are deaf to the delight of Cockney, the honey of Jamaican English, the word joy of Newfoundland talk, the humorous practicality of Prairie phrases, the peculiar lilt of Ottawa Valley speech, the local words like "skookum" that sometimes brighten chat with a person from British Columbia's Lower Mainland.

Word cops are snobs too. What their complaints

"That word is NOT in MY dictionary!"

hide is their prejudice against all whom they perceive to be not of their class, and often not of their race. These elitist moaners huddle together in the warm certainty that they alone use correct English, and all the other, lower orders write and speak twaddle. One of my tests for word cops is to read their plaintive missives and see if I can imagine the writers of such letters throwing down their pens, turning off their e-mailing keyboards, and going to volunteer at literacy programs in their neighbourhoods that teach basic reading and writing to the functionally illiterate. Ha!

Consider the title phrase of this envoi: "Is you is or is you ain't usin' English?" Did you understand what it means? Yes. Is it grammatical? In spite of what word cops might answer, it is grammatical. A basic grammar may even be genetically inherited. We may be born with a neurological "grid" that predisposes humans to think grammatically. "Is you is or is you ain't" happens to be a dialectical use of the verb "to be" in certain interrogative instances. Now, certainly, it is not the grammar of Standard English. But SE began as a dialect too, as the speech and writing of a group of powerful, educated Londoners centuries ago. There is a complicated, binding relationship between dialect and snobbery, as George Bernard Shaw pointed out at the turn of the century in his drama *Pygmalion*, later turned into the Broadway musical, *My Fair Lady*. Shaw had fun with the fact that even a Cockney flower girl could rise to the heights of British society if she did one small thing: switch her verbal codes from Cockney to those of the ruling British elite. The lesson of *Pygmalion* is still valid. Use your natal dialect, but beware. If you or your children wish to advance into the ruling, professional elite, you will have to learn Standard English. If school does not make you a graduate literate in Standard English, you may well be doomed to flip burgers and push mops. A life will be lost, not only a life of earning, but also a life of learning. You must acquire Standard English in order to learn what the modern world most values: the ability to keep learning, because most knowledge worth having will be expressed in a formal standard variety of your native tongue. The average person is capable of, and usually does learn at least two dialects: his home speech and his standard language.

I remember being made painfully aware of my own southern Ontario rural dialect on my first day of college. I promised to meet someone on Saturday night. But I said, according to her, "Sair-dee" night, using a rural Canadianism, quite common too in British dialects, wherein intervocalic *t* is replaced first by a glottal stop and then sometimes the stop disappears completely in a glide as the two, now contiguous, vowels blend into each other. Nowadays I still occasionally say "Sair-dee," but instead of blushing, I smile. That's me and that's my idiolect, my own private mixture of dialect and standard language.

Insulting a person's dialect is snotty and often racist. On the other hand, a dialect speaker who wants to better his or her chances is foolish to remain ignorant of Standard English. All social, ethnic, and regional dialects of English have their validity. I draw the line at schools that preach total freedom: no spelling, no grammar, no reading—just let the pupils speak in whatever dialect they brought to school in the first place. But, even that is permissible, as long as the teacher points out to pupils and parents that this refusal to master SE will handicap their children. In *Paradigms Lost*, critic John Simon wrote: "Everyone has a right to his ignorance and no one is compelled to become educated. But everyone is then also entitled to suffer the consequences of choosing not to become educated."

Dialects suffer many prejudices. Dialects are branded as rural, old-fashioned, substandard, corrupted, and ignorant. They are not. But they won't help you get a job at IBM.

Of course, human nature being what it is—an urge to power—users of dialect can also be crafty in exploiting the guilt of SE speakers. I once attended a public lecture at Convocation Hall on the central campus of the University of Toronto in order to hear a famous British writer talk about her work. A few minutes into her fascinating talk, a member of the audience rose to interrupt her with these exact words: "You oppressin' me by using big words I don't know." The writer looked down from her podium with a friendly smile and replied: "The solution to your problem is the use of a book called a dictionary." I applauded and then stopped, worried lest I be branded a racist. Then I began to applaud again. Geez, I better look around this envoi. Perhaps I'm oppressin' some reader? It is clear why I call this last chapter an envoi, isn't it? Envoi is the apt word. An envoi is the concluding part of a book or poem, in which the author's final thoughts are expressed. The word stems from the French verb *envoier* 'to send on one's way,' itself reaching back to the Latin word *via* 'roadway.' Envoi is not italicized because it is quite at home in English, and has been kicking around our language since A.D. 1398 when Chaucer used it.

Language is rules. But language is also play, and from playful use of language arise neologies. Dialect is a lush seed-bed of new words, from which the standard language often plucks fresh terms to invigorate its vocabulary. I coined a clumsy neology today: "deficitcation," an act of excretion on an entire country and way of life in order to rid that country of a deficit. It won't last. But neither did "lunain" coined in 1971 when man landed on the moon. Lunain was the lunar surface, as terrain is the earthly one. The word cops among us would banish all such playfulness and variety from English. To thwart them, I shall remain a word-nut. Although grim rule-keepers armed with nutcrackers pound at the gates of linguistic diversity, let us keep them in their place, forever outside, envious noses pressed to the bars, while inside the noisy dance of words rings forth, until the day lights and the shadows flee away.

Day dawns in an engraving by Gustav Doré.

SELECTED BIBLIOGRAPHY

BOOKS

Akrigg, G. P. V., and Helen B. Akrigg. *1001 British Columbia Place Names*. 3rd ed. Vancouver: Discovery Press, 1970.

Avis, Walter S., C. Crate, P. Drysdale, D. Leechman, M. H. Scargill, C. J. Lovell, eds. *A Dictionary of Canadianisms on Historical Principles*. Toronto: Gage, 1967.

Bahlow, Hans. *Deutsches Namenlexicon*. Munich: Suhrkamp Taschenbuchverlag, 1972.

Ballantyne, Robert M. *The Pioneers—A Tale of the Western Wilderness*. London: James Nisbet, 1872.

Bardsley, Charles W. *A Dictionary of English and Welsh Surnames, with Special American Instances*. Baltimore, MD: Genealogical Publishing Co., 1968.

Barney, Stephen A., with Ellen Wertheimer and David Stevens. *Word-Hoard: An Introduction to Old English Vocabulary*. New Haven, CT: Yale University Press, 1977.

Baugh, Albert C., and Thomas Cable. *A History of the English Language*. 3rd ed. London: Routledge and Kegan Paul, 1978.

Beauvillé, Guillemette de. *Les noms de famille en France tirés des noms de métiers, de charge et de dignités*. Paris: 1957.

Ben Abba, Dov. Signet *Hebrew/English, English/Hebrew Dictionary*. New York: New American Library, 1977.

NOTE

I have chosen not to list every dictionary, grammar, linguistic treatise, and field note carved on a coconut, such as I consulted, particularly the hundreds perused in tracing the more obscure origins of surnames. While such a list completed would bloat up the bibliography to a plumpness most appealing to pomposity, I happily have no need of an apparatus criticus *that might choke a horse, since I am bussing no academic butt here. Therefore, along with books about Canadian and English words, I list only some surname references that readers may find useful should they want to begin their own searches for the meaning of a family name.*

Benyukh, Olesj, and Raisa Galushko. *Ukrainian-English: Hippocrene Standard Dictionary*. New York: Hippocrene Books, 1994.

Bergeron, Léandre. *Dictionnaire de la langue québécoise.* Montréal: VLB Éditeur, 1980.

Black, G. F. *The Surnames of Scotland*. New York: New York Public Library Reprints, 1946.

Bryson, Bill. *Made in America: An Informal History of the English Language in the United States*. New York: Avon Books, 1996.

Burgess, Anthony. *A Mouthful of Air: Language and Languages, Especially English*. Toronto: Stoddart, 1993.

Burns, Peter, LL.B. *Copyright and Trade Mark Law in Canada.* Toronto: Coles, 1978.

Canadian Encyclopedia. 4 vols. Edmonton: Hurtig, 1988.

Cantwell, Robert. *The Real McCoy: The Life and Times of Norman Selby*. Princeton, NJ: Auerbach, 1971.

Carroll, Jock. *The Shy Photographer*. New York: Bantam, 1964.

Carver, Craig M. *A History of English in Its Own Words*. New York: Harper Collins, 1991.

Chambers, J. K., ed. *Canadian English: Origins and Structures*. Toronto: Methuen, 1975.

Claiborne, Robert. *Our Marvelous Native Tongue: The Life and Times of the English Language*. New York: New York Times Book Co., 1983.

Colombo, John Robert, ed. *Colombo's Canadian Quotations*. Edmonton: Hurtig Publishers, 1974.

Cottle, Basil. *The Penguin Dictionary of Surnames*. 2nd ed. Harmondsworth, Eng.: Penguin Books, 1978.

Cowan, David. *An Introduction to Modern Literary Arabic*. Cambridge: Cambridge University Press, 1958.

Creighton, Donald. *Dominion of the North: A History of Canada*. Rev. ed. Toronto: Macmillan, 1957.

Dauzat, Albert. *Dictionnaire des noms de famille et prénoms de France*. Paris: Larousse, 1951.
_____. *Les noms de famille de France*. 3rd ed. Paris: Larousse, 1977.

Davies, Trefor R. *A Book of Welsh Names*. London: Sheppard Press, 1952.

de Felice, Emidio. *Dizionario dei cognomi italiani*. Milan: Mondadori, 1978.

Devine, P. K. *Devine's Folk Lore of Newfoundland in Old Words, Phrases and Expressions: Their Origins and Meanings*. St. John's: Robinson and Co., 1937.

Eberhard-Wabnitz, Margit, and Horst Leisering. *Knaurs Vornamenbuch*. Munich: Drömersche Verlagsanstalt, 1985.

Ekwall, Eilert. *Concise Oxford Dictionary of English Place-Names*. 4th ed. Oxford: Oxford University Press, 1960.
_____. *English River Names*. Rev. ed. Oxford: Oxford University Press, 1968.

Fair of Speech: The Uses of Euphemism. Ed. D. J. Enright et al. Oxford: Oxford University Press, 1985.

Ferenczi, Sándor. *Sex in Psychoanalysis*. New York: Dover Reprints, 1960.

Fucilla, Joseph. *Our Italian Surnames*. New York: Chandler, 1949.

Gair, Reavley, et al., eds. *A Literary and Linguistic History of New Brunswick*. Fredericton: Goose Lane Editions, 1985.

Garner, Hugh. *Cabbagetown*. Toronto: Ryerson, 1968.

Gorr, Shmuel. *Jewish Personal Names: Their Origin, Derivation, and Diminutive Forms*. Ed. Chaim Freedman. Teaneck, NJ: Avotaynu, 1992.

Graves, Robert. *Food for Centaurs: Stories, Talks, Critical Studies, Poems* (includes "A Toast to Ava Gardner"). New York: Doubleday, 1960.

Gray, John. *Dazzled: A Novel*. Toronto: Irwin, 1984.

Griggs, Terry. *Quickening*. Erin, ON: The Porcupine's Quill, 1990.
_____. *The Lusty Man*. Erin, ON: The Porcupine's Quill, 1995.

Guggenheimer, Heinrich W., and Eva H. Guggenheimer. *Jewish Family Names and Their Origins: An Etymological Dictionary*. Hoboken, NJ: Ktav Publishing House, 1992.

Hamilton, William B. *The Macmillan Book of Canadian Place Names*. Toronto: Macmillan, 1978.

Holmgren, Eric J., and Patricia M. Holmgren. *Over 2000 Place Names of Alberta*. Rev. ed. Saskatoon: Prairie Books, 1973.

Humphreys, W. J. *Weather Proverbs and Paradoxes*. Baltimore, MD: Williams and Wilkins Co., 1923.

Jameson, Anna Brownell. *Winter Studies and Summer Rambles in Canada*. Originally published: London, 1838. Reprinted, Toronto: McClelland & Stewart, 1923.

Kaganoff, Benzion C. *Dictionary of Jewish Names and their History*. New York: Shocken Books, 1977.

Kálmán, Béla. *The World of Names: A Study of Hungarian Onomatology*. Budapest: Akadémiai Kiadó, 1978.

Kneen, J. J. *The Personal Names of the Isle of Man*. Oxford: Oxford University Press, 1937.

Laurence, Margaret. *A Bird in the House*. Toronto: McClelland & Stewart, 1970.
_____. *Heart of a Stranger*. Toronto: McClelland & Stewart, 1976.

Le Menn, Gwennole. *1700 Noms de famille bretons*. Saint-Brieuc, France: 1982.

Lévy, Paul. *Les noms des Israélites en France: histoire et dictionnaire*. Paris: 1960.

Lewis, Charlton T., and Charles Short. *A Latin Dictionary: Founded on Andrew's Edition of Freund's Latin Dictionary*. Impression of 1st ed. 1879. Oxford: Oxford University Press, 1958.

Liddell, Henry George, and Robert Scott. *A Greek-English Lexicon*. 9th ed. Oxford: Oxford University Press, 1953.

Lutz, William. *Doublespeak: How Government, Business, Advertisers, and Others Use Language to Deceive You*. New York: Harper & Row, 1981.

MacLennan, Hugh. *Barometer Rising*. Toronto: Collins, 1941.
_____. *Seven Rivers of Canada*. Toronto: Macmillan, 1961.

MacLysaght, Edward. *The Surnames of Ireland*. Dublin: Irish University Press, 1969.

Mardon, Ernest G. *Community Names of Alberta*. Lethbridge: University of Lethbridge, 1973.

McConnell, R. E. *Our Own Voice: Canadian English and How It Is Studied*. Toronto: Gage, 1979.

McNaught, Kenneth. *The Pelican History of Canada*. Harmondsworth, Eng.: Penguin Books, 1969.

Merriam-Webster New Book of Word Histories. Ed. F. C. Mish. Springfield, MA: Merriam-Webster, 1991.

Mills, A. D. *A Dictionary of English Place Names*. Oxford: Oxford University Press, 1993.

Mitchell, W. O. *Jake and the Kid*. Toronto: Macmillan, 1947.
_____. *Who Has Seen the Wind*. Complete text ed. Toronto: McClelland & Stewart, 1991.

Montgomery, Lucy Maud. *Anne of Green Gables*. Boston: L. C. Page Company, 1908.
_____. *Anne of the Island*. Boston, MA: The Page Company, 1915.

Morlet, Marie-Thérèse. *Dictionnaire étymologique des noms de famill*e. Paris: Perrin, 1991.

Morton, Desmond. *A Short History of Canada*. 2nd rev. ed. Toronto: McClelland & Stewart, 1994.

Mossé, Fernand. *A Handbook of Middle English*. Trans. James A. Walker. Baltimore, MD: Johns Hopkins Press, 1952.

Naumann, Horst. *Familiennamenbuch*. Leipzig: Bibliographisches Institut, 1989.

The New Shorter Oxford English Dictionary. Oxford: Oxford University Press, 1993.

Orkin, Mark M. *Canajan, Eh?* Don Mills, ON: General, 1973.
_____. *Speaking Canadian French: An Informal Account of the French Language in Canada*. Rev. ed. Toronto: General, 1971.

Ormsby, Margaret A. *British Columbia: A History.* Toronto: Macmillan, 1971.

Oxford Companion to the English Language. Ed. Tom McArthur. Oxford: Oxford University Press, 1992.

Oxford English Dictionary. Ed. James A. H. Murray et al. Oxford: Oxford University Press, 1884–1928; corrected reissue, 1933.

Oxford English Dictionary. 2nd ed. Ed. R. W. Burchfield et al. Oxford: Oxford University Press, 1989.

Oxford Russian Dictionary. Rev. ed. Ed. Colin Howlett et al. Oxford: Oxford University Press, 1995.

Partridge, Eric. *A Dictionary of Slang and Unconventional English*. London: Routledge, 1984.
_____. *Origins: A Short Etymological Dictionary of Modern English*. 4th ed. London: Routledge and Kegan Paul, 1966.

Pearen, Shelley J. *Exploring Manitoulin*. Toronto: University of Toronto Press, 1992.

Pinker, Steven. *The Language Instinct*. New York: W. Morrow, 1994.

Poteet, Lewis. *The Second South Shore Phrase Book*. Hantsport, NS: Lancelot Press, 1985.

Pratt, T. K. *Dictionary of Prince Edward Island English*. Toronto: University of Toronto Press, 1988.

Quirk, Randolph, and C. L. Wren. *An Old English Grammar*. 2nd ed. Methuen's Old English Library. London: Methuen, 1957.

Rayburn, Alan. *Naming Canada: Stories about Place Names from* Canadian Geographic. Toronto: University of Toronto Press, 1994.

Reaney, P. H., and R. M. Wilson. *A Dictionary of English Surnames*. 3rd ed. Oxford: Oxford University Press, 1995.

Robb, H. Amanda, and Andrew Chesler. *Encyclopedia of American Family Names: The Definitive Guide to the 5,000 Most Common Surnames in the United States, with Origins, Variations, Rankings, Prominent Bearers and Published Genealogies*. New York: HarperCollins, 1995.

Rogers, David. *Dictionnaire de la langue québécoise rurale*. Montréal: VLB Éditeur, 1979.

Rudnyckyj, J. B. *Canadian Place Names of Ukrainian Origin: Onomastica 2*. 3rd ed. Winnipeg: Ukrainian National Home Association, 1957.
_____. *Manitoba: Mosaic of Place Names*. Winnipeg: Canadian Institute of Onomastic Science, 1970.

Ruhlen, Merritt. *The Origin of Language: Tracing the Evolution of the Mother Tongue*. New York: Wilet, 1994

Scargill, M. H. *A Short History of Canadian English*. Victoria: Sono Nis Press, 1977.

Schaar, J. van der. *Woordenboek van Voornamen*. Utrecht: Het Spectrum, 1981.

Schimmel, Annemarie. *Islamic Personal Names*. Edinburgh: Edinburgh University Press, 1989.

Service, Robert W. *Ballads of a Cheechako*. Toronto: William Briggs, 1909.
_____. *Songs of a Sourdough*. Toronto: William Briggs, 1907.

Shakespeare, William. *The Oxford Shakespeare*. Ed. W. J. Craig. London: Oxford University Press, 1966.

Shipley, Joseph T. *The Origins of English Words: Discursive Dictionary of Indo-European Roots*. Baltimore, MD: Johns Hopkins University Press, 1984.

Simon, John. *Paradigms Lost: Reflections on Literacy and its Decline*. New York: Clarkson N. Potter, 1980.

Simpson, Thomas. *Narrative of the Discoveries of the North Coast of America*. London: Richard Bentley, 1843.

Skinner, Henry Alan. *The Origin of Medical Terms*. 2nd ed. Baltimore,MD: Williams and Wilkins, 1961.

Smith, Elsdon C. *American Surnames*. Philadelphia, PA: Chilton Book Co., 1970.
_____. *New Dictionary of American Family Names*. New York: Harper & Row, 1973.
_____. *The Story of Our Names*. New York: Harper, 1950.
_____. *Treasury of Name Lore*. New York: Harper & Row, 1967.

Sontag, Susan. *Against Interpretation, and Other Essays*. New York: Farrar, Straus and Giroux, 1966.

Stearn, William T. *Botanical Latin*. New ed. Toronto: Fitzhenry & Whiteside, 1983.

Story, G. M., W. J. Kirwin, J. D. A. Widdowson, eds. *Dictionary of Newfoundland English*. 2nd ed. Toronto: University of Toronto Press, 1990.

Stowe, Harriet Beecher. *Uncle Tom's Cabin: or, Life among the Lowly*. First published, 1851. Vintage Books / The Library of America ed. New York: Random House, 1991.

Theophrastus. *Enquiry into Plants* (includes *De signis tempestatum* "Weather Signs"). 2 vols. Ed. and trans. Sir Arthur Hort. Loeb Classical Library. London: Heinemann, 1916.

Tibón, Gutierre. *Diccionario etimológico comparado de nombres proprios*. Rev. ed. Mexico City: Fondo de Cultura Económica, 1986.

Tuleja, Tad. *Namesakes: An Entertaining Guide to the Origins of More than 300 Words Named for People*. New York: McGraw-Hill, 1987.

Updike, John. *Couples*. New York: Knopf, 1968.

Unbegaun, B. O. *Russian Surnames*. Oxford: Oxford University Press, 1972.

Waldrop, M. Mitchell. *Complexity: The Emerging Science at the Edge of Order and Chaos*. New York: Simon & Schuster, 1992.

Webster's Third New International Dictionary of the English Language. Springfield, MA: G. and C. Merriam, 1976.

Wehr, Hans. *A Dictionary of Modern Written Arabic*. 3rd ed. Ed. J. Milton Cowan. Ithaca, NY: Spoken Language Services Inc., 1976.

Withycombe, E. G. *Oxford Dictionary of English Christian Names*. 3rd ed. Oxford: Oxford University Press, 1977.

JOURNAL AND NEWSPAPER CITATIONS

Anthony Jenkins, "Street Slang: The unvarnished, really offensive Toronto," *The Globe and Mail*, March 25, 1995, Focus section.

Canadian Trademarks Journal (June 1995–January 1966).

S. O. Scott and D. A. Mulligan, "The Red River Dialect," *Beaver*, Outfit 282 (Dec., 1951), p. 42.

ILLUSTRATION CREDITS

pp. *i, v, ix*, 111, 127, 279, 287, 291, 295, and 298, Carol Belanger Grafton, *Old-Fashioned Illustrations of Books, Reading & Writing*, Dover Publications

p. *vii*, Grafton, *Pictorial Archive of Decorative and Illustrative Mortised Cuts*, Dover Publications

pp. *x*, 27, 95, 98, and 125, Grafton, *Children: A Pictorial Archive from Nineteenth-Century Sources*, Dover Publications

pp. *xiii*, 13, 36, 41, 47, 51, 157, 160, 179, and 199, Jim Harter, *Animals: A Pictorial Archive from Nineteenth-Century Sources*, Dover Publications

pp. *xv*, 65, 74, 75, 92, 131, 137, 209, 210, and 271, Harter, *Men: A Pictorial Archive from Nineteenth-Century Sources*, Dover Publications

pp. 1, 10, 20, 115, 167, 189, 192, and 276, Harter, *The Ultimate Angel Book*, Dover Publications

pp. 3, 16, 50, and 72, Harter, *Transportation: A Pictorial Archive from Nineteenth-Century Sources*, Dover Publications

pp. 4, 178, 217, 219, and 225, Grafton, *Old-Fashioned Nautical Illustrations*, Dover Publications

pp. 8 and 98, Grafton, *Old-Fashioned Illustrations of Children*, Dover Publications

pp. 11 and 19, *Assorted Images, Volume 1*, compact disc by Harter Image Archives pp. 23, 48, and 62, *Dining and Drinking*, Hart Picture Archives

pp. 25, 28, 43, 45, and 57, Grafton, *Naughty French Spot Illustrations*, Dover Publications

pp. 29, 35, 80, 208, and 228, Harter, *Women: A Pictorial Archive from Nineteenth-Century Sources*, Dover Publications

pp. 29 and 114, Harter, *Music: A Pictorial Archive of Woodcuts & Engravings*, Dover Publications

pp. 30, 67, and 193, Grafton, *Old-Fashioned Sports Illustrations*, Dover Publictions

p. 34, Grafton, *Cuts for Antique Sales and Auctions*, Dover Publications

pp. 37, 56, 253, 266, and 271, Harter, *Hands: A Pictorial Archive from Nineteenth-Century Sources*, Dover Publications

pp. 42, 215, 216, 242, 244, 245, and 248, Grafton, *Old West Cuts*, Dover Publications

pp. 46, 133, and 141, Edmund V. Gillon, Jr., *Picture Sourcebook for Collage & Decoupage*, Dover Publications

p. 60, 106, 152, and 258, Stanley Appelbaum, *Advertising Woodcuts from the Nineteenth-Century Stage*, Dover Publications

pp. 69 and 91, *Harter's Picture Archive for Collage & Illustrations*, Dover Publications

pp. 94 and 119, Grafton, *Old-Fashioned Animal Cuts*, Dover Publications pp. 118, 146, 181, and 184, Grafton, *Victorian Spot Illustrations, Alphabets & Ornaments*, Dover Publications

p. 137 and 188, *Holidays*, Hart Picture Archives

p. 180, William Rowe, *Machinery & Mechanical Devices: A Treasury of Nineteenth-Century Cuts*, Dover Publications

INDEX

"I don't think that's covered in this index."

"You do so know that root, Bill. Why, it's a
common verb in colloquial Outer Mongolian."

"I'll stick this quill in my left eyeball if I have
to index one more word."